CRISIS

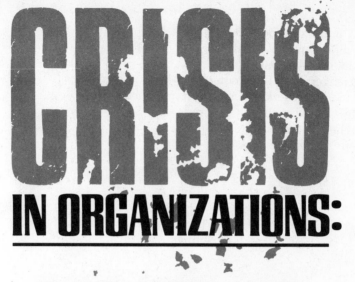

IN ORGANIZATIONS:

Managing and Communicating in the Heat of Chaos

LAURENCE BARTON

Department of Management
University of Nevada, Las Vegas

COLLEGE DIVISION South-Western Publishing Co.

Cincinnati Ohio

Acquisitions   Editor: Jeanne R. Busemeyer
Production Editor: Susan C. Williams
Production House: Julia Chitwood
Marketing Manager: Scott D. Person
Cover Design: Sarah Frederking Design/ Tom Hubbard
Internal Design: Russell Schneck Design
Photo Researcher: Kathryn A. Russell
Internal Photo Credits: See page vii.

EC66AA
Copyright © 1993
by SOUTH-WESTERN PUBLISHING CO.
Cincinnati, Ohio

Library of Congress Cataloging-in-Publication Data

Barton, Laurence.
    Crisis in organizations : managing and communicating in the heat
of chaos / Laurence Barton.
        p.   cm.
    Includes bibliographical references and indexes.
    ISBN 0-538-81818-2
    1. Crisis management.   2. Communication in organizations.
3. Organizational change.   I. Title.
HD49.B37   1993
658.4––dc20   92-12552
                                                               CIP

1 2 3 4 5 6 7 8 9 MT 0 9 8 7 6 5 4 3 2

Printed in the United States of America

For my parents with love and admiration

ABOUT THE
AUTHOR

L aurence Barton is Associate Professor of Management at the University of Nevada, Las Vegas. He previously taught management communication at Harvard Business School and public relations at Boston College and Tufts University.

A consultant to industry on crisis management and organizational communication, Dr. Barton's clients have included Arthur D. Little Inc., the Internal Revenue Service, NYNEX, Swiss pharmaceutical company Ares-Serono, Mirage Resorts, Korean conglomerate Lucky-Gold Star, and numerous others. Dr. Barton is a recipient of a major research grant from the U.S. Department of Energy; he has developed an innovative crisis communication software program that prepares managers for a variety of common and uncommon organizational disasters.

His articles have appeared in the *New York Times*, *Parade Magazine*, the *Boston Globe*, and *USA Today* as well as scholarly journals including *Business Forum*, *Industrial Management and Data Systems*, *Management Decision*, *Long Range Planning*, and numerous others. Dr. Barton is in demand as a guest lecturer by corporate audiences on topics related to crisis management and strategic communication; he has lectured around the world on these issues.

Dr. Barton received an A.B. degree, magna cum laude, from Boston College in speech and communications, the M.A.L.D. in law and diplomacy from The Fletcher School of Law and Diplomacy at Tufts University, and a Ph.D. in international relations and public policy from Boston University.

He and his wife Judy live in Las Vegas. They are the parents of two children, Matthew and Mark.

PREFACE

In the early 1950s, Richard Nixon's political career was enormously bright. Because of his Senate record, he was selected by Dwight D. Eisenhower as the Republican vice presidential running mate. In the middle of the nomination process, Nixon was accused of misusing campaign funds. In the heat of chaos, he managed this public crisis by giving a televised, masterfully delivered speech that stressed his innocence and honesty, and reassured a skeptical public. As a result, his party and the nation embraced him. In his 1962 book *Six Crises*, Nixon said that turning adversity into a triumph was the greatest test of a manager.

Two decades later, however, Nixon seemed to have forgotten the very lessons of crisis management that had earlier salvaged his career. In the midst of Watergate, he waffled. He shunned the public and the press. He engaged in conspiracy. He became unaccountable in a democratic society that demanded accountability. After a relatively productive five years in office, Nixon now lost the confidence of Congress, the media, and the people. His career was permanently tarnished. A major factor in this fall from grace was Nixon's inability to manage the new crisis.

In corporate environments, Richard Nixons abound. This book illustrates how managers can become adept at managing unexpected, negative events so as to protect their own reputations and the entire organization. The events may not be as cataclysmic as Watergate. Nevertheless, an industrial accident, unexpected labor dispute, or product recall can produce chaos in an entire organization. Although such crises cannot always be prevented, they can be mitigated. Crises must be managed well.

About This Book

The introduction to this book discusses the types of crises you may face as a manager. The following eight chapters deal in depth with important characteristics of certain crises and the crucial skills needed.

Chapter 1, "The Rise of Public Opinion: Crises Are No Longer Private," discusses the influence that organized public opinion has played in our society and the role of the mass media in disseminating and interpreting news. The chapter also focuses on the important role news organizations play in reporting news about business and industry, and how corporations use information to influence that reporting and enhance their credibility with consumers.

Chapter 2, "Chaos and Management," surveys several dozen well-known crises that have changed the world. Although the vast majority of crises never become front-page news, they nevertheless create havoc for investors, consumers and employees.

Chapter 3, "A Preneed Assessment of Crisis Planning," shows how an organization can assess its managerial strengths and weaknesses and how these factors can enhance or impede an organization's response to crisis. By measuring vulnerability to disaster, managers can better evaluate the organizational dynamics that will influence their decisions.

Chapter 4, "Complex Crises," gives an intensive and detailed examination of several prominent and serious organizational headaches, which you may one day find yourself managing. For example, false rumors can weaken a company's market share, and a single product recall can destroy public confidence in a manufacturer.

Chapter 5, "Communication as a Management Tool," considers managerial communication in effective crisis management. Each manager should understand the basic elements of communication: audience, goal, source, and message. The tools and strategies used in public relations are also discussed in detail.

Chapter 6, "When the Crisis Has an Environmental Impact," explores the increasingly important role of disasters that harm the natural environment. Whether caused by natural forces (such as earthquakes and floods) or human error (such as oil spills and chemical leaks), the management decisions in these crises can help rapidly contain the damage, or they can prolong effective resolution.

Chapter 7, "How Organizations Cope: Crisis Training Managers for Worst-Case Scenarios," discusses the role of the organizational team in crisis planning. Also included is a discussion on how individual workers may react under adverse conditions, such as when they witness a violent crime on company property. By anticipating such calamities and being prepared to offer professional psychological help to employees, managers can handle residual problems and resulting low productivity.

Chapter 8, "The Crisis Management Plan," provides a concrete outline for developing a crisis management plan. The chapter analyzes both effective and poor crisis responses in recent years, and suggests ways to develop preventive measures.

At the end of each chapter is a short case study. These example cases illustrate the many factors a manager must consider when confronting crisis. Often there is no "right" or "wrong" solution, but you are challenged to identify the *best* response given the dynamics of the case. Such case analysis is good practice for real management challenges both today and in future years.

The book concludes with four appendixes. Appendix A presents an interdisciplinary case that requires you to consider a number of factors, including organizational dynamics, political realities, and financial conditions. Appendix B provides information on the role of the Federal Emergency Management Agency (FEMA) in assisting corporations and institutions in the midst of crisis. Appendix C presents a sample crisis management plan (CMP). Appendix D gives an overview of the program and facilities at the Center for the Study of Crisis Management at the University of Nevada, Las Vegas.

Today's society is litigious. Most managerial decisions are documented, which raises concerns about how regulators, the press, and consumers or investors may later evaluate the individual and group management of the crisis. Many of the book's cases thus test your managerial writing skills. You will also be challenged in terms of public speaking, meeting skills, answering questions at press conferences, and planning corporate strategy.

At several points in the book, you will follow a group of managers at a hypothetical company, Arlington Plastics, that is writing its own CMP. The comments of these managers reflect statements heard by researchers in observing many corporate groups struggling with this task over the past several years.

Acknowledgments

This book could not have been completed without the assistance of many talented people.

I am grateful first to Janet Murrow, who graciously agreed to review the book. An accomplished war correspondent in World War II, Mrs. Murrow witnessed numerous crises during that period of history. During the horrific bombings of London in 1941–1942, she and her late husband, Edward R. Murrow, found themselves directly in the center of one of the greatest crises of the twentieth century. Working for CBS Radio and other organizations, she witnessed, reported, and analyzed numerous political crises and corporate debacles in the years to follow. I am most appreciative for her kind encouragement and comments.

I am especially grateful to the manuscript reviewers, whose comments and suggestions strengthened the presentation. My thanks are extended to

Dr. Sherron Kenton
Emory University

Dr. Robert E. Brown
Bentley College

Dr. John P. Leland
Purdue University

Dr. Don Leonard
Arizona State University

I was assisted in the enormous task of tracing hundreds of disasters, crises, and miscellaneous industrial accidents over the past four decades by three researchers: Kimberly Harrell, Michelle Burke, and Adam Stockton. Many individuals in corporations and institutions around the world responded to my requests for advice, documents, and insight on the topic of crisis management; I am deeply indebted for their generous assistance.

Constructive advice on the manuscript was also offered by Dr. Ed Goodin and Dr. Norval Pohl of UNLV, Dr. Donald Fishman of Boston College, and Steve Leahy. My editor at South-Western Publishing, Jeanne Busemeyer, provided encouragement and direction throughout the project.

Partial support of my research was obtained from the First Interstate Bank Center for Business Leadership in Las Vegas.

Finally, my wife Judy and children Matthew and Mark were wonderfully supportive throughout this project, including those heated moments when crisis engulfed my word processor.

Laurence Barton
University of Nevada, Las Vegas

The author welcomes comments and case material for consideration in future editions. You may contact Laurence Barton at P.O. Box 71858, Las Vegas, Nevada 89170-1858, or phone (702) 367-1007.

CONTENTS

INTRODUCTION 1

Drawing a Line Between Problems
and Crises 2

The Many Sides of Crisis 3

Can Chaos Bring Out the Best in an
Organization? 3

Or Does Crisis Bring Out the Worst? 4

Accurate Information Is an Asset 5

Predicting Problems Requires Strategy 6

Crises That Managers Confront Outside
the Workplace 7

Learning by Error 8

Does the Size of an Organization Matter? 8

Why Managers Need Crisis Management
Skills 10

What Have We Learned? 12

CHAPTER 1
**THE RISE OF PUBLIC
OPINION: CRISES ARE NO
LONGER PRIVATE** 14

The Development of Modern Public
Opinion 16

Public Relations Is Born 17

Crisis and the Messenger: The Role of
Reporters 18

Modern History and Crisis 20

The Great War 20

Winston Churchill at the Helm 21

John F. Kennedy: An Amalgam of Intelligence
and Rhetoric 21

Collision Course: The Integrity of the Press
and the Reputation of Managers 22

The Reporter at the Center of Crisis: Edward R.
Murrow 24

The Dawn of Regulation and Organized
Protests 26

The Proactive Company, the Reactive
Manager 27

CASE STUDY: Talk About Fireworks! 28

CHAPTER 2
**CHAOS AND
MANAGEMENT** 31

The Strategy of Crisis Management: A Team
Approach 33

Senior Administration 34

Technical Operations 34

Public Affairs 34

Public Relations 35

Consumer Affairs 35

Investor Relations 35

Advertising 36

The Fault, Dear Brutus, Is Not in Our Stars 37

Three Mile Island: The Impossible Accident
Becomes Possible 38

General Haig: The One Statement That Will
Haunt Him Forever 40

Exxon: A Barrage of Bad Judgment 41

Why Companies Write Crisis Management
Plans 41

Pandemonium: The AMTRAK Collision and a
Tested Crisis Team 42

INTERVIEW: Frank Moy, Jr.

St. Elizabeth's Hospital of Boston and the AMTRAK
Disaster 43

CASE STUDY: This Quarterback Was Sacked   45

3 A PRENEED ASSESSMENT OF CRISIS PLANNING   48

A Question to Ponder: What's the Worst That Could Happen to Us?   51

One Firm's Crisis Planning Begins: Arlington Plastics   53

Size Correlates to Preparedness   57

How Managers Assess the Role of Crisis Management   57

The Litmus Test of Crisis: Assessing Risk   59

Ownership of the Company   59

Risk Exposure: Size of Organization and Adequate Insurance   62

Warning Signals   62

Communications Channels   64

Risk Associated with the Product or Service   65

Public Awareness of Company   66

INTERVIEW: Lori Heyman

This Manager Confronted Two Crises in Two Months   68

CASE STUDY: More Than Milk and Bread?   69

4 COMPLEX CRISES   72

A Crisis in Investor Confidence: Sell That Stock!   73

The Strategic Importance of Investor Relations   74

Issues That Concern Investors and the General Public   74

Chrysler and Odometers   75

Ralph Nader Challenges Industry Giant GM   77

AT&T Courts NCR Acquisition   78

Tactical Maneuvers Before and During a Financial Crisis   80

Product Investigations In the Public Interest   81

Product Defects and Recalls   81

Consumer Reports and Chrysler   83

The Tylenol Recall   84

Rely Tampons: When Market Leaders Receive the Greatest Scrutiny   85

Sudafed: Was Burroughs Sleeping During the Tylenol Crisis?   85

Perrier: Managing a Recall Across the Atlantic   86

Recall Readiness and Aftermath   90

Product Boycotts   92

Averting Disaster: Taking Charge of a Recall   93

These Rumors Are Worth Listening To   95

The Power of Rumors   97

Violent Crimes on Company Property: The Story of ESL   98

INTERVIEW: Ralph "Pete" Erben

Guiding a Corporation Through Tragedy   100

Neighbors and Crisis: The NIMBY Syndrome   103

Not So Neighborly?   105

You Might Get "Slapped"   108

Strike One!   109

The United Airlines Strike   112

Must-do's When Preparing for a Strike   113

Service Disruption   114

INTERVIEW: Virgil Dissmeyer

What Do You Mean, My Bank No Longer Exists?   116

CASE STUDY: These MagiCans Weren't So Magical   118

5 COMMUNICATION AS A MANAGEMENT TOOL   121

Communication *Is* Strategy   122

Audience   123

Goal   124

Message   126

Source   126

Support and Information   127

Feedback   127

Communicating in a Crisis   128

Press Releases   128

Press Kits   129

News Conferences   129

Meet the Press: Preparation Is the Key   132

Video News Releases (VNRs)   136

AP Managers Discuss Their Communication Program   140

INTERVIEW: Phil Levy

A Television News Producer on Crisis Communication   144

CASE STUDY: "These Sodas Are Being Manufactured by the Ku Klux Klan"   147

CHAPTER 6
WHEN THE CRISIS HAS AN ENVIRONMENTAL IMPACT   150

A Legacy of Neglect Leads to Policy Responses   151

Love Canal: A Neighborhood at the Nucleus of Crisis   153

Asbestos: A Commonly Used Product Is Found to Cause Cancer   154

Information as a Crisis Response Tool   155

If You Pollute, You Will Pay   157

Chernobyl: A Complete Accounting Could Take a Century   159

Regulatory Enforcements May Help Avert Crises   160

Initiatives to Address Environmental Abuse   161

Avoiding Disasters: Is Ecoterrorism the Answer?   162

INTERVIEW: Zygmunt J. B. Plater

Legal Landscape: The Environment and the Law   165

CASE STUDY: When an Earthquake Strikes   167

CHAPTER 7
HOW ORGANIZATIONS COPE: TRAINING MANAGERS FOR WORST-CASE SCENARIOS   170

The Crisis Management Team   172

Attorney   173

Public Relations Coordinator   173

Technical Experts   173

Financial Officer   173

Telecommunications Manager   174

Regulatory or Public Affairs Expert   174

CEO or Representative   174

Phase One: Fact Finding   175

Phase Two: Scenario Development   176

The Role-Play in Action   177

Timing and Location   178

Synergy: A Meeting of Minds   182

Phase Three: Communicating Our Message   182

The Crisis Management Control Center   184

Stress and Crisis: The Individual Response   187

Personal Crisis and the Workplace   188

INTERVIEW: Mark and Susan Braverman

Violence and Trauma at Work: Another Crisis for Management   190

CASE STUDY: We Can't Find Our CEO!   193

CHAPTER 8
THE CRISIS MANAGEMENT PLAN   196

Introduction   197

The Crisis Team   201

Crisis Assessment   202

Documentation Discussion   203

Proprietary Information   204

Action Steps   205

Media Relations   208

Financial and Legal Considerations   211

Logistics of Crisis Management   212

Evaluation Methods   212

CASE STUDY: There Are No Fatalities
on Flight 30 . . . Oops   215

**APPENDIX A: TEST YOUR CRISIS
MANAGEMENT SKILLS**   217

**APPENDIX B: THE ROLE OF THE
FEDERAL EMERGENCY MANAGEMENT
AGENCY (FEMA) IN PREPARING FOR
CRISIS**   219

Federal Emergency Management Agency
(FEMA)   219

Why FEMA?   219

FEMA's Value to the Corporation   219

Disaster Scenarios   220

The Crisis Manager's Responsibilities   220

Resources   221

**APPENDIX C: SAMPLE CRISIS
MANAGEMENT PLAN**   223

**APPENDIX D: NEW AVENUES IN
DISASTER PLANNING: THE UNLV
CENTER FOR THE STUDY OF CRISIS
MANAGEMENT**   227

BIBLIOGRAPHY   229

COMPANY INDEX   239

NAME INDEX   241

SUBJECT INDEX   245

Introduction

Just imagine being in the shoes of *Exxon Valdez* captain Joseph Hazelwood when his Third Mate called him in a panic that fateful day of March 23, 1989, and muttered "Captain, I think we are in serious trouble!" After realizing that oil was spewing from his ship into Alaska's Prince William Sound, Hazelwood turned to his Chief Mate and said "I guess this is one way to end your career." ❑

Christopher Manes, *Green Rage: Radical Environmentalism and the Unmaking of Civilization* (1990)

Crisis. The very word evokes feelings of insecurity in all of us. Indeed, all our lives have been changed by personal and professional crises, in relationships as well as world events. It would be hard to find a manager anywhere in the world who is not familiar with the assorted calamities that have afflicted Exxon, Union Carbide, NASA, and Chernobyl.

Teachers spend a huge amount of time showing future managers how to read balance sheets, comprehend management information systems, supervise an assembly line, or export products. Yet we have largely failed to send future managers through crisis boot camp. Unexpected, negative events impact small and major industries alike, and crises can and have devastated thousands of companies. The role of managers is to manage people and projects; yet problem solving is rarely taught and often is just picked up on the job, sometimes with little or no formal direction from senior management. As a result, many organizations—and their managers—never fully recover from a single embarrassing, and costly, gaffe.

The purpose of this book is to show you the dynamics of preparing for and managing worst-case scenarios. Failure can be a superb teacher. By analyzing how managers have coped successfully (and unsuccessfully) in a wide variety of cases, you will gain insights on decision making during difficult periods in the life of an organization. You will also better understand how various audiences (stockholders, news media, regulators, customers) shape decisions in the midst of chaos. By the end of the book, you will thoroughly understand the tools managers need to anticipate crisis in their organizations. You will also have become capable of assessing the many risk factors that contribute to the potential crisis. Finally, you will be able to develop an effective crisis management plan (CMP). Such a plan can be of enormous help to you—and your career—in the future.

DRAWING A LINE BETWEEN PROBLEMS AND CRISES

Problems are commonplace in business. What differentiates crisis from the routine or even extraordinary management dilemma is very much open to debate. A good place to begin is with the following definition:

> A crisis is a major, unpredictable event that has potentially negative results. The event and its aftermath may significantly damage an organization and its employees, products, services, financial condition, and reputation.

The term *crisis* is heavily overused. We have the AIDS crisis, the Mideast crisis, the ozone layer crisis, and even the federal deficit crisis. All are important. Each needs our attention. But for our purpose, we will consider only those that fall under the preceding definition.

Problems can be addressed in a *limited* time frame without arousing public attention and without draining the human resources of an organization. By contrast, the magnitude of crises often takes *considerable* time to grasp; management may need to rely not only on many segments of the organization itself but also on outside consultants.

We expect problems—they are truly inevitable in the life of any person or organization. Some crises also share this characteristic—we know, for instance, that earthquakes and hurricanes occur and that these events are caused by natural forces that are largely out of our control. Nevertheless, we plan for natural disasters by way of measures such as community preparedness programs, concrete flood barriers, and reinforced school buildings so that when crisis does strike, damage to life and property is minimized. What makes natural crises so distinctive is the recognition that their timing is virtually impossible to predict.

THE MANY SIDES OF CRISIS

Crisis recognizes no boundaries. It strikes corporations, nonprofit organizations, government agencies, houses of worship, utilities, cooperatives, and families. It strikes our personal lives with disease or accident without a moment's notice. Likewise, the organizations we work for or support—multinational corporations, small stores, churches, superpower governments—are all susceptible to crisis.

The impact of a crisis can often be reduced if individuals take the time to understand the relationship of crisis to their specific organizations. They also need to do advance planning, use human talent properly to weather any storm, and evaluate action *after* a crisis so that future problems can be avoided or at least minimized in scope.

Some managers use crisis to their advantage—their swift and effective decision making may save millions of dollars in lost revenue and preserve their company's reputation. Others, as you will see, crumble under the burden of crisis containment. They lose focus, underdelegate or overdelegate, or simply underestimate the significance of the disaster they face. These managers—those who have complete access to data, are prepared and minimize the damage caused by crisis, and those who earnestly prepare but still fail to cope completely with crisis—are the polar extremes of crisis management.

CAN CHAOS BRING OUT THE BEST IN AN ORGANIZATION?

Most people are familiar with Johnson & Johnson's superb handling of product tampering with its Tylenol line in 1982. Most experts agree that the company weathered this crisis well, that Johnson & Johnson's crisis management team had rehearsed and planned for problems in advance, and that diligent leadership contributed to a return of public confidence. Johnson & Johnson's team received worldwide praise for their efforts. Analyst Marion Pinsdorff notes that the Tylenol poisonings received the most press coverage of any news story since the assassination of President Kennedy in 1963. Today, sales of Tylenol actually exceed its pre-crisis market share.*

The Tylenol case is one of the few exceptionally well-handled management crises available for study. The full resources of a complex multinational corporation were focused on product reliability and public concern. Johnson & Johnson was recognized as a corporation with a conscience, with a swift and effective decision-making team, and with a reserve of public goodwill that allowed product reintroduction.

But Johnson & Johnson is an exception. On balance, corporate America has been slow to recognize its vulnerability to crisis. A number of companies and individuals could have been spared significant trauma and financial damage over the past quarter-century if a concerted effort had been made to anticipate failure. The cumulative knowledge amassed from mistakes can be of great value to new managers and students of business. As a result of well-publicized management failures (many highlighted in this book), training programs, role-playing seminars, and credible literature are increasingly being used. Crisis management is a new field of management science; it is also one of the most compelling, complex, and challenging.

OR DOES CRISIS BRING OUT THE WORST?

Sometimes crisis brings out the worst possible management styles. When *Challenger* exploded in late 1986, NASA refused comment for a full five hours. Agency executives initially refused to give background briefings to reporters, which further fueled rumors spread by uninformed self-appointed "analysts." University of Southern California professor Ian I. Mitroff, a pioneer of crisis management, commented on the crisis:

> Virtually all major crises are caused by a mixture of human and technical elements. The immediate "cause" of the disaster was a faulty O-ring, a poor engineering design that led to a catastrophic technical break. However, the real precipitating cause of the accident was a bureaucratic organization that deliberately blocked repeated warning signals.[1]

As a result of NASA's actions, both public confidence and positive media reporting about the agency waned. A disillusioned public and angry members of Congress complained about NASA's actions after the incident, and the *Wall Street Journal* remarked,

> Still, the space agency's fumbling has been all the more stunning because of its longtime reputation as one of the slickest self-promoters in Washington.... NASA does have an emergency public affairs plan. But after years of its preoccupation with promoting the shuttle program and after 24 successful flights, the agency was clearly caught off guard.[2]

*Although 6,000 criminal leads were provided to the police, an arrest was never made. One individual, James W. Lewis, was convicted in 1984 of trying to extort $1 million from Johnson & Johnson. He is currently serving two consecutive 10-year sentences at the federal penitentiary at Fort Leavenworth, Kansas, where he remains a prime suspect in the deaths.

Expecting an eventual crisis could have allowed a swifter response. Similarly, when Exxon's *Valdez* tanker dumped nearly 250,000 barrels of oil into Alaska's Prince William Sound in March 1989, Exxon's chairman was accused of seeming to be uncaring about the actions (or absence of actions) by the company, its tanker, and crew. The *New York Times*, in a rare public rebuke on a news page, suggested,

> The biggest mistake was that Exxon's chairman, Lawrence G. Rawl, sent a succession of lower-ranking executives to Alaska to deal with the spill instead of going there himself and taking control of the situation in a forceful, highly visible way. This gave the impression that the company regarded the pollution problem as not important enough to involve top management.[3]

More about Exxon later; here, notice the element of public relations strategy in managing this crisis.

Deep into the recession that began in late 1990, *Business Week* reported that the nation's third-largest insurance company, Equitable, faced enormous problems with customers and regulators when false rumors swept the country that the company was headed for imminent bankruptcy. In this case, the magazine noted,

> Executives at Equitable Life Assurance Society of the U.S. took the talk so seriously that they launched a major effort to kill it: memos to employees, letters to customers, and statements to the media. They even enlisted the New York State Insurance Department to certify that all was well.[4]

Sometimes you need a swat team to control *perceptions* that a crisis is imminent, as well as to control a real crisis. Regardless of the situation, planning is important, and good planning requires quality data.

ACCURATE INFORMATION IS AN ASSET

Information—data—is crucial to planning. A manager may have no idea of when a business crisis will take place, but certain signals can help. A manager can read articles from trade journals, speeches, a management report, or other research data to learn how other firms are coping with a given problem. Let's say terrorist threats are on the rise in a country where your employees live and work, or a leading activist group may have targeted your organization at home. Every day, organizations face these and many other crises. How managers use the information available to them can help them *avert* crises as well as *mitigate* their impact.

Like millions of homeowners on the West Coast, major grocery chains in that region, such as Safeway, must consider many factors in meeting customer demands in the event of an earthquake. Safeway, however, has a large management staff as well as engineering consultants who can help minimize damage and return the company to some level of normalcy as rapidly as possible. The homeowner cannot afford ready access to these professionals and must try to minimize the impact of crisis "on the fly." Both groups—food chains and homeowners—may need to work with regulators, insurance agencies, emergency personnel, and others in the midst of chaos. Their plight is the same; the scope of damage *differs*. Yet both learn of the crisis at the same time and with the same vulnerability to nature. No matter how much access to data they enjoy, the inevitable crisis can only be partially abated.

PREDICTING PROBLEMS REQUIRES STRATEGY

Unlike the expectation of earthquakes in active fault zones, not all crises can be predicted. Despite this fact, managers have a good opportunity—even a *responsibility*—to prepare for crisis by frequently reviewing data that are readily available about their organizations. Some of these data may be objective (sales figures), and some may be derived from opinion (marketing studies, feasibility reports). Yet regardless of the source, managers make daily judgments as to the *quality* of the data used to influence their decisions. It is difficult, if not impossible, to make a decision if this information is flawed, incomplete or badly biased.

Similarly, managers must have adequate data, both objective and biased in nature, to guide them in preparing for, and ultimately containing, crisis situations. This is essential for *strategic management*, which *challenges managers to find the best possible solution based on an objective evaluation of all information and available options.*

Managers also need to know what crises to plan for. The types of organizational crises are varied and complex; just consider these scenarios:

- Computer breakdowns
- Terrorism
- Product tampering
- Hostile takeover attempt
- Challenges to proprietary data
- Embezzlement
- Environmental accidents (chemical leak, explosion)
- Shootings or crimes at a plant or company location
- Unexpected resignation or termination
- Recall of product due to safety considerations
- Industrial accidents
- Protests by neighbors or consumer advocates
- Critical media advertisements placed by competitors
- A company's product being mentioned negatively in a research or medical journal

Corporations are increasingly hiring psychologists to intervene immediately after some of these types of crises in the workplace. Specially trained professionals address the trauma of workers after an experience such as seeing several co-workers gunned down by a madman with an Ouzi. Lost productivity, illness, depression, increased workers compensation claims—all are important but often neglected consequences of personal trauma.

The attention afforded this aspect of crisis management is likely to increase in the years ahead. An estimated 800 to 1,400 Americans are murdered at work every year, and tens of thousands of others are injured on the job.[5] Decades ago, few if any managers worried about their safety in the office. Today, nearly 70 percent of all letter bombs in Europe are addressed to the chief executive officers of major companies.* One-third of all terrorist activity in the world is directed at corporations, not embassies or consulates.[6] The continual threat of fear via intimidation constitutes yet another kind of crisis. Recent events may prompt us to wonder how well prepared small and large corporations are for such events, and whether management has planned an adequate response for chaos. *Business Week* (December 16, 1991) reports that in 1988 nearly 1,000 felonies and 2,700 misdemeanors were committed in New York City hospitals, including the murders of patients, nurses, and doctors.

CRISES THAT MANAGERS CONFRONT OUTSIDE THE WORKPLACE

Managers also face personal crises. When a manager is troubled by a sudden, negative event at home, that may influence his or her ability to cope with the job. Some researchers have indicated, however, that one's ability to cope with the pressure of such events may help strengthen resolve (and temperament) during a crisis on the job. Common personal crises include

- Accidental death
- Divorce
- Suicide by a loved one
- Foreclosure, bankruptcy, or insolvency
- Disease or serious illness
- Marital or relationship stress
- Injury as a result of assault and battery
- Car accident

A major difference between crises on and off the job is the number of people affected, but a second difference is that at home managers sometimes receive strong, personalized support, counsel, and encouragement—a benefit corpora-

---

*Note to Readers: *Time* magazine reports that "dozens of American corporate executives have been calling the FBI to say they are worried that workers they have fired will come back to kill them . . . Agent John Douglas, the agency's top behavioral-science expert, advises that all such threats must be taken seriously." (*Time*, January 13, 1992, p. 9)

tions often fail to offer. At work, managers often feel that crisis will be controlled by someone else, that the shock and aftermath is better absorbed by an institutional shield. This notion is not quite "passing the buck" as much as it reflects the naive belief that the larger the organization, the greater the ability to withstand crisis. If that were the case, however, companies such as Chrysler, Exxon and Union Carbide would have better survived several corporate crises that were notoriously mismanaged.

LEARNING BY ERROR

We can learn from the mistakes that managers of many organizations have made. These people, who manage farm cooperatives, airlines, factories, retail operations, and hundreds of other concerns, are usually decent, hard-working, and highly skilled. Unfortunately, both technical and academic management training has failed to include holistic planning for crisis—and managing crisis fallout. Managers who have made mistakes in planning for and handling crises can now look back and offer sage advice. Their experiences are shared in the following pages.

DOES THE SIZE OF AN ORGANIZATION MATTER?

Let's say a crisis for a small jewelry store in Bangor, Maine, is triggered by a fire that destroys a showroom and most inventory. Looters steal items that were being repaired or held for special family occasions. Obviously, the complexity of response required for this crisis differs from the response demanded of Exxon in Alaska when its tanker dumped 11 million gallons of oil into the ocean.

In the Bangor case, the manager must coordinate details with insurance representative and customers. Managers of one jewelry store interviewed indicated they did not know how many insurance policies they had, or what insurer covered what—the building, the customers' goods, the store's inventory, and expensive tooling equipment. The Bangor newspaper is empathetic but nevertheless highlights the destruction prominently—this is the big story in Bangor for at least several days. Customers demand immediate and accurate answers to their questions. ("Where's my ring? It's a family heirloom! How much insurance do you have? Who's your attorney?") Despite the publicity, management trusts that normal operations will resume without a loss of goodwill within a relatively short time; it may relocate to a vacant store within days if possible. This crisis will be centered and controlled within the first week to ten days after the calamity.

In the case of the *Exxon Valdez*, however, almost $3 billion was spent on the cleanup while an international debate raged over the social responsibility that such multinational companies exercise. At the height of the *Valdez* incident, Exxon was in true chaos. Although company officials held twice-daily news conferences to release updates on their efforts to contain environmental damage, they simply did not realize the enormity of news coverage the story had received around the world.

Hundreds of environmentalists arrived in Alaska to try to save some of the fragile species threatened by oil in the ocean and on beaches. Exxon officials from the company's New York corporate office who flew to the site had little knowledge of Alaska, its laws, and elected officials.[7] The governor of Alaska conceded that he didn't know if he had the authority to direct Exxon to do *anything*.[8] And the Coast Guard, responsible for ensuring tanker compliance, lacked a sophisticated radio communications system in the area.

To make matters worse, evidence suggested that the captain of the tanker was intoxicated at the time of the accident and was not on the bridge. The captain had a history of alcohol-related problems, but Exxon's control system did not prevent him from again taking command of a huge tanker.

Exxon officials tried to cope with protests, frantic phone calls, and demands for access to records. A few of them even received death threats. Organized protests were staged outside Exxon-owned facilities around the world, and editorials chastised the company for the catastrophe.[9] On site in Alaska, matters were even worse. A few days after the ship first leaked oil, one official for Alyeska, a consortium of six companies (including Exxon) that controls the Trans-Alaska Pipeline, noted,

Source: Copyright *San Francisco Chronicle*. Reprinted by permission.

Exxon was widely criticized by editorial writers and cartoon artists for the damage caused by the March 1989 oil leak of its *Valdez* tanker. Thousands of customers cut up their credit cards and mailed them to Exxon headquarters to protest the way Exxon was managing the crisis.

The crowds are getting angrier and nastier. *Valdez* has become a black hole, sucking in every nut and screwball in the universe. Some of these clowns tried running our people off the road. I told our employees, 'Don't drive Alyeska's red Suburbans, drive your own cars.'[10]

When regulators demanded action, that was one thing. But the impact of individual consumers in demanding that management become environmentally responsible was not as easily measured. In addition to the thousands of Exxon customers who reportedly cut up their credit cards and returned them to Exxon, untold numbers of others simply stopped buying Exxon gasoline. Certainly the Valdez fiasco continues for Exxon today, with litigation still pending; residual negative public relations could last for decades. Exxon's situation was so overwhelming that traditional means of managerial response were simply not adequate.

It is clear that the burden of the disaster fell properly on Exxon, although the company was hardly alone in mismanaging the crisis. In the end, the company faced a no-win situation, because the environmental damage to one of America's most spectacular coastlines was so acute. In his detailed book In The Wake of the Exxon Valdez, one of Alaska's leading environmental experts, Art Davidson, concluded, "The billions of dollars that Exxon threw willy-nilly at the spill brought to mind a well-known scenario all the king's horses and all the king's men—and, above all, all the king's money—couldn't put Humpty together again." [11] Thus, Exxon paid in terms of image and capital: on October 9, 1991, Federal Judge H. Russel Holland finally accepted a plea bargain from Exxon; the oil company agreed to pay $1.03 billion in claims and charges for its actions. That agreement concluded the largest case by the government against a company in U.S. history.

Exxon went through a crisis that could not and would not subside in a week to ten days. Yet there are similarities in the cases of the Bangor jewelry store and Exxon. The management within both organizations should have (1) been prepared for crisis, (2) reviewed and rehearsed their options in advance, (3) developed a written implementation plan, and (4) identified communications channels that would have given them greater access to specific audiences quickly, before public confidence was eroded. Although they both cared about their reputation and profit, each failed to anticipate crisis and to plan for its containment.

WHY MANAGERS NEED CRISIS MANAGEMENT SKILLS

For those who think that the main lessons of crisis management are already learned, let's look at a few more trends and examples.

The Environmental Protection Agency (EPA) now offers a $10,000 bounty that leads to the conviction of those who violate Superfund statutes (Superfund is the statute that controls cleanup of hazardous wastes). Over the past three years, there has been a 170 percent increase in criminal prosecutions of environmental crimes.

Most of those convicted claim they had no idea they were about to be charged by the U.S. government and profiled as a violator in the news media. Tens of thousands of U.S. businesses are affected by Superfund regulations, although most of them may be unaware of that fact until it is too late.[12] And in a major study released in July 1991 by the consulting firm Arthur D. Little, some 74 percent of 1,000 persons surveyed said that executives should be held *personally* liable for their companies' environmental offenses. Those who were interviewed said that corporate environmental crimes are more serious than antitrust violations, insider trading, and violations that could cause worker injury. The annual celebration of Earth Day is now appropriately viewed as considerably more than a public relations stunt organized by a few activists. There is virtually no U.S. business that can deny that environmental matters now influence its budget, policy, and strategic marketing.

Sometimes it seems that past experience hasn't been given enough consideration. One would think that Burroughs Wellcome, one of the world's premiere pharmaceutical manufacturers, would have, given Johnson & Johnson's crisis with tainted Tylenol capsules, adequately prepared for the follow-through necessary in the event of product tampering. Yet despite pharmaceutical makers' public praise of Johnson & Johnson's crisis procedures, Burroughs found itself buried in criticism after two deaths in March 1991 related to tainted Sudafed capsules. The *Wall Street Journal* compared Johnson & Johnson and Burroughs and found Burroughs coming up short: "The company set up a toll-free number to answer questions, but never advertised it. It suggested in its first news release dated March 3 that customers return all Sudafed 12-hour capsules, but didn't back that up with widespread information on refunds or exchanges."[13]

One of the more interesting trends in crisis management was reported on by *ComputerWorld* Magazine (July 7, 1986). Executives at Lloyds Bank International were excited about the prospects of building a new headquarters next to the Thames River in London; they commissioned a study to determine the likelihood that a flood could damage a large computer room planned for the basement of the facility. The results of that analysis shocked senior management: actuarial experts told Lloyds that the greatest risk to the new facility was *not* flooding, but (given the location, visibility, and prominence of the firm) a terrorist bomb attack. If such a study had not been completed, the steps needed to prepare for such a crisis might never have been taken. Today, virtually any corporation that values its information and retrieval systems must consider the possibility that a natural or terrorist-inspired disaster could create havoc for operations. The existence of the Irish Republican Army, Basque ETA, Bader Meinhoff group, and an assortment of other extremist groups is potentially devastating for business and industry.

The following chapters discuss in more detail how management can minimize the damage that results from crisis. Specific steps that organizations can take to *avert* crisis are also highlighted. Information is provided on how any organization can assess its risk of crisis, where it is most vulnerable in terms of people and products, and how it can communicate its pro-active stance to a variety of parties.

WHAT HAVE WE LEARNED?

Spectacular failures—whether the chaos occurs at a Union Carbide plant in Bhopal, India, in a Wall Street boardroom, or in the White House—have taught us that crisis management requires planning. This book examines how many different organizations have coped with unexpected change. Some have fared comparatively well; others were sold or liquidated because they never were able to regain public esteem, generate enough new capital, or overcome the stigmas associated with their name. Here are some of the questions (and answers) presented in the rest of the book:

- *Why do some companies do better than others at containing crisis?* (Some proactively prepare for crisis by writing crisis management plans and rehearsing their response to problems well in advance. Others react in a vacuum of information and fail to contain the crisis.)

- *Which aspects of managerial science are most helpful in preparing for an inevitable crisis?* (Understanding the importance of public opinion in the marketplace is a good beginning. Equally relevant are public relations skills, understanding organizational behavior, and developing a sense of social responsibility.)

- *How can you test crisis skills you have developed on and off the job so they are ready to be used at the company you work for?* (A large number of corporations, particularly multinational groups, use role-playing scenario games as a crisis management tool. A hypothetical crisis is announced to a group of corporate executives, and for the next several hours, or longer, they are asked to react and manage a crisis. Throughout this scenario, new information is continually provided by the game organizers, along with assorted, realistic surprises and turns in events. Just weeks before Iraq invaded Kuwait in August 1990, managers at Shell Oil, for instance, used such a managerial tool to rehearse how their company would respond to war in the Middle East.)

- *What do those managers who have managed a crisis, and can discuss their responses, have to say about the predicaments they faced?* (They regret not having been exposed to crisis management when they were formally trained in management. Some crises help the careers of executives if their judgments and actions are proven correct. In many other cases, however, lessons in effective crisis management came much too late and produced a national embarrassment.)

- *How can a manager train a team that can cope well enough with crisis to minimize damage to the organization's future?* (Balance—in terms of background and professional skills—is a good beginning.)

- *Why is a crisis management plan (CMP) important? Why should students pursuing an MBA or other graduate degree, and managers in almost every field of endeavor, care about crisis management?* (A single crisis could alter your life and career. A CMP lets you test how you will treat people inside and outside your organization during moments of intense stress. It will challenge you to consider issues and individuals with whom you have had little contact. One day it could be the tool you use to save lives, protect assets, and retain or even enhance your company's image.)

It would be incorrect for the reader to assume that the managers and subordinates discussed in this book were somehow ignorant, myopic, or uncaring in confronting serious management crises. Over the past quarter-century, management has learned *much* from the disasters that have struck both large and small organizations around the world. Many people now in a decision-making capacity did not have formal training in the management sciences. Twenty years ago, formal management training programs still largely ignored the role of mass opinion and regulation. As a result of mistakes made by some of these people, we can learn how to cope under chaotic conditions in the future.

ENDNOTES

1. Ian I. Mitroff, "Crisis Management: Cutting Through the Confusion," *Sloan Management Review,* (Winter 1988): p. 17.
2. Matt Moffett and Laurie McGinley, "NASA, Once a Master of Publicity, Fumbles in Handling Shuttle Crisis," *Wall Street Journal,* December 14, 1986, p. B1.
3. John Holusha, "Exxon's Public-Relations Problem," *New York Times*, April 20, 1989, p. 1B.
4. Larry Light, "Killing a Rumor Before It Kills a Company," *Business Week,* December 24, 1990, p. 23.
5. Thomas Hales, M.D. et al, "Occupational Injuries Due to Violence," *Journal of Occupational Medicine* (June 1988): 483.
6. Diane Plummer, "Crisis Communication," paper presented to IABC London Conference, July 16, 1987, p. 1.
7. Art Davidson, *In the Wake of the Exxon Valdez* (San Francisco: Sierra Club Books, 1990), p. 58.
8. Ibid.
9. Ibid., p. 48.
10. Ibid.
11. Ibid., p. 297.
12. G. Glynn Rountree, "The Current Legal Climate," *Aerospace Industries Association Newsletter,* 3 (1990): p. 4.
13. Joanne Lipman, "Sudafed Maker Faulted for Failing to Follow Through After Recall," *Wall Street Journal,* March 11, 1991, p. B6.

1

The Rise of Public Opinion: Crises Are No Longer Private

Every newspaper when it reaches the reader is the result of a whole series of selections as to what items shall be printed, in what position they shall be printed, how much space each shall occupy, what emphasis they shall have. There are no objective standards here. It is in a combination of these elements that the power to create opinion resides. ❏

Walter Lippmann, in *Public Opinion* (1922)

C risis is nothing new to corporate America. But the very nature of crisis has changed as technology, the rise of formal public opinion, and the general literacy of the masses have developed since the eighteenth century. Indeed, the rise of public opinion in the twentieth century is significant prior to any in-depth discussion of crisis management. Public opinion and crisis management are inevitably linked; how an organization is viewed by the masses is a clear reflection of its value, the amount of respect it commands, and whether it can withstand short- or long-term damage.

Some managers have learned how to shape public opinion brilliantly and to use it to their advantage in crisis. Lee Iacocca of Chrysler Corporation is a notable example. When Chrysler was on the verge of bankruptcy, he told Congress that losing one of the "Big 3" U.S. automakers could trigger a collapse of the entire economy. Congress responded with the single largest loan guarantee program in modern history. Yet it has not always been easy for a CEO or prominent figure to nurture public opinion; certainly some of our greatest lessons come from the failure of others.

Although public opinion has always existed in every society, it has often been controlled or negated by censorship, military rule, or propaganda. The former Soviet bloc is an example. With the recent democratization of Eastern Europe, millions of people now find themselves exposed to a sophisticated, multimedia barrage. Cable television, electronic mail, information services, teleconferencing, demographic surveys, and opinion polls had been largely unknown to them. When public opinion was measured in early plebiscites in any of these countries, it was often found to run contrary to the desires of the ruling authorities. Thus, whenever despots wanted to change public opinion, they either tried to change it through government propaganda or, if that failed, by mass annihilation. The inability of world leaders such as Joseph Stalin, Mao Tse Tung, and Idi Amin to change public opinion provoked these heads of state into purging malcontents in the former Soviet Union, China, and Uganda, respectively.

Easy access to information, boosted by modern communication technology, has changed how we view world leaders and how we learn about catastrophes. Today, Cable News Network (CNN), which reaches 52 countries twenty-four hours a day, gives up-to-the-minute information on the latest airplane hijacking, coup d'état, or mass murder. In earlier centuries, when plagues swept across Europe and killed millions, government officials had no way to communicate with the masses about these diseases. Today, a single case of cholera may rate a front-page headline in a community; an inoculation program benefitting thousands can begin the very next day.

In February 1991, when ground war broke out between Iraq and the United States and her allies, the lingering eight-month crisis took on sharp new significance for government officials, soldiers, families, and other parties. Before February, the deployment of troops was viewed by many as a modest excursion to protect the oil interests of the United States. Now, with the death of soldiers, networks sought to broadcast virtually every move by either side. News conferences by both Iraqi and U.S. military leaders contradicted statements, corrected (or perpetuated) falsehoods, and set up rounds of instant strategic analysis. SCUD missiles fired against Israel or Saudi Arabia were public knowledge within seconds of being launched.

THE DEVELOPMENT OF MODERN PUBLIC OPINION

Of course, public opinion has not always been influenced by CNN, exit polls, telephone surveys, and "sound bites." A good case in point is the twenty-sixth U.S. president, Theodore Roosevelt. Historian Edmund Morris notes that Roosevelt became both the most admired and despised man in the country—simultaneously—due to his fiery handling of crises faced early in his career as New York City police commissioner and later as the nation's chief executive.[1] As a result, the presidency was transformed from an office largely beyond the comprehension of most individuals into the nation's center for problem solving .[2]

Most people, in fact, did not even know what the president looked like or what policies he espoused until the mass media began to demystify the man and his job. Roosevelt matured as a president as the very news media that showcased his energy and his politics also matured. Opinion leaders, industrialists, and others who challenged the president (including developers who did not want Roosevelt

Source: From *The American Presidency in Political Cartoons,* edited by Thomas C. Blaisdell, Jr., and Peter Selz. Published by Peregrine Smith Inc., 1976. Used with permission.

This cartoon, "A Nauseating Job, But It Must Be Done" (artist unknown), originally appeared in The *Saturday Globe* in 1905. It sarcastically depicts President Teddy Roosevelt inspecting the deplorable conditions at Chicago's meat-packing houses, news of which first surfaced from muckraking journalism by Lincoln Steffens.

to preserve major sections of the western United States for national parks) faced a popular president and an institution that was no longer obscure or beyond their comprehension.

The role of the mass media in reporting national affairs, including the activities of major corporations and their owners, helped to propel the careers of both presidents and industrialists, including names now synonymous with successful businesses, such as Du Pont, Kellogg, Edison, Ford, and Hershey.

In the years following the presidency of Theodore Roosevelt, the nation's population swelled with massive immigration, mostly from Europe. Laws began to reflect more cultural and ethnic diversity, and corporations became interstate powers. Management emerged as an academic discipline.

Now universities began to teach courses in business and finance; a variety of rules, norms, and theories evolved. By the mid 1920s, with the proliferation of monopolies and national chain stores and the arrival of radio networks, Americans had become less separated by distance and ethnic backgrounds. It seemed that the United States could become a civilization making its own contributions to industry, literature, and other arts. Washington, D.C. became the formal center for the nation's business and for "public opinion." Now, no one—politician, executive, entertainer—could ignore the fact that the masses were linked by a common language, court system, and press.

PUBLIC RELATIONS IS BORN

In the seminal work on public relations published in 1923, Edward L. Bernays asserted that corporations could no longer deny the existence of public opinion. He argued that the responsibility of corporations was to educate employees, stockholders, and the masses, and also to understand the *pulse* of these groups and to be prepared for crisis and public recrimination.

Bernays's book, *Crystallizing Public Opinion,* served as the first guidebook for managers who witnessed these considerable societal changes. The book tells managers that the lack of adequate preparation for crisis is a recipe for disorder. In the years to follow, Bernays served many of the world's leading corporations as a paid strategist in both proactive and reactive communications. Bernays was listed in 1990 by *Life* magazine as one of the most influential Americans of the twentieth century. He continues to lecture and counsel clients today—in his hundredth year of life.

The era when Bernays and his contemporaries flourished as commentators on the role of public opinion also was a period of extraordinary growth in the federal government. In 1911, in a landmark decision, the U.S. Supreme Court asserted that the public interest would be best served by breaking up Standard Oil, the largest oil enterprise ever created. In the following years, similar decisions affecting the operations of large industries—thrift institutions, railroads, telecommunications—were issued by courts throughout the country. The companies involved in the break-up of monopolies were forced to consider how the press would report such news to the public. If the coverage was favorable, the reaction might be minimal, or it could even result in a tremendous increase in stock value. If unfavorable, however, the product could lose its market share, costing the firm millions of dollars.

The government also became concerned with ensuring the rights and safety of individuals. To ensure compliance with court rulings both at the federal and state level, new government agencies were launched to protect the public interest—in weights and measures, in prescription drug quality, in establishing minimum standards for construction of homes and commercial buildings, and for the regulation of publicly owned corporations.

With increased power concentrated in Washington and various agencies, and with public opinion now galvanized by a "penny press" that brought news of corporations and politicians to the masses for relatively little money, major companies hired "press officers" to cultivate positive coverage in leading magazines and newspapers.

Ivy Lee, of Georgia, became one of the first professional public relations strategists. In 1906 he designed a successful strategy to turn public opinion against striking miners. When scandals erupted over concentrated power and wealth in the nation's railroad system, he successfully urged major operators to begin scholarship and welfare programs in the communities where they operated. Another earlier pioneer who understood the value of positive public opinion was AT&T vice president Arthur Page, who urged the company to underwrite film programs for schools and colleges and distribute telephone company subcontractors more evenly to poorer communities and lower-income vendors. And he successfully urged AT&T to let large numbers of people purchase stock in the company.

Companies began spending considerable sums to publish annual reports that explained their operations, goals, and financial status. Occasionally, news conferences and "briefings" were held to announce new products or acquisitions. The importance of the news media and of reporters could no longer be ignored.

CRISIS AND THE MESSENGER: THE ROLE OF REPORTERS

Concurrent with the growth of corporate public relations, two other significant trends also emerged during this era: the increasingly important role played by reporters, and the emergence of regulatory control at all levels.

Muckraking—the process in which reporters serve as self-appointed societal advocates—reached its peak in the early 1900s. One dedicated muckraker, Lincoln Steffens, directly attacked widespread corruption in Minneapolis and printed portions of notebooks kept by city hall "swindlers" who accepted bribes for favors. Steffens's colleagues in other cities detailed the horrible conditions in meat-packing houses throughout the North and the threat to public health from the lack of sanitary regulations. By 1903, business and industry found itself increasingly incapable of defending many organizational policies, given the persuasive and exhaustive reports appearing in such journals as the *New York Times*, *Colliers*, and *McClure's*, all of which boasted large circulations.

Now the term *consumer* began to enter public discussion. Editorials demanded change in various industries. Doctors and scientists were often interviewed and provided clinical perspectives to business stories. In many cases, public indignation was so strong that federal intervention was necessary to clean up several shady industries, including oil, natural gas, rental housing and pharmaceuticals.[3]

Steffens's most famous and lasting work, *The Shame of the Cities* (1904), required that he personally confront two members of the mob to verify the authenticity of his data. On several occasions between 1904 and 1910, his life was threatened by these gangsters. Because of such bravery, Steffens now became a revered figure. Many public individuals would not meet with him or agree to an interview for fear that their statements would lead to devastatingly negative press. In fact, President Theodore Roosevelt, who had earlier encouraged reporters to ferret out and expose corruption, was now concerned that "muckrakers" such as Steffens were becoming even more powerful than the government itself. Although the president and Steffens were close friends (and met frequently at their barber), Roosevelt increasingly distanced himself from reporters for fear that they might criticize his policies.

Even Roosevelt, himself a former reporter, could not escape the significant trend underway in the new century—the emergence of a fierce, strong, editorially independent press. Companies and politicians found it increasingly difficult to escape the intense scrutiny of reporters, and crisis management, (although the term was not yet coined) was very much on the minds of executives and local and federal officials. Making other important revelations about corruption at New York's Tammany Hall, price fixing by several railroads, and improper union activities, the news media had emerged as a crusading vehicle of the public interest, often as effective as the ballot box itself. (In later years, some would claim it had become *more* potent.)

Certainly by the time of the Great Depression in 1929, the rise of public opinion as a viable force in corporate America was well established. Surveys were routinely used to gauge public opinion on issues of the day. Editorial comment, usually reserved for the editorial page, was now often printed on the first page alongside the news. Aggressive publishers such as William Randolph Hearst and Joseph Pulitzer now freely integrated their political prejudices into their editorial product. A legion of distinguished historians of journalism have suggested that the Spanish-American War, for instance, was largely fought because major U.S. publishers such as Hearst and Pulitzer found new readers, and new power, by pursuing crisis headlines. David Halberstam, in his exhaustive media analysis *The Powers That Be*, notes,

> The Spanish-American War, rich as it was in the jingoism of the era, was exactly what Hearst and Pulitzer loved, and they moved in what seemed like battalion strength, they filled gunboats with reporters, photographers, illustrators (when Frederick Remington, the great artist, had complained that there was too little action, Hearst had wired back that *he* would furnish the war, and Remington would furnish the pictures). They loved a story like this, rich as it was with blood and flag. Their coverage was full, lavish and properly gory.[4]

Had the press begun to *make* events, as well as *report* them?

MODERN HISTORY AND CRISIS

The twentieth century offers us many events for reflecting on the meaning of crisis management. These include two world wars and hundreds of smaller conflicts and regional battles; the assassinations of many world leaders, including U.S. president John F. Kennedy, Egyptian president Anwar Sadat, and Martin Luther King, Jr.; the slaughter of students at Kent State, Tiananmen Square, and elsewhere; and certainly hundreds of individual disasters that wreaked havoc on public corporations, small communities, island nations, and space agencies alike.

The Great War

The first truly great calamity of our century, World War I, was called The Great War because the scope of that crisis was so immense that it still defies explanation nearly eighty years later. Eight million people lost their lives during the four years of active fighting.[5] What makes World War I such an intriguing prologue for our discussion of modern crisis management is that the size of the event was simply staggering—challenging people who lacked the benefits of modern technology and communication to grapple with an endless string of crises. The first multifront, massive war in human history was certainly not limited to heads of state and their subordinates.

The mass media, especially the daily newspapers, reported up-to-date news of this widening entanglement, including the introduction of lethal chemical warfare, the new destructive force of machine guns (capable of causing 60,000 casualties on a single day) and modern propaganda systems used to demoralize enemy soldiers and their families.

Individuals were mobilized as a citizenry; a sense of group consciousness was developed by political leaders, the press, community leaders, and others. Newspaper headlines of the day did not mince words, such as this offering from a London daily:[6]

WHAT CAN I DO?
How the Civilian May Help in This Crisis:
Be cheerful.
Write encouragingly to friends at the front.
Don't repeat foolish gossip.
Don't listen to idle rumors.

In the end, World War I was victorious for the Allies not only because of their military prowess, but, also, as many historians have argued, because of their shrewdness and skill in giving citizens a sense of responsibility and preparedness. (One of the most popular posters of the Great War depicted a worried father of the future being asked by his children "Daddy, what did *you* do in The Great War?")

Public opinion, of course, is a curious thing—it can be mobilized for the good of society, but it can also generate hate. The press and public opinion have supported great leaders as well as violent demagogues in the twentieth century.

Winston Churchill at the Helm

Few individuals have faced so many personal and professional crises concurrently than British Prime Minister Winston Churchill; even fewer have been so able to rebound from adversity, ready to capture the respect and admiration of even ardent opponents at home and abroad. Certainly Churchill was no quitter:

> Pursued by creditors—at one point he had to put his home up for sale—he remained solvent only by writing an extraordinary number of books and magazine articles. He was disowned by his own party, dismissed by the BBC and Fleet Street and the social and political establishments as a warmonger, and twice nearly lost his seat in Parliament. Churchill stood almost alone against Nazi aggression and the British and French pusillanimous policy of appeasement. Despite his personal and political troubles, Churchill managed to assemble a vast, underground intelligence network—both within the British government and on the Continent—which provided him with more complete and accurate information on Germany's rearmament than the government was able to gather.[7]

Churchill also wrote a brilliant five-volume series on modern history, called *The World Crisis.* His cool head and managerial skill kept Churchill at the helm when the storm broke out in deadly earnest. Allied leaders found that World War II and its management were marked by highly developed technology, theory, and implementation.

John F. Kennedy: An Amalgam of Intelligence and Rhetoric

Managers who have failed at successfully managing a crisis tend to remember and apply the painful lessons during their next encounter. President Kennedy is a notable example. The young president suffered his greatest public embarrassment in 1961—the miserably orchestrated and ill-fated invasion of Cuba at the Bay of Pigs served as the low point in his presidency. He later noted that he had delegated too much, trusted too much, and lacked focus in assessing and making decisions.

Kennedy had the chance to apply this knowledge, gained from failure, a year later. In the Cuban missile crisis, evidence indicated that a series of nuclear warheads were being stored 90 miles off the coast of Florida. Professor Graham Allison of Harvard notes that this and similar crises are shaped by assumptions, evidence and options. Kennedy's ability to focus was central to his skillful handling of this particular crisis. The president contemplated all the options suggested by his advisers, and after thoughtful reflection his decisions were shaped by one principal factor: he had to convince Soviet premier Nikita Khrushchev that *only* the withdrawal of Soviet missiles from Cuba could prevent a potential Armageddon.[8]

Few managers and leaders in our lifetime ever handle such dangerous decisions as those confronted by the crisis management team that Kennedy assembled. Allison argues,

> Never before had there been such a high probability that so many lives would end suddenly. Had war come, it could have meant the death of 100 million Americans, more than 100 million Russians, as well as millions of Europeans. Beside it, the natural calamities and inhumanities of earlier history would have faded into insignificance.[9]

The Cuban missile crisis was administered fiercely by the nation's CEO—the crisis came close to consuming his every waking minute. Kennedy had matured in his ability to cope with crisis. Every president, like every manager in industry, tends to see his decision-making skills mature during his tenure in office. Noted historian Theodore H. White reflects on Kennedy's handling of this crisis and provides a wonderful analogy for every manager who aspires to cope well under stress:

> Like all presidents, he was groping. They all do as they try to reach for controls of the levers and pedals in their first few months—as a buyer gingerly tests the brakes and gas pedals of the new car he has driven off from the dealer's. Kennedy, however, was groping not only for control of unfamiliar instruments; he was pushing out into an unknown stream, guiding the power around the bend into a new country, new times, and the unexplored landscape of the 1960's.... After the instant disaster of the Bay of Pigs and the taut confrontation with the Russians on access to Berlin, by his first autumn in office he had brought his instruments well in hand and, then, gradually, moved to the mastery of the missile crisis and the test-ban treaty.[10]

When managers remain focused on their primary objective—solving a crisis in a timely fashion and working skillfully to help others (including opponents) avoid public embarrassment, the chance of resolving the crisis can be significantly enhanced. Kennedy was careful not to box in the Soviets to the point where an ultimatum would prompt a decision on mass annihilation; rather, he used tools of business communication—memos, telephone messages, and meetings—to help the Soviet leaders see that the only feasible solution was to remove nuclear warheads and to send them back to the Soviet Union. Meanwhile, the press opened up the crisis to public opinion.

COLLISION COURSE: THE INTEGRITY OF THE PRESS AND THE REPUTATION OF MANAGERS

In a democratic society, the press plays an especially important role both in opening up crises for examination and resolving them. In one respect, the press serves as the vanguard of the public trust. The function of news reporting, in newspapers and the electronic media, is to document decisions and events of wide public interest. This ranges from policy development in Washington to corporate takeovers to revolutions in distant lands. But reporters are often hampered by a variety of factors. In many cases, the sources of news—politicians, business leaders, and others—seek to put the best "spin" or angle on every story; they work to avoid criticism or any issue that could show them, or their organization, in a negative light.

A reporter trained in journalism learns how to balance that bias with equity; he or she will seek out other sources of opinion for a fair presentation on the issue. A principal precept of U.S. schools of journalism is that you should be able to read any story in a newspaper, or listen to a news broadcast in its entirety, and *not* know the personal opinion of the reporter by the time you conclude the story.

When a reporter or editor does wish to express his or her opinion on an issue, the editorial page serves as a robust sounding board of ideas. Here the editorial staff can question the motives of people in the news. They may print a cartoon that satirizes prominent individuals in a crisis or controversy. Or they may print letters-to-the-editor from readers who disagree with various opinions printed in recent days or who wish to make contrasting statements.

During a crisis, people are even more hesitant to speak with reporters than they were before a problem surfaced. They may feel threatened by the barrage of questions they will be asked when they may have few answers. They may be concerned that if they make mistakes they will be roundly criticized by the public and special interests. They may fear litigation. Or they may be worried that in the heat of chaos they could show their anger or frustration in public.

When they don't speak to reporters, managers block the flow of information. With deadlines approaching, reporters are faced with essentially two choices; they can drop the story altogether (which is highly unlikely) or they can proceed with the story, identifying and quoting *alternative* sources of information. The problem, of course, is that the "experts" used may have little knowledge about the actual events being discussed, or may criticize the central party's responsiveness. Only *one* side of the story may reach the mass media.

So it is important that executives learn that the news media are not the enemy. Reporters are not trained to "hunt" their subjects and expose them to humiliation, and the news industry is not in the hands of a concentrated few who seek to destroy companies or reputations. There are sloppy reporters, and not all journalism is balanced, but most reporters are ethical and thorough in their reporting. They work with the material in front of them. They rely on sources who are willing to speak. They thrive on a multitude of ideas and varying opinions. In doing so, the media helps society evaluate and debate the crucial issues of the day.

It is not accidental that some of the twentieth century leaders who have best weathered crises had backgrounds as competent communicators. Churchill was a reporter before he was a statesman; he became one of the most prolific writers of the twentieth century. Kennedy also served as a newspaper reporter before serving in Congress; he wrote two books, one of which (*Profiles in Courage*, 1956) won the Pulitzer Prize. Communication involves listening, speaking, writing, and reading; the most effective and efficient communicators are adept at all four skills.

The Reporter at the Center of Crisis: Edward R. Murrow

The most celebrated broadcast journalist of the twentieth century, Edward R. Murrow, championed the use of radio for news and commentary while Great Britain was under siege in World War II. As a result of Murrow's skillful reporting, which influenced not only the U.S. people but lawmakers and diplomats as well, the reporter became a confidant of President Franklin D. Roosevelt and Churchill. In fact, Edward and Janet Murrow dined with Franklin and Eleanor Roosevelt on the evening of the Japanese attack on Pearl Harbor, December 7, 1941.[11]

Even before Pearl Harbor, Murrow openly pleaded with the U.S. people to come to the aid of England; he worked feverishly to remind his listeners that Western civilization, not merely Great Britain, was faced with a grave crisis.

Murrow's nightly newscasts from the rooftops and underground shelters of London cannot be compared to the terse, impersonal method used today to report military crises or disasters. Murrow's popularity with millions of listeners, and the respect that he earned from his peers, was primarily based on two attributes. First, his use of language was so personal, so vivid, that listeners thousands of miles away felt that they were sharing the threats, the bombings, the devastation—and the occasional laugh—with Murrow. Second, Murrow never pretended to be distanced from the nature of the crisis. He did not hide his subjectivity; instead he aggressively worked to convince the U.S. people that the crisis that had befallen Great Britain would soon fully engulf the United States on its own soil unless intervention was swift and complete. (Fifty years later, CNN reporter Peter Arnett used the same approach in reporting from the rooftops of Baghdad during the 1990–91 Gulf War. In fact, he was compared to Murrow by almost every U.S. major news organization.)

Reporters throughout World War II faced an ethical and professional dilemma. Should they report the news objectively, or should they "spice" the news with their own opinions in addition to information provided by government agencies such as the U.S. Office of War Information? Murrow routinely praised Churchill and Roosevelt for their leadership in the midst of chaos. He expressed open dismay at pacifists such as industrialist Joseph P. Kennedy, Sr., and others who advocated nonintervention in European affairs.

After Pearl Harbor, as the inevitability of war was recognized by all, reporters were subject to arrest if they printed classified military information. Almost all print reports and broadcast scripts were censored by defense officers. Murrow was one of several distinguished reporters from World War II who excelled at their craft despite this censorship and later became important figures in cases of crisis management.

In an era in which patriotism ran high, Senator Joseph McCarthy of Wisconsin had built a career on breeding national paranoia against Communists; his Senate hearings were classic cases of witch-hunting at its worst. The Army hearings in 1954 lasted 36 days and occupied television for 187 hours. This man single-handedly created a series of crises for government employees and many others. One mention in a McCarthy-inspired report or hearing could lead to public humiliation and professional blacklisting.

CBS newsman Edward R. Murrow is shown in March 1954, shortly after he publicly challenged Senator Joseph McCarthy for his witch-hunting tactics in connection with the Army-McCarthy hearings.

On March 8, 1954, Edward R. Murrow became the first nationally respected figure to publicly challenge Senator McCarthy. His decision to do so created the prospect of a crisis for several parties: for himself (McCarthy was considered a hero by millions for having "exposed" Communists in positions of responsibility); for the show's sponsor, Alcoa Aluminum; and for CBS and its chairman William S. Paley.

Murrow's brilliant half-hour documentary painted the senator as a demagogue; Murrow used Senator McCarthy's own recorded statements in the broadcast to seriously damage his public credibility. Murrow became the first broadcast journalist of the twentieth century to test the power of television for a cause beyond passive news, boxing, game shows, and comedy. In doing so, he helped launch the independence of the broadcast press and created a prototype for documentaries. Certainly his caustic attack during that broadcast raised an immediate credibility crisis for Senator McCarthy:

> The actions of the Junior Senator from Wisconsin have caused alarm and dismay amongst our allies abroad and given considerable comfort to our enemies. And whose fault is that? Not really his. He didn't *create* this situation of fear, he merely *exploited* it; and rather successfully.[12]

CBS chairman Paley supported Murrow and his broadcast, although he was reportedly rattled by the forceful words Murrow chose for a news broadcast. Despite some outcry that no one person should have the power to criticize others in such an unedited fashion on the national airwaves, common sense prevailed. In the following days, over 100,000 supportive letters and phone calls flooded CBS and Congress. Alcoa Aluminum received only a few complaints; company managers' fears of a boycott for its products never materialized. The *New York Times* praised Murrow for "crusading journalism of high responsibility and genuine courage."[13]

McCarthy faced the biggest crisis of his political career, and he failed. Instead of developing a crisis strategy focusing on issues, he chose to personally attack Murrow as a traitor. Few agreed with that assessment; Murrow was an icon for most Americans due to his superb reporting skills during World War II—people remembered him on London rooftops dodging German bombs, and they admired both his intellect and honor.

Invited by Murrow and CBS to tape a response, McCarthy had not taken the time to learn the basics of television: he did not smile, his makeup melted under the hot lights, and his body nervously twitched throughout his taped rebuttal. Suddenly, reporters who had previously flocked to him for interviews were not interested; major trade associations that had begged for convention appearances sought alternative speakers; editorials, letters to editors, and general press coverage now questioned the senator's motives.

McCarthy died three years later, broke and an alcoholic. Obituaries treated him more as an anomaly rather than one of the towering political figures of the decade. Murrow, on the other hand, had been since 1954 host of "See It Now," a weekly news program that influenced the creation of CBS's "60 Minutes" more than two decades later. He had continued daily radio broadcasts and also covered the Korean war for radio and television.

Crises occasionally provide a showcase for new talent to shine; they also occasionally provide a forum for individuals who do not understand crisis to write their own professional epitaphs, as with McCarthy. He had managed to create a crisis for others, yet when he was personally challenged, he was incapable of managing one.

The growing sophistication and independence of the U.S. press developed and changed the nation and its government. These two powers in our society would shape the content and conscience of public policy for the rest of the century.

THE DAWN OF REGULATION AND ORGANIZED PROTESTS

At the beginning of the century, even after the passage of the Sherman Antitrust Act (1890), U.S. business was mostly unregulated. Indeed, with the exception of a handful of agencies regulating the national distribution of some prescription products and lending practices, few organizations had broad jurisdictional powers governing industry. For the most part, only scandalous press exposés prompted public outcry.

From 1909 to 1930, the federal government assumed a unique character that it maintains to this day—it has an interest in, if not regulatory control over, many aspects of U.S. industry: interstate trade, communications, brokerage, food, manufacturing, pharmaceuticals, aviation, and others. The alphabet soup of agencies and their precursors grew in influence in the following years. USDA, FAA, OSHA, FDA, HUD, FCC, and others—all became familiar aspects of life in a modern society.

By the 1960s, the United States had witnessed a new phenomenon—the emergence of organized, sophisticated mass protest. The influence of mass media, especially television news and documentaries, in shaping not only public opinion but also policy at the state and federal levels, was unprecedented. Civil rights groups protested publicly to draw attention to inequitable treatment, and college students rallied on campuses to argue—sometimes militantly—that the Vietnam War was both illegal and illogical. Again, public opinion was not changed *solely* because of these protests, but it was certainly shaped by the steady stream of messages and pictures of protesters willing to be arrested for demonstrating their outrage.

By the early 1970s, corporate America could no longer ignore mass public opinion. A number of major corporations created "public affairs" departments designed to link corporate goals with the good of society. The corporate practices of contributing portions of income to charities, sponsoring science fairs in high schools, contributing computers to elementary schools, and thousands of other initiatives were aimed at eliminating the impression that the business of America was *solely* business—ideally, it was also the good of the community. A secondary factor in this new spirit of cooperation by business and industry was the evolution of mass protest. Demonstrations, boycotts, and protests—all took on a new flavor when the mass media began reporting, with horrifying detail and clarity, cases of air and water pollution, substandard construction, or the inhumane treatment of animals used for food and cosmetics.

Damages and fees assessed by the courts in the wake of such allegations often hampered corporate profits, and consumer boycotts became commonplace in the United States. Companies such as Nestlé, Nabisco, Starkist, Citibank, and others have all been targets of orchestrated, well-financed boycotts over the past thirty years from a variety of special interest groups, including environmentalists and abortion rights activists. For the managers of these corporations, what typically began as a modest public outcry later became a major crisis.

Such developments raise an important question: Why have some corporations and institutions responded well to new pressures added by citizen activism, while others have ignored—at great loss, both in terms of actual dollars and a tarnished public relations image—the evolution of this societal change?

THE PROACTIVE COMPANY, THE REACTIVE MANAGER

In several recent best-sellers, prominent business analysts have asserted that those companies that successfully attract and keep top-caliber talent and introduce innovative, successful products to the marketplace all tend to share some of the same qualities that we as individuals look for in colleagues and friends—respectability and reliability. But even in the most orderly and peaceful of environments, crisis can create havoc for individuals and companies. In his best seller, *It's Not My Department!* Peter Glen observes,

Most people don't get motivated until they get into a crisis. Some stop smoking when their doctor tells them they've got three months to live. Madeline Pflaumbaum started Mothers Against Drunk Driving after her daughter was killed by a drunk driver. Rick Hansen pushed his wheelchair forty thousand miles around the world after he was paralyzed from the waist down in an accident. People stop having unsafe sex or using dirty needles when someone they know dies of AIDS. Greg Louganis dove to win gold medals right after he cracked his skull on the diving board.

Nike's people got motivated after success made them smug and they started repeating themselves. Reebok suddenly pounded them out of the lead. Nike woke up and started fighting, invented the slogan "JUST DO IT," and recaptured first place.[14]

Proactive companies—those which continually assess public sentiment by way of marketing campaigns, do their homework, and rehearse for trouble—will be more adequately equipped when crises occur.

The essential message of Thomas J. Peters' *In Search of Excellence: Lessons from America's Best-Run Companies* (1982) and similar books is that companies with vision excel; short-sighted ones stagnate and lose direction in the marketplace. No company can effectively prepare for every type of accident or calamity. But there are basic skills and principles that we *can* use, and *must* integrate into our management science, if our organizations are to flourish in today's increasingly competitive global marketplace.

CASE STUDY: TALK ABOUT FIREWORKS!

One of the nation's largest and most respected fireworks manufacturers and distributors is Grucci, Inc., a $4-million-a-year company located on Long Island, New York. Since 1929 the Grucci family has produced custom-made fireworks displays for shows that have brightened skies in almost every major city of the world, including the 1980 Lake Placid, New York Olympic Games.

On November 26, 1983, a major explosion ripped through the Gruccis' plant, killing the oldest son in the family and his cousin. Twenty-eight other people were seriously injured. The plant was destroyed, and suburban neighborhood homes located hundreds of yards away were seriously damaged. By almost any standard, the plant was a "sleeper" facility—it had quietly coexisted for years in the neighborhood without arousing concern by residents about their safety.

Now the plant explosion had changed the dynamics of Grucci's future as well as its relationship with neighbors, city and state officials, customers, and the press. As a family-owned company, serious questions were debated by members of the family regarding whether the company should dissolve or rebuild. Yet of more immediate concern were the complex issues of crisis management that evolved.

Let's assume you are vice president of operations for Grucci. It is the day after the explosion, and company owner Felix Grucci, Sr., has asked that you prepare a comprehensive plan of crisis management. Address in detail what steps the company should take, and what additional resources may be necessary given this initial list of problems now piled on your desk:

1. Calls from the *New York Times, Newsday, Daily News, Good Morning America!* and most other major news media, seeking interviews with a company spokesperson. The reporters have left messages stating that if you will not speak, they will find someone who will—and they cannot be responsible if the story is "not balanced" due to your lack of response.

2. An official from the New York State Department of Public Safety has called and asked for a meeting in the next twenty-four hours to review the status of permits Grucci has for the plants and to begin a comprehensive investigation into the cause of the explosion.

3. Two attorneys representing area homeowners have called to seek information for a filing they are preparing against the firm for structural damage caused to their homes. You have heard from other sources that a score of other attorneys representing other concerns are in the preliminary stages of filing similar complaints.

4. Twelve corporate and organizational customers have called and inquired as to the status of their orders. They are unaware of the scope of the damage, have paid their deposits, and are expecting a complete fireworks display for their upcoming programs.

5. A neighborhood association has quickly galvanized and is calling for a protest in front of the leveled plant in three days. They want assurances from Grucci that the company will not rebuild on that site out of concerns for their future well-being.

The magnitude of these tasks is considerable. Even though your exposure to the topic of crisis management may be minimal at this point (as it unfortunately is for most managers), let's test your ability to identify just some of the issues that a manager at Grucci would need to consider in such a crisis. On a piece of paper, list some of the issues that Grucci must confront in order to take control of this situation. A good way to begin is to consider the various audiences that Grucci may need to communicate with, including customers, both current and prospective; regulators, both state and federal; news media; and neighbors of the manufacturing facility. ❑

ENDNOTES

1. Edmund Morris, *The Rise and Fall of Theodore Roosevelt* (New York: Ballantine, 1979), p. 497.
2. Ibid., p. 503.
3. John Tebbe, *The Media in America* (New York: Crowell, 1974), p. 288.

4. David Halberstam, *The Powers That Be* (New York: Knopf, 1979), p. 209.

5. Paul Fussell, *The Great War and Modern Memory* (London: Oxford University Press, 1975), p. 8.

6. Ibid., p. 17.

7. William Manchester, *The Last Lion: William Spencer Churchill Alone, 1932–1940* (Boston: Little, Brown, 1988), inside cover.

8. Graham T. Allison, *Essence of Decision: Explaining the Cuban Missile Crisis* (Boston: Little, Brown, 1971), p. 247.

9. Ibid., p. 1.

10. Theodore H. White, *In Search of History: A Personal Adventure* (New York: Harper & Row, 1978), p. 496.

11. A. M. Sperber, *Murrow: His Life and Times* (New York: Freundlich Books, 1986), p. 210.

12. Ibid.

13. Ibid., p. 438.

14. Peter Glen, *It's Not My Department* (New York: Morrow, 1990), p. 26.

2

Chaos and Management

Adolph Coors Co. last week inadvertently spilled at least 150,000 gallons of beer in Clear Creek, Colorado, killing at least 17,000 fish, Colorado officials said.

The spill, which occurred early in the week, wasn't investigated by state wildlife officials until Thursday, making an accurate count of dead fish difficult. State officials said the company faces fines of as much as $10 per dead fish plus fines of as much as $50,000 for violating water standards for five days. ❏

The *Wall Street Journal*, May 13, 1991

Crisis is no stranger to large organizations, and almost every organization should design a crisis management plan (CMP) that can be applied on a moment's notice. (In Chapter 8, the specific components of a CMP are discussed in detail.) Examine this roster of major crises since 1983 and consider for a moment the impact on organizations, consumers, and the news media:

- Perrier Water's benzene incident leads to product recall (1990)
- Strike by Hormel workers; razor blades found in some products (1985)
- Bombing of IBM office in Purchase, New York (1984)
- A. H. Robins files for Chapter 11 amidst claims that its Dalkon IUD caused miscarriages and deaths (1985)
- Walkway of Hyatt Regency Hotel in Kansas City collapses (1985)
- False rumors that Procter and Gamble's logo reflects Satan-worshipping management (1986)
- Audi vehicles accelerate without explanation (1987)
- DuPont Hotel fire in Puerto Rico leaves ninety-five dead (1986)
- 10,000 cubic meters of contaminated water enters the Rhine River due to accident at Sandoz Chemical plant (1987)
- Dean Witter stockbroker charged with bilking investors of $2.6 million (1989)
- Employee of ESL (Sunnyvale, California) kills seven, injures five in office shooting (1988)
- Morton Thiokol struggles to explain company's role in NASA's *Challenger* disaster (1986)
- Massive oil spill from the *Exxon Valdez* along coast of Alaska (1989)
- Texaco slapped with a $10.5-billion judgment in court battle with Pennzoil (1987)
- Hitachi officials indicted for stealing trade secrets from IBM (1988)
- Union Carbide disaster at Bhopal, India, kills over 2,000 (1984)
- Walkout of 6,300 Greyhound bus drivers (1990)
- Arrest of Michael Milken and the bankruptcy of Drexel Burnham Lambert (1990)
- Explosion of Pan Am Flight 103 over Lockerbie, Scotland, caused by terrorist bomb (1988)
- The federal takeover of Charles Keating's Lincoln Savings and Loan (1990)
- Brinks is robbed of 3.5 tons of bullion gold at Heathrow Airport (1983)
- Tylenol pills are poisoned, resulting in seven deaths (1982)
- Tampon makers Johnson & Johnson, Kimberly-Clark, Procter & Gamble, and others face a toxic shock syndrome crisis (1985)
- MGM Hotel fire in Las Vegas (1980)

- The verdict in the Rodney King-LAPD trial triggers violent protests resulting in the deaths of more than fifty people and more than one billion dollars in damage to Los Angeles businesses (1992)

- Belgium's Heizel Stadium soccer riots kill thirty-nine, wound four hundred fifty spectators (1985)

- Bank of Boston is accused of money laundering, complicity with organized crime (1985)

- Bank of America unexpectedly closes one hundred thirty-two branches employing 2,200 people in ninety California communities (1984)

- Twenty-four customers of Luby's Cafeteria in Killeen, Texas, are shot to death during a lunch-hour massacre (1991)

- Dow Corning targeted in FDA breast implant probe (1992)

- Eleven adults and children perish in fire in attempt to evict members of radical group MOVE at its Philadelphia headquarters (1985)

- At least 150,000 people die in cyclones and floods in Bangladesh (1991)

- Thousands are estimated to have been killed or injured in explosion at Soviet Chernobyl nuclear power plant (1986)

- Sudafed capsules are tainted with cyanide, leading to two deaths (1991)

- Veryfine Products and other apple juice manufacturers face public scrutiny when the safety of using apples treated with alar is questioned (1989)

- Japanese stock market scandal creates crisis for hundreds of corporations implicated in schemes to cover up trading losses (1991)

- Gorbachev is target of coup; corporations worldwide reassess their investment status in Soviet Union (1991)

- Chicago flood causes $1 billion in property damage; area businesses lose $435 million in sales in first week (1992)

And that is just a sample. Could it happen to you?

THE STRATEGY OF CRISIS MANAGEMENT:
A TEAM APPROACH

Crisis management should involve *all* departments of an organization. It should draw on all available resources. When managers must respond to myriad audiences and problems under stressful conditions, they need to know the theories and practical dimensions of organizational behavior, organizational communication, ethics, strategy, and public relations. To utilize such knowledge in a coordinated approach, you need to build a team.

In most mid- to large-sized organizations, major crises are managed by a senior-level executive. Many organizations try to divide the duties of crisis management within their organizational structure. That often results in a struggle, sometimes motivated by ideology, questions of staffing or experience, or office politics over just who will be singularly responsible for managing chaos. It is not uncommon in a meeting in which a crisis is being assessed, for instance, to have the heads of several company divisions present data arguing that they and their staffs are best equipped for managing a crisis. An effective team typically includes the managers discussed in the following sections.

Senior Administration

A vice president for administration or operations usually serves as the link between (1) the chief executive officer (CEO) or chief financial officer (CFO) and (2) the various directors and managers within a company. This senior manager is responsible for ensuring that the stated management plans of a company for any quarter or year are being met in a timely fashion, and he or she usually has a strong working knowledge of both finance and operations. Such managers have typically achieved their positions by rising up through managerial ranks within the organization, or by having been recruited from a competing firm because of proven administrative talents. Senior administrators are typically trained in both the technical operations of a company as well as in the administrative functions (accounting, finance, public relations, human resources) of management.

Technical Operations

Technical operations managers usually supervise the highly specialized work of an organization. In an oil company, this may include the vice president responsible for research and drilling; in a telephone-manufacturing plant, it would be the person who oversees materials procurement and production. These people often have a depth of technical knowledge not shared by other managers, yet sometimes they lack a broader exposure to organizational objectives. A large multinational organization such as IBM has thousands of technical operations managers on its payroll because of the complexity of that organization and its diversified product line.

Public Affairs

The public affairs manager typically manages contact between the organization and external nonmedia audiences. For example, state and federal regulators, city health officials, and local nonprofit organizations such as a hospice center or the League of Women Voters all have a vested interest in the activities of local industry. The primary objective of public affairs managers is to retain the goodwill of the public (often through publicity and media efforts) by encouraging the company to interact in the community. These individuals traditionally develop specialized knowledge of legislative affairs and state and congressional policies. They may not have considerable experience in the technical or operations side of an organization, but are adept at cultivating positive relations with lawmakers on behalf of the organization.

Public Relations

The public relations manager serves as a central coordinator for proactive and reactive relations with the news media, both print and electronic. Such executives seek to place favorable stories profiling a company or its products with the general or trade press, and they also respond to inquiries from the media.

In a typical week, a public relations manager may write and send several news releases to major newspapers, produce a video news release that is sent to area television stations, and respond to reporters calling for information on the company. In many instances, this director has training and experience as a journalist and thoroughly understands the nuances of press relations. Like their public affairs counterparts, public relations managers may lack a specific technical background in the company's product area and thus must rely on the technical staff to translate complicated issues into lay terms for the general public.

Consumer Affairs

A consumer affairs manager is less concerned with legislators, news media, and operations than with how individuals and groups feel about the image and products of a company. Because most organizations receive many customer inquiries, including complaint letters and phone calls, or inquiries for information from students, neighbors, or consumer groups, companies need consumer affairs specialists who are adept at promptly and accurately responding to consumer questions. To respond quickly and well, the organization may provide a toll-free 800 number to consumers or may sponsor educational fairs and community gatherings. It will be alert to tracking specific complaints should a recall become necessary because of a product defect or production problem.

Investor Relations

A small, family-owned business or privately held company may not be overly concerned with stockholders, but imagine the difficulty in acquiring and retaining the goodwill of investors who own a piece of a company such as McDonald's, which in 1991 had over 362 million shares in the hands of millions of investors! Managers at a company such as McDonald's are concerned not only about individuals who own several—or several thousand—shares of stock, but also about institutional investors, who in any one day could buy or sell millions of shares of stock, thus driving the value of the company up or down, sometimes single-handedly. And although the federal government and various stock exchanges (New York Stock Exchange, NASDAQ, American Stock Exchange) have worked to prevent manipulation of stock prices, any significant piece of news reported about a company on the CNBC can and does affect a stock price.

The investor relations manager monitors the "pulse" of investor confidence. This work includes, among other duties, organizing focus groups to hear investor concerns, responding to individual inquiries for information, writing and distributing the organization's annual report to stockholders, and ensuring that the company complies with federal and state investment regulations.

Advertising

A director of advertising is concerned with making sure that a consistent image and message is applied in all paid advertisements, including the rapidly growing field of direct mail. In many cases, companies hire an advertising agency to devise an advertising strategy and to recommend the best mix of advertising outlets (television, radio, billboards, magazines, newspapers, cable, and so on).

Advertising for a regional food manufacturer, for example, focuses on hometown newspapers and radio and television stations. But for a diversified company such as Kraft Foods, advertising requires specialized talent in producing successful strategies for Hispanic cable channels, black community newspapers, overseas markets, and elementary school cafeteria directors, to name but a few. This diversification presents a significant challenge because Kraft will want to appeal to the specialized tastes of each group while also seeking to maintain a consistent corporate image. What is more important, in the event of a crisis, the advertising team must understand the information needs of each target audience and have the ability to reach them effectively.

In the ideal management setting, the aforementioned executives of an organization work well together to handle crises. (Some organizations will use variations of this group when composing their own crisis management team, as explained in Chapter 7.) Managers know where their responsibilities begin and end. They do not seek to circumvent each other, and they work cooperatively, sharing information and encouraging teamwork. Through company value systems, staff meetings, and daily interaction, these managers fit themselves to the company's culture and their individual roles within that "big picture." Through trial and error, they have learned to delegate. Many are masters of persuasion, rarely alienating other managers who may be negatively affected by their suggestions.

This is the *ideal* organization. Most organizations are far from ideal, however. Sometimes chaos erupts because of events that may seem beyond the reach of management, yet such moments can be effectively controlled. Organizational behavior is often influenced by stress, which is fueled by sales quotas, staff disputes, government regulation, hostile takeovers, negative press reports, and loss of clients. Managers must be trained in how to cope with such managerial headaches, which can, if not controlled, turn into crises of greater proportions.

Crises aren't stationary. Managers often tend to grope for answers and solutions that may be either the most expedient or least expensive. Sometimes the "quick fix" can solve an immediate dilemma, but it often fails to provide a lasting remedy. Crises can and do recur, which is often a symptom of fundamental organizational dysfunction. For this reason, executives need to ask their crisis team to look at crisis management as a *strategic challenge*. They need to ask, Where are we vulnerable? What small problems could become larger ones if they are not corrected? What crises have our competitors faced that could one day strike our organization? What might happen in the short term? In the long term?

Signs are often evident before a major organizational crisis, but not always. Even if an event has not taken place but is just possible, management should take steps necessary to minimize damage to the organization's reputation and operations. Recognizing that need, many organizations try to formalize operations with policies and massive procedures manuals for the company; in other organizations, senior management may have less formal methods to keep a team cohesive.

THE FAULT, DEAR BRUTUS, IS NOT IN OUR STARS

Many successful, major corporations have survived both small and significant corporate crises because their senior management team was unified. In some cases, the personalities of the individual team members contributed to a united front that enhanced rapid, effective decision making. In other cases, managers set aside their philosophical differences in favor of achieving a success in time of adversity.

Yet many companies fail in handling their crises—they aren't prepared or can't coordinate their responses, their managers act or speak impulsively, sometimes on the basis of inaccurate data. In over 120 cases studied, from 1984–1990, managers were criticized by the public or press for failing to present a coordinated response to a crisis. Such situations can be described as organizational behavior crises, because the situations were made worse by the actions of one or more managers. Although their actions or statements were usually an attempt to appease a reporter or regulator, for instance, the ramifications of those acts actually further complicated the crises because the information the managers presented was false, incomplete, or misleading.

Of the 120 cases studied, three broad problem categories emerged. Individual managers

- Spoke without authorization, usually without understanding organizational culture, procedures, or norms (43%).
- Presented incorrect data or misspoke based on faulty information presented to them by others in the organization (27%).
- Took action that in turn complicated the crisis. Usually the steps they took were intended to help resolve the crisis, but were perceived differently (22%).

Other circumstances accounted for another 8 percent.

What causes companies to fail the test of crisis? If we can answer this question, we can perhaps learn how to manage crises well. Let's look at some case examples.

Three Mile Island: The Impossible Accident Becomes Possible

Few cases are as illustrative and disturbing as the Three Mile Island (TMI) accident of March 1979. A gas bubble was building within this major nuclear plant, threatening to spew radiation into the air, with a potential major loss of life far beyond Harrisburg, Pennsylvania. Just one week before, *The China Syndrome,* a major movie that portrayed public utility executives as corrupt and ill prepared, opened to wide acclaim around the country. Awareness of nuclear power as a potential threat to people was at its peak in the United States.

As the nation watched in horror, the White House struggled with then Governor Richard Thornburgh to determine who was in charge, what contingency plans existed, and how a massive evacuation would be implemented, if necessary. For the first time, the nation's vulnerability to nuclear catastrophe was more than theoretical. In many ways, luck—rather than effective crisis management—prevailed.

Although plant managers worked feverishly to respond to press inquiries about public safety, the sheer volume of media attention could not be adequately addressed by the limited staff of General Public Utilities Service Corporation, owners of the facility. Writing in *Public Utilities Fortnightly* in 1990, GPU's former director of public affairs, Kenneth McKee, reflected on how unprepared the company was to deal with the media:

The Three Mile Island nuclear power plant near Harrisburg, Pennsylvania, experienced an accident on March 28, 1979, that resulted in a major release of radiation. There was another release of radiation on March 30. People within a radius of ten miles from the power plant were asked to stay indoors.

Suddenly, perhaps for the first time ever, the nuclear experts were at a loss for words. To fill that vacuum, that dearth of information, too many well-intentioned but self-appointed experts from around the globe anxiously stepped forward to make their views heard. Voila! We had an international news story and the beginning of chaos.

... Few had seriously considered crisis communications and its vital role in crisis management. As an example, the plant operator, Met-Ed, had only two or three persons experienced in dealing with the media. They were assigned to headquarters, a distance of more than two hours travel from TMI. At the plant site, there was only one person available to speak with the public—and he was a tour guide with very little media exposure.[1]

McKee notes that at the height of this crisis, soon to become front-page news around the globe, there was only one public telephone at the TMI facility—the next was several miles away. He wrote as many as three news releases a day to cope with the ever-changing nature of the crisis. Rumors about a potential accident that could kill millions were sweeping the country. "Cover-ups" were being discussed on radio talk shows. With the press frustrated over its inability to get the story out, multiple representatives talking to the press, and the public concerned over what to do, President Jimmy Carter asked plant managers to refrain from speaking to the press about the status of the plant. He then asked Nuclear Regulatory Commission (NRC) experts to coordinate media affairs from that moment on.

The TMI crisis offers a host of lessons in crisis management. Ultimately they involve the absence of preparation, but they also involve organizational behavior. What were the plant operators' priorities? Why had they failed to adequately prepare for a crisis of this magnitude? If staff members had expressed concerns in previous years, how were they handled? The answers to these questions remain unanswered more than a decade later, but new insight is being added incrementally.

For example, an NRC official told *Time* magazine, "We had a hell of a time trying to find out what was going on. The whole commercial phone system was jammed. We couldn't get through."[2] In an exhaustive analysis of the causes of the TMI crisis and of the crisis management by plant managers, *Time* argued that the NRC was astonishingly slow in sending expert engineers to the scene and that agency managers tripped over themselves when they tried to handle organizational responsibility. In a rare public rebuke, the nation's largest newsweekly asserted, "Experts from the NRC should be on duty in the control room of every reactor round the clock, armed with full authority to take over at the first sign of trouble, order a shutdown if that seems necessary, direct all emergency procedures for closing the plant—and damn what it may cost."[3]

Shared responsibility is part of the answer. Although it is easy to point the finger at the executives who managed TMI, the ultimate responsibility for this calamity was shared: federal regulators had not done their job, state officials were unprepared for an accident, and the nuclear industry had failed to contemplate all possibilities and train some managers for the heavy burden they would bear if the public panicked at news of a potential nuclear catastrophe.

General Haig: The One Statement
That Will Haunt Him Forever

Summoned to meet with reporters in the minutes after the assassination attempt on President Ronald Reagan on March 30, 1981, Secretary of State Alexander Haig was asked how the nation and its allies would respond if the President were seriously wounded. "I'm in charge here," he responded, much to the astonishment of the press and—understandably—the American people. The U.S. Constitution provides that the order of succession to the presidency first goes to the Vice President, then to the Speaker of the U.S. House of Representatives. With Reagan in surgery at George Washington Medical Center and given the chaos in the White House, Haig's statement was his political epitaph.

Just one week before the assassination attempt, President Reagan had personally ordered Vice President Bush to direct all crisis management functions in the White House.[4] Haig had openly opposed that decision and threatened to resign as U.S. Secretary of State. So the week before the presidential shooting, the White House was reportedly in confusion over who would be coordinating the many domestic and foreign functions if such a crisis were to occur. Upon learning that Bush, not he, would be the White House's crisis manager, Haig, despite a distin-

Source: Copyright 1989 by Herblock in the *Washington Post.*

guished career of thirty-six years in government and military service, was reportedly "brooding" both in public and private.

In the days and weeks after making the statement, Haig was widely criticized for speaking too abruptly, without consulting with then Vice President George Bush, and for attempting to usurp authority. As *Time* magazine reported, Haig's blunder not only caused a crisis of confidence for the White House, but generated concern over Haig's state of mind:

> Even Haig's friends were taken aback by the televised discomfiture of the four-star general who had steered Richard Nixon through his last crisis. "I've never seen him like that before," said a State Department colleague who has known Haig for years. "He was cracking emotionally." ... "I can understand his perception of the need to reassure," said Democratic Senator Joseph Biden, a persistent Haig critic. "But the Secretary's actions had an entirely opposite effect."[5]

Haig's remarks at the White House news conference were undoubtedly well intentioned as he sought to calm the people of the United States and the nation's allies. But that one statement gave the appearance that he had usurped power and was playing the very role he had been ordered to avoid.

Exxon: A Barrage of Bad Judgment

After the *Exxon Valdez* oil spill in March 1989, Exxon officials appeared myopic in deciding who would speak for the company and who would travel to Alaska to take managerial control of the disaster. The company first dispatched Frank Iarossi, the president of a subsidiary company called Exxon Shipping, to Alaska. Then Exxon sent William Stevens, the president of another group, Exxon USA.

Not until three weeks after the spill did the chairman of Exxon, Lawrence G. Rawl, travel to Alaska to assess the damage himself. Top executives refused to comment on the growing environmental nightmare for almost a week. When company officials did speak, it was often with incomplete information. The *New York Times* quoted one Exxon spokesperson as actually saying the damage to the environment was "minimal." The *Times* also commented on the organizational behavior questions that loomed behind the incident: "In Exxon's case, the company may not have been well prepared for the glare of publicity in part because it has been inward-looking in recent years. Emphasizing cost cutting and pushing decision making down to operating levels, Mr. Rawl has rarely spoken to the press, securities analysts or business organizations."[6] The overall corporate response showed a lack of preparation for crisis, and the behavior of individual managers made the whole company look uncaring.

WHY COMPANIES WRITE CRISIS MANAGEMENT PLANS

Many large organizations have proactive strategies—they have anticipated crisis and produced documents and planning models that will help them weather catastrophic events. In one study of 166 surveyed firms, about 55 percent reported that they had prepared a CMP. The numbers were significantly higher for firms with over $10 billion in sales (92 %) as opposed to firms with sales between $100 million and $1 billion (35 %).[7] The reasons these firms gave for launching a CMP included

- Recognition of the potential for a disaster resulting in injury of people or property (53%)
- A previous company crisis where a plan did not exist (13%)
- Assuring the continuation of business during a crisis (12%)
- Forming a consistent crisis response across a company (11%)
- Recognizing the importance of dealing with the media during a crisis (10%)

The following incident shows how proactive crisis management can avert a cluster syndrome, in which one crisis begets another.

Pandemonium: The AMTRAK Collision and a Tested Crisis Team

In an accident involving injuries and death, the actions of emergency room physicians, technicians, ambulance personnel, nursing staff, and others are of paramount importance. Their ability to handle massive crises must be planned, tested, and coordinated with the efforts of industry and government representatives.

Frank M. Moy, Jr., director of community relations for St. Elizabeth's Hospital of Boston, Massachusetts, understands well how important emergency medical care is. This 350-bed institution is a tertiary teaching hospital and, as a result, offers advanced care techniques, especially in life-threatening situations. That care proved particularly valuable on Wednesday morning, December 12, 1990 when an AMTRAK commuter train collided with a stopped commuter train in Boston. The impact was so severe that the twisted wreckage punctured the subway ceiling, even cracking the street above. The train's operating system that records speed and other variables was damaged, so important evidence was lost. Ambulance and rescue personnel sent the injured to nine neighboring hospitals, including 12 people to St. Elizabeth's.

Although no one was killed, over 280 people were injured, some of them seriously. When the accident was announced by area radio and television stations, switchboards at all nine hospitals were jammed by concerned families and loved ones of potential victims. Some lawyers reportedly roamed the halls of the various hospitals, handing out business cards. According to Moy, one reporter tried to disguise himself as a doctor and sought access to the room where the AMTRAK driver, Richard Abramson, was recovering from multiple injuries. The reporter was caught and escorted from the property. For families, emergency personnel, the news media, and others, the AMTRAK accident demanded complex crisis management.

INTERVIEW

Frank Moy, Jr.
St. Elizabeth's Hospital of Boston and the
AMTRAK Disaster

Hospital administrator Frank Moy, Jr., (above, right) says that physicians, nurses, and administrators worked as a team when dozens of injured patients needed immediate care after the AMTRAK collision. Moy attributes his crisis management style to the founder of modern public relations, Edward L. Bernays (above, left). Bernay's role in crisis communication is discussed in Chapter 1.

Here are Frank Moy's impressions of how managers at AMTRAK and St. Elizabeth's responded in a crisis.

Q *Before we discuss the AMTRAK accident, could you explain your role within the organization?*

A I report to the Senior Vice President of Development and Public Affairs. That is fairly common in nonprofits such as hospitals, colleges, or museums. Community relations is a fairly broad rubric—I'm responsible for cultivating goodwill with local community groups, in listening and responding to neighbors, and in trying to serve as a general ombudsman for the hospital. As a result, it's a very broad responsibility on my shoulders. I love it—I've been here for ten years. In any given day, I interact with our president, with the medical staff, with employees, local business owners, neighbors, maybe a reporter, and sometimes with our patients.

Q *What kinds of crises have you faced in the past as a manager of a department?*

A Looking at it retrospectively, I suppose they are relatively small crises, but at the time, they were major problems! I think that's something that many managers don't really sit down and assess. Over the years, we've had neighbors threaten to file lawsuits against us for wanting to build or expand or update sections of the hospital. We've had prominent people in the hospital as patients who wanted their identities protected, or we have received suicide victims, but their names sometimes are compromised. We've had people threaten to protest out front over one issue or another. For the most part, we handled those minor crises very well. In a pinch, the team comes together, we discuss different ways of coping, and somehow we move on. Some [crises] last longer than others in terms of the damage they do.

Q *What contributes to that?*

A I think part of it is the significance of the crisis. If you have a group of angry neighbors who don't want to see construction in their neighborhood, they will prolong the initial sting of a crisis with letters to an editor, protests, phone calls to newspapers, whatever they can do. Much of that is understandable—they need a forum to vent frustration. It's commonplace with every major institution. Largely even those who cause a crisis for us are very reasonable, kind people. They want to speak out. And it's my job to listen to them and, wherever possible, see if we can work with them.

Q *What made the AMTRAK crash a different kind of crisis?*

A Wow, what a difference! When you sit at a desk as a manager and you are writing memos, answering the phone, going to meetings and solving problems, it can be routine. Imagine a phone call telling you that several hundred people are hurt and that all the resources of the city are being exerted to ensure their care. It all clicked for us. We've been through many miniversions of AMTRAK before; maybe a bus overturned, or workers were exposed to a poisonous gas from a plant leak, or there was a plane crash.

But this was much bigger—the injuries were serious, there were many of them, and we had to take care of them in rapid order with the limited staff we had on hand. You don't have time to phone a dozen emergency room physicians and nurses and say, "Gee, could you come in?" These people need care now, their families need to be called now, the media wants answers and numbers now, and the regulators are already crawling all over the place wanting to talk to anyone. It has the potential for being pure chaos. What we found was that with an emergency plan in place that we had tested in advance, a central communications office was able to maintain contact with all of the parties involved, from families to regulators to curious citizens to emergency personnel.

Q *Would you describe it as controlled chaos?*

A No, it never got even close. I'm convinced that when you have a crisis like this, people pull together in a natural and systematic way. Our staff is skilled at their job; they knew how to prioritize patient needs, they knew who would call families. You have no time for petty squabbling over who does what. Professionals pull together and do their job.

Q *What was working with the AMTRAK personnel like?*

A Like everyone, I had read stories about different AMTRAK accidents over the years, and often the reports told of disaster—these managers did not know what to do. We didn't see that.

This was a management team that clicked, that walked around with their notebooks of checklists and procedures of what to do and what to say and how to approach almost every conceivable situation that came our way. We were impressed with their crisis manage-

ment abilities. In the end, the driver sent personal notes to the doctors, nurses, EMC people, everyone. He wrote "God bless them all!"

Q *What specifically impressed you?*

A On receiving the names of the injured, AMTRAK officials personally called relatives. They visited with each patient in our wards. They provided them with the AMTRAK representative's name and phone number and told them that if they needed anything, twenty-four hours a day, they were available and at their disposal. I saw them spending considerable time with each person in a caring fashion; this was no "quickie" conversation.

In the days that followed, flowers and small gifts were received by the patients. AMTRAK was positioned by their staff as caring and compassionate, as much of a victim of the crash as was the person lying there with pins in their legs. You might say it was crisis management at its best. When reporters were asking patients for comments, I really think they expected people to unload on AMTRAK's poor management. Instead, people largely took it as an unavoidable accident. There was very little finger pointing. As a result, AMTRAK didn't take much of a public relations lambasting.

Q *You mentioned their crisis management plan.*

A It works. From what I saw of it, almost every conceivable situation, question, or problem was addressed in the crisis folder they brought with them. Their managers had read it in advance; they were very savvy.

Q *What about the hospital? You face crises every day—do you have a crisis management plan?*

A I suggested to our president that we develop one. It's underway right now. In the end, I hope we can emulate the success that other organizations have enjoyed with that kind of foresight. ❑

CASE STUDY: THIS QUARTERBACK WAS SACKED

Victor Kiam was a jewel in the crown of American industry; in 1980 he bought Remington Corporation from Sperry Rand Corporation for $25 million and within a decade had turned the shaver manufacturer into a thriving $250 million-a-year company.

Kiam, a Harvard Business School graduate with extraordinary sales acumen, had successfully sold everything from brassieres to toothpaste earlier in his career. By 1984, at the helm of Remington, he had appeared in a series of commercials for the company's shaving products—he personally offered a refund to anyone who didn't like his shavers. Within a few years, Remington captured 40 percent of the U.S. market share for men's razors.

Competitor Norelco, concerned over a diminishing market share, introduced a series of new shavers and sales promotions in 1990 aimed at jostling Remington's wave of success. For Kiam, the timing couldn't have been worse. Kiam had bought the New England Patriots football team in 1989 for $80 million. After the purchase, the team nosedived both in terms of performance—its 1990 record was the National Football League's (NFL) poorest, 1–15—and in ticket sales, losing between $5 and 6 million annually. Eventually the NFL was forced to assume control of the Patriots' board of directors to keep the team from going bankrupt.

The U.S. market share of Remington razors now slipped to less than 30 percent, largely, in Kiam's own words, because "a lot of things were falling through the

Victor Kiam bought Remington Corporation in 1980, and in 1989 he bought the New England Patriots football team.

cracks." He told *Business Week* (February 25, 1991) that "The company got too big for my entrepreneurial style." Some Remington products flopped, and new product development was mediocre at best.

Kiam's popularity was waning with both Remington consumers and Patriot fans. Then on September 17, 1990, Lisa Olson, a 26-year-old sports writer for the *Boston Herald*, and one of about 500 female sports writers in the United States, complained to NFL officials that she had been sexually harassed by several Patriot players. She claimed that they had taunted her by exposing themselves during a postgame locker room incident, and seven months later she sued both Kiam and the players.

In the aftermath of the Olson incident, Kiam's reactions were at best muddied. Although he paid for a full-page newspaper ad that apologized for any misunderstanding, Kiam also told *Boston Herald* editors that "Your paper's asking for trouble sending a female reporter to cover the team."

Then the *New York Times*, on September 28, 1990, reported claims that Kiam had referred to the well-regarded reporter as a "classic bitch." Kiam, now in receipt of thousands of angry letters and faced with a crisis of credibility, fired back. He hired a New York press agent, Howard Rubenstein (whose clients included such notables as Leona Helmsley). But the controversy continued. Just when the "bitch" incident was calming down, Kiam reportedly told an off-color joke about Olson at a February

Sports writer Lisa Olson interviews Patriot player Irving Fryar.

4, 1991, sports banquet in Stamford, Connecticut. Once again, Victor Kiam's personal and business style was in the news. Eventually the NFL fined the Patriots team $50,000 for the Lisa Olson incident, and most of the team's front office was fired.

Business Week is the largest-circulation business publication in the world. Typically, *Business Week* stories combine hard news with minimal commentary. After the derogatory sports banquet reference to Lisa Olson, however, *Business Week* decided it was time for a potent warning. On February 25, 1991, beginning a full-page article headlined "Victor Kiam, the Self-Sacking Quarterback," *Business Week* remarked, "One of these days, Victor Kiam may learn to keep his mouth shut." The article went on to review Remington's lackluster performance, numerous debacles with the Patriots, and Kiam's blunt, apparently sexist persona.

In many circles, Kiam is regarded as a talented and adept business manager. Despite the lack of success with the Patriots, he believes that Remington will rebound. Certainly neither Remington nor the Patriots are going to collapse as a result of the Lisa Olson incident; yet the blistering *Business Week* attack could prompt stockholders, employees, and colleagues to wonder whether or not Kiam is the best leader for both organizations. When *Business Week* takes aim at your CEO and most visible spokesperson, you have a crisis of confidence underway.

Assume you are the chairperson of Remington's board of directors, and you have just read the *Business Week* article. Write a candid and complete memo to Kiam that mandates him to refocus public attention on Remington's quality products and away from his controversial comments. ❑

ENDNOTES

1. Kenneth C. McKee, "The Lessons of Three Mile Island," *Public Utilities Fortnightly*, November 22, 1990, p. 15.
2. "Now Comes the Fallout," *Time*, April 16, 1979, p. 26.
3. "Looking Anew at the Nuclear Future," *Time*, April 16, 1979, p. 33.
4. "Trouble on the Team," *Time*, April 6, 1981, p. 8.
5. "I Am in Control Here," *Time*, April 13, 1981, p. 40.
6. John Holusha, "Exxon's Public-Relations Problem," the *New York Times*, April 20, 1989, p. D4.
7. Joseph Z. Wisenbilt, "Crisis Management Planning Among U.S. Corporations: Empirical Evidence and a Proposed Framework," *SAM Advanced Management Journal* 54 (1989): 34.

CHAPTER

3

A Preneed Assessment of Crisis Planning

On February 29, 1984, Federal District Judge Miles Lord summoned three senior executives of the pharmaceutical manufacturer A. H. Robins to his Minneapolis courtroom amid charges that thousands of women had suffered due to use of the company's intrauterine birth control device, the Dalkon Shield. His words stunned the court:

"And when the time came for these women to make their claims against your company, you attacked their character. You inquired into their sexual practices and into the identity of their sex partners. You ruined families and reputations and careers in order to intimidate those who would raise their voices against you. You introduced issues that had no relationship to the fact that you had planted in the bodies of these women instruments of death, of mutilation, of diseases.... Another of your callous legal tactics is to force women of little means to withstand the onslaughts of your well-financed team of attorneys.... You have taken the bottom line as your guiding beacon and the low road your route." ❑

From "A Plea for Corporate Conscience,"
Harpers, June 1984

T he three executives of A. H. Robins should never have been in court. Indeed, the 12 million Dalkon Shields that were sold by 1972 should never have even made it to pharmacy shelves throughout the world. The plastic, nickel-sized device was implanted in the uteruses of an estimated 4 million U.S. women between 1971 and 1974. Almost immediately, complaints of infections were being received by Robins; these were followed by complaints of septic abortions, infertility, damaged Fallopian tubes, and scores of other maladies.

With so many Dalkon Shields in use, generating tens of millions of dollars in revenue for the company, Robins executives found themselves on the defensive. They challenged each new medical report issued by the Centers for Disease Control and the questions that hundreds of private physicians and researchers were raising about the product's safety. This approach backfired.

By 1980, over 4,300 lawsuits had been filed against Robins. The company was so financially troubled that it eventually had to be acquired by American Home Products in December 1989. American agreed with the bankruptcy court to funnel some $2.35 *billion* into a trust fund to settle the lawsuits, which now swelled to over 6,500 claims. How could this have happened? Robert F. Hartley, in his book *Management Mistakes and Successes*, notes that

> Robins continued to ignore reports of major problems—such as massive bleeding, pelvic inflammatory diseases, miscarriages, and even deaths—that kept coming in over the years following the introduction of the Shield. . . . The Robins Company maintained that its product was safe—and it proclaimed so publicly. But evidence suggests that the company knew otherwise. Internal memos indicated that the company knew of potential danger less than a month after it acquired rights to the Shield. And more internal company memos were to surface during subsequent litigation: two to three truckloads of incriminating papers.[1]

Their crisis management strategy was "Deny everything, at all costs." It cost plenty.

Unfortunately, the Robins case is not uncommon. Neither small companies nor multimillion-dollar enterprises are immune from crisis. In some cases, simple errors become major headaches. In other situations, such as the Robins case, complicity and intimidation became an active part of daily management to the point where they destroyed a venerable business whose other products had saved lives and helped countless patients. Would a more farsighted strategy have saved Robins?

Many experts believe that without a visionary strategy that articulates business goals, identifies resources needed to achieve them, and anticipates setbacks and crises, any organization is doomed to mediocrity, if not failure. Henry Mintzberg, in the *California Management Review*, says that organizations need strategy[2]

1. To define the organization.
2. To focus effort and help coordinate activity.
3. To set direction for themselves and to outsmart competitors, or at least enable themselves to maneuver through threatening environments.

Karen Hicks (left), president of the Dalkon Shield Information Network, and Fran Cleary protesting against Robins outside the federal courthouse in Richmond, Virginia.

4. To reduce uncertainty and provide consistency.

These four themes need to be addressed by business strategists.

Moreover, there is a relationship between strategy and crisis. Crisis is characterized by *surprise, a high threat to important values, and a short decision time.*[3] To avert or handle crisis well, strategy must be long-term enough to anticipate crisis and to manage its aftermath.

Many organizations focus on "fixing" the problem rather than on developing plans that could minimize or avert organizational damage. Researchers and managers have routinely examined the aftermath of crises without realizing that since crisis is inevitable, proactive strategies could have averted embarrassment and, in some cases, loss of life. Managers tend to focus on the surprise aspects of crisis—reacting to the unknown human and dollar damage, the harm to reputation and future profit, the frustration of grappling with angry publics or regulators. In Exhibit 3-1, Ian Mitroff identifies preventive actions that can minimize damage caused by a lack of management preparedness. The exhibit illustrates that the interdependency of managers and a variety of internal and external parties is most evident in a crisis situation.

EXHIBIT   3-1   Preventive Action Families

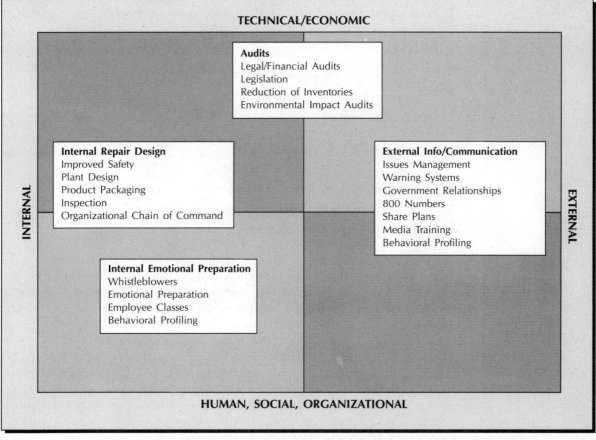

A QUESTION TO PONDER: WHAT'S THE WORST THAT COULD HAPPEN TO US?

Some organizations use contingency planning out of necessity (Heinz, Kellogg, and General Mills must rely on contingency plans if certain foodstuffs and grains become unavailable due to drought or crop disease). Other organizations engage in contingency planning because it offers insight into new models of thinking. For example, U.S. military colleges routinely encourage cadets to develop contingency battle plans that are later openly debated in front of senior and junior officers. Any student of crisis management will want to consider the following questions:

1. What kinds of organizations should be prepared for crisis?
2. What resources can be reasonably allocated to developing a crisis plan?
3. Which managers within an organization are the most appropriate to plan for crisis and contain its fallout?

Reilly lists six core components in crisis readiness:[4]

1. The organization's ability to respond quickly to a crisis.
2. Information available to managers about the organization's crisis management repertoire.
3. Managers' access to the organization's crisis management plans, resources, and tools.
4. The adequacy of the firm's strategic crisis planning.
5. The organization's media management ability in a crisis.
6. The perceived likelihood of crisis striking the organization.

In a study of corporate managers, Reilly found only a few who felt their organizations were ready for crisis. Note that Reilly concentrates on the organization and not on the specific talents, attributes, and qualifications of managers within an organizational team. Managers may come and go, but the organization as a whole can prepare for, and survive, crises.

Developing a worst-case scenario can be especially useful. Managers should ask themselves "What's the worst event that could happen to us? What is the likelihood of that happening? Has it happened to others?" This overview allows us to assess the vulnerability of an organization to a potential disaster.

Let's take a closer look at vulnerability and risk. The vulnerability of a business to a serious crisis—one that could impair its future operational ability—is increased when situational variables change in the output or direction of an organization. Some of the factors that especially increase susceptibility to crisis are

1. Opening a new or expanded facility where machinery, systems, and procedures may not be adequately tested.
2. Opening a new division in a satellite location, causing a temporary period in which communication systems may be erratic and control measures affecting decision making need refinement.
3. Launching a new or modified product that has received careful review in limited testing, but that, because it has not had wide use, could be susceptible to breakage, leakage, or other problems.
4. Expanding into the international marketplace, possibly placing the company's reputation at odds with local customs and regulations if there has been inadequate review and planning for assimilation into the community.
5. Undertaking a scientific or technological project with some risk factor (such as fumes, nuclear waste, or toxic components) without training managers in

departments throughout the company as to the background of the project
and how problems should be addressed in a timely manner.

6. Avoiding the early warning signs of a potential crisis, including patterns
   of complaints by customers or regulators, or problems similar to competitors' problems that could be indicative of industry-wide failings or short-
   comings.

ONE FIRM'S CRISIS PLANNING BEGINS: ARLINGTON PLASTICS

Throughout the remainder of the book, we will occasionally follow the attempt of
managers at one firm to develop a crisis management plan. For the sake of discussion, let's consider the ideal management team of a mid-sized manufacturing
organization, Arlington Plastics (AP).* The company produces specialized mold-
ing forms for plastic manufacturers and distributors; many makers of plastic cups
and containers, toys, office equipment, and electronic goods use AP molds. For six
years, the company has successfully responded to consumer demand for its goods
and services. The following managers are eager to tackle competitive challenges:

- *John, CEO.* Master's degree in business administration. Fifteen years in industry, highly proficient in finance and budgetary considerations. Founder
  and owner of this company.

- *Marie, Vice President of Operations.* Bachelor's degree; twelve years' manufacturing experience. Promoted three times over six years.

- *Roberto, Vice President for Human Resources.* Bachelor's degree; eighteen years
  of personnel expertise. With AP two years.

- *Laurie, Director of Advertising and Public Relations.* Master's degree in journalism. With AP four years.

- *Donald, Director of Tooling.* High school graduate, seeking community college
  degree. Twenty years industrial experience, frequently promoted. With company since it first opened.

- *Luis, Director of Order Placement.* No formal education. Proficient in tracking
  orders and deliveries. Five years with AP.

We will assume that AP's theoretical management team has not made a sophisticated examination of crisis management. Although admittedly it is difficult to
make further assumptions, it would not be surprising to find managers at such a
firm arguing that contingency planning sounds like an academic principle with no
direct impact on company operations and that their days are filled with more
pressing matters.

---

*Arlington Plastics is a fictitious entity and any similarity to real persons or situations is purely
coincidental.

With 6 senior managers and 48 other employees, this company has flourished because it has a quality product line, reasonable prices, and responsible management. Although a major crisis has not yet confronted the owners and operators of Arlington Plastics, they have an opportunity to consider both contingency planning and crisis management in a thoughtful manner. Such planning does not necessarily require outside intervention by strategic specialists, CPAs, legal counsel, or even a public relations agency. Indeed, with AP a combination of skills, knowledge, and proven experience exist that can help the organization prepare its first crisis management plan.

AP managers need to first consider what kinds of crisis could affect their company. Senior managers are typically more seasoned at strategic and business issues, well honed through the trials and errors of their past work. Middle-level managers share some of these talents but may have less exposure to both macro and micro decision making. The junior officers and technical directors have limited management exposure but offer a wealth of specialized information in their areas of expertise. In many ways, AP is analogous to hundreds of thousands of mid-sized companies.

Read how AP managers introduced and discussed the subject of preneed crisis assessment planning at one of their weekly meetings.

John: Good morning. This is a difficult subject to broach with you, but the trade group we belong to, the Manufacturers Research Institute, urged in its last newsletter that all members should discuss how we'd handle a corporate crisis in the event we were a victim of a tragedy of some sort or another. We have just completed the quarterly reports and we have a small break; I think it's an appropriate time to tackle some crisis planning.

Roberto: You mean an explosion or something?

John: Yes. An explosion, a major client leaving us for a competitor, a shooting of workers, such as some plants have seen—whatever.

Luis: Shooting? Do you have some information about this plant that I've missed?

John: Seriously. We need to tackle this thing. What conceivably could go wrong, and how should we respond? Have we ever assessed where we are vulnerable as a company? That's what I want to tackle.

Marie: We should make a list of all possible items, see how likely they are, and probably designate someone to develop a contingency plan. That's what the association recommended. Nobody's saying we'll have a madman come in and shoot workers, but if it does happen, we'd better be prepared. That's the extreme case. But extremes happen.

Laurie: Management is people, products, competition, regulation, and—I forget the last one. Why not begin with those categories?

John: Customers, too. We'd better not forget them.

After discussing crises for about forty-five minutes, AP officers develop a list of potential calamities their company could face. The following chart emerges:

People
Death
Disease (such as AIDS)
CEO or major executive resigns from the company
Nervous breakdown on or off job
Plant accident
Romance on the job
Libel or slander
Violence
Sudden dropoff in sales, or a recession
Someone arrested on or off site

Products
Faulty product and/or recall
Unusually large price increase
Product becomes obsolete
Patent infringement here or abroad
Product review that criticizes AP
Product shelf life is too long, hurting future sales

Plant and Facilities
Fire
Flood
Earthquake

Competition
Price undercuts AP substantially
Heavy advertising blitz and/or sales jump
Attempts to purchase AP
Major legal challenge
Libel against AP in advertising/marketing

Regulation
Levy of fine or imprisonment for some action
Shutdown for OSHA or other violation

Customers
Boycott by customers
Cancellation of a major order
Product recall
Customers seek overseas suppliers

The discussion continues:

Laurie: These aren't all crises. We need criteria to refine the list of possible disasters. A crisis is something sudden, unexpected ... an event with so much negative fallout that it could have a lasting impact on the organization or on us personally.

Donald: Then let's refine it down to the point where we meet those criteria.

A discussion ensues among the managers. The group members agree that the following is a reasonable list of crises for AP:

People
Unexpected death of owner or officer
Major breakdown of critical piece of equipment that cannot be repaired immediately
Major plant accident caused by explosion, etc.

Products
Product recall

Plant and Facilities
Fire

Competition
Unexpected lawsuit, such as patent infringement

Regulation
Unexpected sanction by local, state, or federal agency

Customers
Cancelation of a major contract (possibly causing layoff of workers, shutdown of plant, pay cuts, closure)

The officers of AP had reduced their list of crises by 75 percent. They had refined the topics to be more specific, realizing that to prepare adequately for every unexpected event was beyond their means if they were to complete their everyday duties. Although the second list is by no means perfect, it presents them with a reasonable assessment of where they are managerially at risk in the event of crisis. The discussion continues:

John: I'd like to suggest that we break into teams and that each group come back next week with a list of suggested actions and remedies that might help the company if these events were to occur. When you come in with your written recommendations next week, we'll have a better idea of how to put together some kind of manual for future use.

Marie: John, what if the press gets hold of a manual? If we admit we might be sued or have a product recalled someday, that could be a real crisis. I'm against this process becoming too public. It's all well and good for us to sit and think about how to respond, but things get leaked. If someone at this table, or an assistant who types the crisis plan, or anyone who leaves our company gives sensitive data away, we're in trouble. That could cause a greater crisis for us than some romance between employees that goes sour.

Laurie: That's unlikely to happen. A huge number of companies have crisis plans, and I'd rather defend to the media the fact that we're prepared than to go before a press conference and represent AP as an overwhelmed, unprepared company while bad news surrounds us.

John: I agree. The number of cases where companies were caught short in a crisis is astounding. We've worked too hard to build the company to let a mishap cripple us.

Donald: Can I suggest that we approach this by management areas? Luis, since you and I work in orders and tooling, we should confront the product area. John and Marie would be ideal with competition and regulation, Roberto is trained with the people angle, Laurie knows how to communicate with customers and the press.

John: (Writes the names on the chalkboard next to the areas of responsibility.) Makes sense. Let's proceed—each of your tackle your areas in the next few days. When we meet next week, I'll ask you for no more than three pages of potential crises and suggested actions we should take. Please edit and polish your work before you submit it. Be sure to include what kinds of resources we may need—lawyers, accountants, asbestos removers, hospitals, whatever. Then we'll review each as a group, refine them, and proceed with a manual that's formatted to company style.

AP is on its way to crisis management assessment and planning. The officers have realized that they cannot tackle every conceivable management dilemma, so they have honed the list down to the most likely, mainly unpredictable, events that could harm the company. This type of preneed assessment is the first step in developing a successful crisis management plan. We will return to their progress later in the book.

SIZE CORRELATES TO PREPAREDNESS

When Joseph Wisenbilt surveyed 166 firms in 1989, over half reported having a CMP in place. It was not surprising that the largest firms, reporting in excess of $10 billion in sales, saw the highest concentration of preparedness (92%). What was discouraging was the low percentage of midsized firms, those reporting between $100 million and $1 billion in sales, with CMPs (35%).[5] For the vast majority of corporations in the country, those with sales significantly below $100 million, the percentage probably drops off even more dramatically. Wisenbilt's survey shows that larger organizations have both the need and the resources to be better prepared for crisis. Smaller organizations have the need, but often lack the resources.

In addition, we need to ascertain whether smaller firms, which were not targeted by the Wisenbilt survey, share the interest of big business in the issue of crisis management. After studying Exhibit 3-2, you will have a better sense of how to use a model or grid to assess the severity of a crisis.

HOW MANAGERS ASSESS THE ROLE OF CRISIS MANAGEMENT

In September 1989, some 800 surveys were mailed to selected firms by region in the United States. Each firm reported gross annual earnings of between $1 and 3 million. A cross-section of industries was targeted: manufacturing, agricultural, advanced technology, and service or consulting (for example, in agriculture or engineering). A surprisingly high rate of response was achieved (68%), primarily because respondents were promised a copy of the results as well as anonymity.

Surveys addressed to operations vice president or director of public affairs asked three specific questions:

1. Has the issue of crisis management emerged as a significant management challenge for your firm in the past three years, requiring discussion, study or action by an executive committee, board, or senior management?

2. Has your firm established a written, corporate policy or plan to respond to company crisis?

3. Has your firm been involved as a defendant in a suit filed by a community, neighborhood or civic association or individual with regard to a case involving a corporate crisis (chemical spill, zoning issue, traffic, pollution, union grievance, etc.) over the past three years?

There is ample evidence to suggest that an organization's location may impact its need and even its interest in formulating a CMP. The responses shown in Exhibit 3-3 confirm the widely held belief that litigation against firms in the West and Northeast (areas dominated by heavy manufacturing, extensive real estate development, and controversial projects such as biotechnology experimentation) represent the highest concentrations of lawsuits filed by angry members of the public.

EXHIBIT 3-2   Crises in Perspective

It's easy to lose your perspective in a crisis situation. A model proposed by Meyers and Holusha* (modified to fit the travel industry) can help you put a crisis in perspective. The model helps you analyze crises according to two criteria—dimension and control.

Dimension. Dimension is the size or amount of resources at risk. Dimension relates to the survival of your company. A crisis such as a fire or a hostile takeover could put your company's existence at stake. A union strike or loss of revenues from currency fluctuations may weaken a company, but probably won't destroy it. You can evaluate the severity of a crisis on a scale of one to ten, where a score of ten implies a grave threat.

Control. Control involves your ability to influence the outcome of a crisis. If you see several possible effective ways to react, your control rating would be high (a score of ten). If there are few or no options to choose from, your control would be low (a score of one).

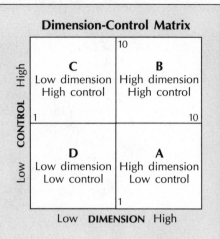

Dimension-Control Matrix

	Low DIMENSION High	
CONTROL High	**C** Low dimension High control	**B** High dimension High control
CONTROL Low	**D** Low dimension Low control	**A** High dimension Low control

Four-Square Matrix
By creating the matrix shown here, with dimension on the horizontal line and control on the vertical line, you can express the relationship between these two criteria presented by the crisis situation.

—*Quadrant A* (low control, high dimension) represents a crisis over which you have little control that threatens to engulf the company. An example would be a small company facing the high litigation costs and possible large judgment of a lawsuit caused by management negligence.

—*Quadrant B* (high control, high dimension) represents a crisis with the same degree of severity, but which gives you more control over the outcome. A typical case would be an attempted hostile takeover of a large, publicly traded company. In creating a takeover defense, you have a choice of actions, but a wrong move could put your company in the hands of the aggressor.

—*Quadrant C* (high control, low dimension) comprises less serious crises that can be managed effectively. A union strike might fall into this category.

—*Quadrant D* (low control, low dimension) also represents less serious events, but these crises offer no options. A convention hotel in Arizona, sitting in the midst of a political boycott, has a crisis in this category. There probably is enough other revenue to keep the hotel alive until the boycott ends, but there are few options in the meantime.

This grid will help you evaluate crisis conditions. To get a clear sense of a crisis, you must first establish where the crisis fits on the grid. Each position suggests different options. In quadrants A and D, your strategy is one of preparing post-crisis plans, because, without control of the crisis, you must figure out how to react to its eventual outcome. For crises in quadrants A and B, senior management should be fully involved because the company's survival is probably at stake. The strategy for crises in quadrants B and C should be active crisis management. Top management probably need not be involved heavily in crises falling in quadrants C and D, because company survival is generally not at stake.

An assessment of both dimension and control, as defined here, is essential to placing a crisis in perspective. This dimension-control framework is designed to help you identify the gravity of a situation and develop a perspective for dealing with it. By using this framework, you will be better able to assess your position and your strategy for dealing with a crisis.

*See: Gerald Meyers and John Holusha, *When It Hits the Fan* (Boston: Houghton Mifflin, 1986), pp. 207–210.

EXHIBIT   3-3   How Managers Assess the Role of Crisis Management

	Issue of Concern	Program Established	Involved in Litigation
Northeast	61 percent	42 percent	8 percent
Southeast	22	11	3
Midwest	21	16	2
Northwest	51	30	16
Southwest	53	27	7
West	79	64	19

Source: These data previously appeared in Laurence Barton's article, "When Managers Find Themselves on the Defensive," *Business Forum*, Winter 1991, pp. 8–13.

The Northwest, where a major debate over the fragile environment has been underway for several years, emerges as a region likely to experience an increase in such lawsuits in the coming years.

Clearly, the size and resources of an organization affect its ability to cope with crisis. Similarly, the location of the organization raises questions involving local issues, neighbor concerns, the ability of various interests to pursue litigation, and others. Location, size, and structure of the organization are three of the major issues requiring consideration in preparing for crisis.

THE LITMUS TEST OF CRISIS: ASSESSING RISK

Managers need to assess their organizations' potential exposure to crisis. Consider the organization you own, work for, or aspire to work for. Regardless of the company, the following assessment factors should be used to evaluate the risk of crisis.

Ownership of the Company

Publicly traded companies have a special burden in the sense that crisis can cause havoc with stockholders. For example, when stockholders of Union Carbide learned about the catastrophic gas leak in Bhopal, India, in 1984, they sold millions of shares of stock within a matter of hours, reducing the value of the company by an astonishing 27 percent. Risk is higher with publicly traded companies principally because the volatility caused by the sheer number of shareholders and their changing moods can create additional trouble beyond whatever other crisis it is experiencing. While Union Carbide officials were trying to cope with problems six thousand miles away, shareholders in the United States and elsewhere were selling millions of shares, reducing the company's net worth, the value of some employees' retirement stock, and the overall image of the company.

Managers of multinational corporations must grapple with a sharp increase in

An injured man is helped during the evacuation of thousands of residents following a leak of methyl isocyanate, a pesticide component, at Union Carbide's plant in Bhopal, India, in December 1984. More than 3,000 people died and another 20,000 were seriously injured.

the number of threats targeting their operations in recent years. Although U.S. corporations have long been key targets throughout the Third World, now Japanese corporations constitute the new elite. Shiniricho Tomioka and Kiochi Oizumi, two Japanese crisis management experts, have documented just some of the more than one thousand violent and/or criminal acts since 1984 directed against Japanese businesses operating overseas (see Exhibit 3-4). Security experts in the U.S., such as Edward Badolato of Falls Church, Virginia, advise companies on preventive measures to protect employees and physical assets.

Privately owned companies are a different story, however. Because there are fewer owners in a privately owned company (and in many cases only one), there is less immediate volatility in the stock price. In fact, stock may not be affected at all because the essential value of the company lies in its assets, not its shares. In growing companies, shares of stock are often incrementally distributed as executives are promoted or as stock options are offered to new employees. But for the most part, a privately held company not governed by the Securities and Exchange Commission and state regulatory offices has less immediate risk concern.

An added dimension of the ownership situation is the natural propensity of both the public and the news media to focus on crisis situations centering around

EXHIBIT .3-4   Major Terrorist Incidents Aimed at Japanese Businesses

Date	Country	Terrorist Act, Victim	Group Responsible
Apr. 1984	France	Bombing, Laboratoire de Sony France	Anarchist group
Sept. 1984	Iran	Wounded, IJPC engineers	Iran–Iraq War
Mar. 1985	Iraq	Bombing, two engineers of Toshiba Air Conditioning wounded	Iran–Iraq War
Apr. 1985	Iran	Kidnapping, employees of an affiliate of NEC	Anti-Iraq government guerilla, PUK
May 1985	The Philippines	Arson, Universal Silk	New Peoples Army
Aug. 1985	Sri Lanka	Murder, boilermaker employee	Unidentified
Sept. 1985	Peru	Bombing, Mitsubishi Corp.-affiliated car dealership	Shining Path
May 1986	Sri Lanka	Bombing, Tokyo Cement Co. factory	Tamil extremists
May 1986	Sri Lanka	Bombing, Air Lanka jet, five Japanese killed or injured	Tamil extremists
July 1986	Iran	Rocket attack, Ishikawajima-Harima Heavy Industries	Iran–Iraq War
Sept. 1986	Iran	Wounded, two Hitachi engineers	Iran–Iraq War
Nov. 1986	The Philippines	Kidnapping, general manager Mitsui Co., Manila branch	Unidentified
Mar. 1987	Peru	Bombing, Bank of Tokyo, Lima Branch	Left-wing, extremist guerillas, MRTA
Mar. 1987	Peru	Shooting, general manager of Bank of Tokyo, Lima branch	Unidentified
Aug. 1987	Peru	Intimidation by bombing, Mitsui Co.	Unidentified
Nov. 1987	Peru	Armed attack, Nissan Peru	Shining Path
May 1988	Taiwan	Kidnapping, child of Japanese radiographer	Unidentified
July 1988	The Philippines	Intimidation, Japan International Cooperation Agency	New Peoples Army
Mar. 1989	Laos	Kidnapping, head of liaison office of Mitsui Co.	Unidentified
July 1989	China	Blackmail, Japan Air Lines, Beijing Branch	Unidentified
Sept. 1989	Thailand	Murder, engineer for Tokyo Engineering Co.	Unidentified

Source: Reprinted with the permission of *Counterterrorism & Security Magazine* (Winter 1990/91), p. 23.

celebrity owners (such as Donald Trump, Merv Griffin, or Leona Helmsley). Lee Iacocca of Chrysler Corporation is a favorite of the business press because of his proven success with that company's astounding turn-around in the early 1980s. Yet when employees of Chrysler were found to be illegally tampering with odometers, the press focused not on the accused executives, but on Iacocca—he was well known, at the helm, and as a manager responsible for the actions of his subordinates.

The same is true for the heads of church and social organizations accused of wrongdoing. Although a subordinate preacher or director of finance may be accused of a sex crime or extortion, it is typically the statements and actions of the head of the organization that are most of interest to the public and the news media.

One would think that every organization knows who has a vested interest in its operations—yet that is rarely the case. Whether publicly or privately held, an organization's director of public affairs should have on hand a list of owners or shareholders, preferably with address labels printed and already on the envelopes. In the event of crisis, this resource will be invaluable.

Risk Exposure: Size of Organization and Adequate Insurance

As noted earlier, larger firms tend to be better prepared for crisis, and well they should. Certainly, the more individuals on an organization's payroll, the greater the amount of earnings generated, or the more products being used in the marketplace, the greater the danger of a calamity. Smaller firms are susceptible to crisis, to be sure, but the overall opportunity for serious crisis that could cripple the company due to lingering damage is greater when a company is well known, widely respected, and has a greater number of publics to accommodate.

Although the insurance coverage protecting both the larger and smaller firm may be equal in terms of depth of coverage, the larger the firm, the greater the risk exposure. Insurance may cover the cost of immediate damage to a factory or neighboring homes, but it may never help a company recoup its image in a competitive marketplace. Smaller companies, many of which exist because there is no competition, can often rebound with greater ease, less publicity, and less scrutiny. The insurance industry recognizes that the greater the assets owned by an individual, company, or organization, the higher the possibility that a catastrophe could place those assets at risk.

At least yearly, the organization's designated risk officer should discuss insurance and catastrophe provisions with the group's insurance agent. Often a company has protected itself against damage to a company plant from earthquake, flood, or other natural disaster. But few ask about protection from lawsuits arising from slander, libel, or copyright or patent infringement, or losses if data is stolen and sold to a competitor or foreign government.

Warning Signals

Many organizations receive early warning signals that a significant crisis could someday face them, but they fail to recognize and heed those signals. Managers need to maintain a system for monitoring emerging problems and controversies before they become an expensive embarrassment. Public relations professionals believe that this type of "issue audit" is an essential part of their work on behalf of a client.

Consider the Los Angeles Police Department, which in March 1991 was severely criticized for the alleged complicity of at least twenty-one officers in the beating of a black unarmed civilian, Rodney King (struck with a nightstick 56 times, kicked 7 times), while a neighbor videotaped the episode. This videotape was shown repeatedly to millions of television viewers. In the days after the beating, city officials, community activists, editorial writers, and others suggested that LAPD Chief Daryl F. Gates had received reports of, and failed to take concerted action on, numerous other cases of harassment and excessive use of force by the L.A. police against civilians, some of whom were stopped on routine traffic matters. In 1989, for instance, a man was handcuffed by two Los Angeles officers who stopped him on Wilshire Boulevard because a light on his license plate was not working. He happened to be a former basketball star—a fact not germane to the case but quite embarrassing, and tending to suggest that less well-known citizens were also treated this way.

With the King case, the public's fury over police misconduct reached a peak. The *New York Times* quoted Karol Heppe, executive director of the Police Misconduct Lawyers Referral Service:

> It's horrible, but I must tell you that we receive complaints in this office of that kind of conduct on a weekly basis, if not a daily basis. The difference this time is that there was somebody there to videotape it. That's the only difference.[6]

Couple that with further findings of the *Times:*

> Complaints of police brutality and racism have continued, and verdicts and settlements against the department have risen over the decades, from $553,000 in 1972 to $6.4 million in 1989 to $8 million in 1990. In one case, a jury found Chief Gates personally liable for $170,000 for a beating some of his officers gave a Hispanic family while searching for a murder weapon. One of the four officers charged in the beating of Mr. King had previously been disciplined for excessive use of force.... In the first two months [of 1991] there was a sharp rise in complaints filed against the police—127 for two months, against a yearly average over the past five years of about 600.[7]

In the days that followed, most national newspapers printed thousands of words on the story, most of them critical of the Los Angeles Police Department because it had failed to take action to prevent such unwarranted violence. Black leaders around the nation were especially indignant, and rightfully so. Geoffrey Taylor Gibbs, board member of the John M. Langston Black Lawyers Association, wrote in a nationally syndicated editorial:

> Can anyone who has seen the [King] videotape or read about the Wilkes incident not wonder what happens to residents of Los Angeles and other cities like Dallas and New York who are not famous athletes or not "lucky" enough to have their encounters with renegade officers recorded?[8]

The Los Angeles Police Department failed miserably at convincing the public that the organization understood the general outrage over the incident. In this connection, consider this definition of public relations by Otis Baskin and Craig Aronoff (emphasis added):

> Public relations is a management function that helps define organizational objectives and philosophy and facilitate organizational change. *Public relations practitioners communicate with all relevant internal and external publics in an effort to create consistency*

between organizational goals and societal expectations. Public relations practitioners develop, execute, and evaluate organizational programs that promote the exchange of influence and understanding among organizations' constituent parts and publics.[9]

In the Los Angeles case, the leader of the organization, Chief Gates, held the primary responsibility for maintaining effective relations with all publics—his officers, city officials, community leaders, and the people of Los Angeles. Some have argued that Gates failed to communicate with all his publics and he failed to understand the role of societal expectations. He was also criticized for failing to communicate any empathy with the victims of this and similar incidents. As a result, he was perceived as having broken the public trust.

Specific departments should routinely monitor phone questions and concerns as well as letters of inquiry. Often only through such communications have trends requiring recalls from toy and auto manufacturers surfaced. For the small company, such warning signals may be received in a less formal manner, but they can still foreshadow a potential lethal catastrophe. Managers should insist that designated individuals or departments log in any complaints and that summaries of those complaints be sent regularly to a central operations manager.

In the aftermath of the acquittal of four LAPD officers in April 1992, a major race riot erupted in south central Los Angeles. Murder, looting, and indiscriminate violence created havoc for industry, government, and schools. Astonishingly, it once again appeared that Chief Gates and his department had failed to anticipate a serious crisis. An amalgam of interests—National Guard troops, Mayor Thomas Bradley, citizens, and the LAPD—tried to bring calm to a city engulfed in chaos. Yet more than fifty people died in that crisis.

Communications Channels

If an organization has not established formal channels of open communication between senior management and all other levels, the risk of a prolonged and very damaging crisis is much greater. In a complex organization such as Citibank, for instance, clear communication channels have been established and refined over the years. If there is a robbery at a branch, a potentially damaging story in a trade or business journal, or a bomb threat, employees at all levels have been instructed on whom to call, what procedures to follow, and what they should and should not say to a variety of individuals and agencies. Such procedures also identify when attorneys, accountants, security agencies, or federal regulators should be informed about a crisis underway.

Organizations should designate in advance who will speak for the organization in the event of a crisis. The person in charge should attend seminars and briefings on crisis management before writing a draft company-wide communication plan for a crisis. She or he should inform all appropriate managers what their role will be in a crisis and how communication will be handled within and between offices. This person may be the same as the spokesperson or may be someone else.

Risk Associated with the Product or Service

Common sense suggests that certain types of organizations have a higher degree of crisis risk than others. Based on an exhaustive review of several hundred crises from 1981 to 1991, the following lists categorize various enterprises in terms of their susceptibility to public crisis:

High-Risk Category

All manufacturers, particularly pharmaceutical and chemical manufacturers

Banks, financial institutions, credit unions, trading institutions

Technologically sensitive firms (e.g., software development, ammunition control, and biotechnology)

Public transportation: airlines, railroads, and bus and subway systems

Hotels and motels, lodging houses, apartment buildings

Nuclear power plants

Food producers and distributors

Nightclubs and casinos

Government agencies

Amusement parks, resorts

Public personalities: politicians, entertainers

Soft drink and juice manufacturers

Helicopter, raft, shuttle boat, and pleasure craft renting

Real estate developers

Public and private utilities and airports

Builders, roofers, concrete suppliers, and structural engineering companies

Medium-Risk Category

Universities, hospitals, nonprofit agencies, churches, museums

Food and retail concerns

Petroleum manufacturers and distributors

Telecommunications companies

Household product manufacturers

Packaging plants

Computer manufacturers and distributors

Engine and heavy metal manufacturers

Elevator manufacturers

Physicians, dentists, chiropractors, and other medical professionals

Aerospace interests

Mall and shopping center operators

Health clubs, YMCAs, YWCAs, zoos, preschools

Restaurants and fast-food chains

continued

Personal hygiene product manufacturers (tampons, lotions, and so on)
Harvesting interests: fishing companies and farming concerns
Liquor, beer and wine, cigarette concerns

Low-Risk Category
Insurance agencies
Foundations, charitable trusts, special interest and community groups
Radio, television, and cable broadcasters
Certified public accountants
Photography and film manufacturers and distributors
Apparel manufacturers
Neighborhood businesses: hair cutters, pet shops, video rental companies, dry cleaners, travel agencies, real estate offices
Newspaper, magazine, and book publishers; commercial printers
Repair shops: automobiles and consumer products
Nurseries, plant and lawn businesses
Law firms
Fraternal, ethnic, and social organizations
Consulting firms
Car rental companies
Mail order and catalog companies
International agencies (such as UNESCO, World Bank)
Graphic design, interior decorating, architectural firms
Research, data collection, survey, and demographics firms

Public Awareness of Company

Mention to an audience the infamous case where several employees were killed at a computer development company in the mid 1980s and many will be unable to recall the name of the firm, ESL. But mention a gunman shooting children and adults outside a fast-food restaurant, and the vast majority of people recall that it happened at a McDonald's in southern California. We human beings tend to retain only certain information, and are more likely to recall the names of well-known companies and products associated with recalls, boycotts, acts of terrorism, or other crises much easier than names of obscure firms about whom we may have no product knowledge or brand loyalty. For instance, we remember the controversies associated with the Soviet-instigated destruction of Korean Airlines flight 007 over the Pacific. Similarly, most people recall how the community of Lockerbie, Scotland, was traumatized after bomb-exploded Pan Am flight 103 crashed onto it, leading to 270 deaths of passengers and people on the ground. Think of other plane crashes caused by natural phenomena, or by mechanical failure, and the names of

CHALLENGE

This true story will challenge your managerial skills and heighten your appreciation for quality crisis management.

Assume it is 1989, and you are president and chief executive officer of New York's Bellevue Hospital. You have just received a panic phone call from a security guard, who informs you that one of your staff physicians, Dr. Kathryn Hinnant, 33 years old and pregnant, has just been raped and murdered on the hospital's property. The guard then informs you that the assailant was Steven Smith, a patient recently discharged from the psychiatric ward of the hospital. After discharge, Smith spent two weeks in the hospital pretending to be a doctor, wearing a stethoscope and surgical garb.

As president of a nonprofit institution that depends heavily on public goodwill and the trust of patients, you quickly realize how devastating this incident could be. Hospital patients, or anyone connected to the hospital, will fear for their safety.

Take a few minutes and identify the various audiences that you must communicate with quickly. Then prepare a brief presentation to the hospital staff and physicians, who are expecting you to meet with them in the auditorium in half an hour. Although you have very little information about the incident itself, your responsibilities demand that you show leadership, empathy, and managerial decisiveness. ✳

Note to Readers: For more information on this crisis and others in the health care industry, read Walt Bogdanich, *The Great White Lie: How America's Hospitals Betray Our Trust and Endanger Our Lives* (New York: Simon & Schuster, 1991).

the airlines and circumstances surrounding those tragedies tend to be more difficult to recall.

There is a difference between what lands an organization on page one of the newspaper and how it is treated once it appears there. Although very few reporters will admit that their stories are shaped by tools of public relations, there is often a certain degree of reliance on, for example, press releases, stock photos provided by the company, and video news releases. In assessing risk, remember that preparedness for dealing with the media is crucial.

To summarize, any organization whose reputation extends beyond traditional "hometown" borders has a compelling management responsibility to rehearse and plan for a crisis. Although like their larger counterparts, local businesses can and do suffer irreparable harm from crises, much evidence suggests that far more lasting damage to reputation and profit is incurred by organizations whose recognizability extends beyond a few miles' radius. If your name is well known to more people, you are more vulnerable to lasting negative press and increased scrutiny by regulators, news organizations, citizen activist groups, and others.

Based on research in the field of crisis management, we know that the preceding are among the most important criteria used to assess the risk of an organization to the negative aftermath of a crisis. Any manager who finds that his or her organization is deficient in one or more of these areas should begin proactive planning.

INTERVIEW

Lori Heyman
This Manager Confronted Two Crises in Two Months

One reason why crises fill our newspapers and broadcasts, of course, is that so few managers prepare. Consider the following interview with Lori Heyman, a former CBS radio reporter. She is now director of U.S. public relations for Alsys, a worldwide software firm that provides sophisticated products to a number of military contractors, NASA, and other interests. Ms. Heyman had to manage several crises in the span of several months, including the sale of her company and resignation of the company president.

Q *You've made the common transition from reporter to public relations director. Given the fact that you reported so many crises as a reporter, have you tried to assess the risk at your new job?*

A It's odd. In the first few months of any job, you become so busy with the details of managing, of meeting new people, of fine-tuning an operation to your standards, and learning the new culture around you, that crisis is the furthest thing from your mind. We could have had a major headache on my second day on the job, but we were lucky.

Q *As a reporter, what did you learn about managers and risk?*

A Whenever I was sent out to cover a story about a politician in trouble or a company in trouble, these people had rarely considered risk. Certainly the vast majority of them didn't think that I'd be at their front door with thirty other reporters and photographers clamoring for their attention.

Most of the time, if there was an FBI indictment, or the state's Consumer Affairs Office charged an auto dealer with massive fraud, or whatever, the company stonewalled reporters and closed the doors—they refused comment. That was the worst possible action to take. People assume you are guilty as hell if you're not even willing to speak to a reporter. Everyone feels that a crisis will happen to someone else. Those that were prepared, with fact sheets, or a spokesperson we could talk with, usually were treated in a fair manner.

When companies weren't ready, we had to call around and scramble and do whatever we could to get *someone* to talk. And believe me, there's always someone—a former employee, competitor, a state regulator looking to be promoted, whatever—willing to talk to reporters. It's not balanced journalism, but it's about as fair as you can get in that situation.

Q *Now that you work in public relations, how prepared is your company for crisis?*

A We just experienced *two!* The founder of our company left after ten years. He was well regarded in the industry, and his name was certainly synonymous with Alsys. His departure was rather abrupt, and we feared that once our clients and potential clients learned that he was leaving, there would be a lack of confidence in our company. There were multiple concerns, about employee morale, bad press, jittery customers. Would some major customers consider his departure the beginning of the end for us? What if this was just the right reason for a trade journal to do an in-depth story on us? In cases like that, *we'd* prefer to be the ones to prompt the story, not them.

Q *Is that really a crisis?*

A Yes! this wasn't a major disaster in that there was a loss of life or anything, but in this company, direction, management—whatever you want to call it—emanates from the top. When you have a change in the top level, that's about as big a crisis as you can get, especially in a very specialized sector of an industry where there are only a few who offer the services we provide. Everyone knows everyone else.

Q *How did you plan and assess the risk?*

A First, I called for a meeting to identify the potential reactions of the press, our customers, and industry observers. Second, we set out specific means to communicate with them in advance so that they heard the news directly from us, not from other parties or a trade journal. Third, we tied in the CEO's departure with the naming of his replacement, so there was some continuity that might buffer any negative news.

Q *How did it work out for you and the company?*

A Amazingly well. Our plan worked as we expected it to. Sure, some people were worried about this person's leaving; I don't think you can pacify everyone. But the vast majority of clients saw the change as a normal event in the life cycle of an organization. I think we really minimized damage by planning ahead.

Q *What was your other crisis?*

A Just one month later, our parent company in France filed for reorganization, or what we'd term Chapter 11 in this country. Talk about a crisis! We received phone calls, faxes, and messages from all over the globe. Although we are a separate division of the parent company, and our business is very healthy, there is an understandable degree of anxiety for our current and prospective clients. They want to know, Are you going to be there two years from now? What's the reason behind the financial problems of your parent company?

This kind of crisis is really complex. Do you announce the problems of your parent company? Ignore them? What do you tell the U.S. industry trade press? Will your competitors use the information against you when they're soliciting contracts? If so, do you sue them if they are engaging in questionable practices? Does the SEC get involved?

We decided to be proactive, and we worked with a few key industry publications in printing stories that clearly differentiated our company from the parent. Our salespeople went out of their way to personally assure major clients of our independence and stability. All of this has happened just in the past two months, but we are doing fine. But what a headache! I'm becoming an expert at crisis management myself.

Q *What other kinds of potential crises might you face?*

A Product defects, corporate sabotage, the selling of company secrets—they're all very real in this industry. In the past year I've spent time developing risk assessment for all these areas, and we're now in the midst of finalizing crisis plans for each of those areas. We may not enjoy the same level of success with each of them as we had with the departure of the CEO, but we'll be in better shape than if we had not looked at risk at all.

CASE STUDY: MORE THAN MILK AND BREAD?

Cumberland Farms is a convenience store chain based in Canton, Massachusetts, with about 1,100 outlets located on the East Coast between Maine and Florida. The profitable chain caters to shoppers who are avoiding major supermarkets and who usually spend under $10 per visit on milk, eggs, and other essentials.

Like many chains staffed by usually young, teenaged clerks handling a large amount of cash on a daily basis, Cumberland Farms has been concerned for many years about the potential for stealing by company clerks. Many stores have installed video surveillance systems to check the activities of both customers and employees, while others use vacuum-based drawers to routinely remove cash and, supposedly, any enticement to steal from cash registers.

Cumberland Farms' approach to potential employee theft may or may not be unusual, but it certainly has been newsworthy. In late 1990, a series of stories began appearing in major newspapers and news magazines reporting that Cumberland officials had allegedly used extortion and coercion to force employees, some of them known to be innocent, into signing admission statements that they had committed grand larceny. One employee, Shirley DiSalvo, nine months pregnant, was arrested in August 1990, in a Delaware parking lot some four years after being accused of stealing $2,900 from a Hobe Sound, Florida, Cumberland Farms. She argued that she had been pressured into signing the admission in 1986 and was innocent. The governor's office arranged for her to be released.

A flurry of reports appeared throughout the country. On September 24, 1990, *Newsweek* reported that "In the last few months, hundreds of other ex-employees of Cumberland Farms have come forward with allegations of coercion and extortion by the convenience store chain." The company denied the charges, but *Newsweek* challenged that statement by quoting former Cumberland investigators who admitted that they intimidated employees into signing false statements. As a result, many employees reported that not only had their morale been impaired, but that they felt scared as a result of the tactics of their employer.

Cumberland Farms has a serious crisis on its hands. Typically located in stand-alone locations in middle-class neighborhoods, the company has flourished because it offers quality products at reasonable prices and without the traffic, lines, and delays of a large supermarket. In many cases, managers and employees are neighborhood residents themselves who are known and liked by their clientele. With each new headline, however, the company, and its honest employees, face a dilemma that includes a crisis of confidence.

Loss prevention is a serious problem for retail America. Serious, too, are charges that any company would knowingly implement a program of intimidation. Consider what steps Cumberland Farms can and should pursue in addressing the following issues:

1. Local newspapers in the hundreds of communities where Cumberland Farms outlets are located may want to put a local "spin" on this national story. In many cases, editors from these journals will read about Shirley DiSalvo and her colleagues in news magazines and want to focus on what cases, if any, have taken place locally. Should Cumberland Farms design a proactive or reactive program in communicating with these local newspapers?

2. Advertising programs for the company may need to be reexamined. If the company is in the midst of a major advertising campaign, or about to launch such an effort, should the content of the message be altered in any way?

Should current or planned advertising be postponed? For how long? What are the pros and cons of such a decision? Should a focus group of random consumers be commissioned to determine the extent of damage, if any, these stories have had on the reputation and viability of the company?

3. Law enforcement officials in many communities began questioning whether cases that they had prosecuted in the past were legitimate or contrived. Some have told the company that they will not prosecute cases in the future unless detailed documents on company policies are produced. How should the company communicate with law enforcement officials so as to maintain their confidence in the future? Is it possible that by communicating with law officials they may attract unnecessary and unwanted attention to this crisis of confidence in the company? ❏

Note to Readers: On May 4, 1992, Cumberland Farms filed for Chapter 11 of the U.S. Bankruptcy Code. The *Wall Street Journal* reported that "a number of former Cumberland employees have filed lawsuits alleging that the company falsely accused them of stealing cash and goods from stores … Cumberland has denied the allegations."

ENDNOTES

1. Robert F. Hartley, *Management Mistakes & Successes*, 3d ed. (New York: Wiley, 1991), p. 359.
2. Henry Mintzberg, "The Strategy Concept II: Another Look at Why Organizations Need Strategies," *California Management Review,* Fall 1987, p. 25.
3. Charles F. Hermann, "Some Consequences of Crisis Which Limit the Viability of Organizations," *Administrative Sciences Quarterly* 8 (1963): 61.
4. Anne Reilly, "Are Organizations Ready for a Crisis?" *Columbia Journal of World Business,* Spring 1987, p. 81.
5. Joseph Z. Wisenbilt, "Crisis Management Planning Among U.S. Corporations: Empirical Evidence and a Proposed Framework," *SAM Advanced Management Journal* 54 (Spring 1989): 35.
6. Seth Mydans, "Tape of Beating by Police Revives Charges of Racism," *New York Times,* March 7, 1991, p. A2.
7. "A Videotape of a Police Beating Puts National Glare on Issue of Brutality" *New York Times,* March 18, 1991, p. A8.
8. Geoffrey Taylor Gibbs, "L.A. Cops Taped in the Act," *New York Times,* March 12, 1991, p. 33.
9. Otis Baskin and Craig Aronoff, *Public Relations* (Dubuque, IA: Brown, 1988), p. 4.

4

Complex Crises

The outcomes of the Ford Pinto and Johnson & Johnson Tylenol cases are now known. Ford executives were defensive until forced to admit that there were problems with the vehicle. Johnson & Johnson executives, on the other hand, remained accommodative throughout the incident, even though our data show that their firm suffered considerable stock market damage. The initial stock market impact on Johnson & Johnson was quite negative, but in the long term the actions of the company's management earned the firm respect and helped it gain back market share in a remarkably short time, given the nature of the problem. Ford, in contrast, suffered reputational damage. It also had to pay large awards to the victims, which hurt the company financially. These cases suggest that it may take many years before the true impact of managerial actions can be understood. ❑

Alfred Marcus and Robert Goodman, "Victims And Shareholders: The Dilemmas Of Presenting Corporate Policy During A Crisis," *Academy of Management Executives* (1991)

To flourish, publicly traded corporations must communicate effectively with a variety of publics. If a company is to maintain a healthy stock price, many individuals—shareholders, brokers, investment analysts, regulators, customers, and others—must receive timely information on the company's status and intentions. This need has led in recent years to a dramatic increase in efforts by companies and corporations to enhance communication with shareholders.

A few statistics provide amplification. According to North American Precis Syndicate, as of late 1991, "There are over 650 companies with more than a billion in assets, more than 550 firms with more than a billion in value of common shares, and more than 600 with more than a billion in sales." Yes, we're talking dollars. These dollar amounts underscore the importance of communication with multiple audiences in the midst of chaos.

A CRISIS IN INVESTOR CONFIDENCE: SELL THAT STOCK!

Organizations use annual reports, annual and meetings, newsletters, and other communication vehicles to keep the public abreast of their progress. When crises occur, these audiences will be closely watching and listening to the statements of managers. If investors or analysts detect corrupt behavior, a pending indictment, poor dividend news, a major product recall, or some other problem, a sense of panic could cripple the company. Nervous individual and institutional investors tend to react in unison when there is news that a company may be in trouble. By selling in large quantities, such investors drive down the value of the stock and, as a result, the value of the organization itself. Stock market analysts, shareholders, business commentators in the mass media—all will actively monitor and comment on the volatility of share prices, prompting some to purchase and some to sell their interest in the corporation.

The ramifications from any loss in investor confidence are multifold. A manager needs to be concerned about many questions, including the following:

1. If investors sell in large numbers, how will various brokerage houses, who recommend stocks to their clients, regard the short- and long-term prospects of the company? How long will it take for the company to rebound? How can the company assure these advisers that the organization has a competent management team that can turn around a short-term crisis?

2. How can the company communicate quickly, personally, and individually with its shareholders to avoid a panic? Given widespread viewing of Cable News Network (CNN), CNBC, and other media that instantaneously report downturns in stock value, is it even feasible to communicate with shareholders quickly and personally?

3. Who is the most appropriate spokesperson for a company when the stock value of the organization is at risk? Should the visible CEO speak on behalf

of the company, or should a technical analyst or public relations spokesperson speak?

THE STRATEGIC IMPORTANCE OF INVESTOR RELATIONS

Investor relations consultants perform an important management function, offering expert advice to companies such as Chrysler, Bally's, AT&T, and NCR. Those who specialize in this area often bring to it an extensive background in investment brokerage firms or in a government regulatory agency such as the Securities and Exchange Commission (SEC). Such professionals advertise routinely in *Barron's, Public Relations Journal, O'Dwyers Public Relations Report,* and other journals. They are experts at communicating salient issues to company investors and many other audiences, and they can help develop a comprehensive strategy to achieve the organization's management and communication goals.

Because these consultants have typically spent many years working in financial markets, they can advise a management team on the importance of communicating effectively and rapidly with stockholders and brokerage houses. Their mission involves developing the content of messages to be sent, identifying the most strategically important vehicles for dissemination (such as direct mail or an open letter in a financial newspaper), and responding to questions raised by financial reporters. They play an especially significant role during leveraged buyout attempts, hostile takeovers, restructuring, and bankruptcy proceedings.

ISSUES THAT CONCERN INVESTORS AND THE GENERAL PUBLIC

The American Stock Exchange, like the other exchanges, has ruled that its members (that is, publicly traded companies) must publicly disseminate any news of its operations that fits into following categories:[1]

- Joint venture, merger, or acquisition
- Declaration of omission of dividends or of the determination of earnings
- Stock split or stock dividend
- Acquisition or loss of a significant contract
- A significant new product or discovery
- A change in control or significant change in management
- Call of securities for redemption
- Borrowing of a significant amount of funds
- Public or private sale of a significant amount of additional securities

- Significant litigation
- Purchase or sale of a significant asset
- Significant change in capital investment plans
- Significant labor dispute or disputes with contractors or suppliers
- Establishment of program to make purchases of company's own shares
- Tender offer for another company's securities

Any of these events signals the need for effective communication. The cases that follow illustrate the impact of investor confidence in an organization.

Chrysler and Odometers

In early 1981, Chrysler Corporation was at a low ebb. Consumer confidence in the company was mediocre at best, sales were lagging behind U.S. and Japanese competitors, and management was under pressure to reinvigorate the company. These tasks were difficult—the company had declined to just $8 million in liquid assets. In their analysis of the case, two public relations experts, Otis Baskin and Craig Aronoff, report that

> Company lawyers held that Chrysler must issue a press release to disclose its near insolvency, but company officials risked being charged by the SEC rather than destroy what little confidence their creditors and customers had left. The release went unissued and the company survived—its potential insolvency made a moot point by its renewed financial health.[2]

Chrysler, of course, is a wonderful "comeback" story of an organization that, in the middle of a financial disaster, found its charismatic and talented CEO, Lee Iacocca, ready to champion its cause. Iacocca had developed personal friendships with a number of influential policymakers in Washington and elsewhere. When he personally pleaded with the U.S. Congress for $1.5 *billion* dollars in loan guarantees to preserve the major auto maker, a tacit threat was implied: without such support, one of America's manufacturing giants would close. This raised the possibility of further penetration into the U.S. marketplace by Japanese auto makers, as well as the bleak prospect that tens of thousands of dismissed Chrysler workers would have no alternative jobs waiting for them.

Despite several major investor crises, Chrysler has survived. Another crisis began in 1986. When a Chrysler executive was stopped for a routine speeding violation, the first chapter in an investor crisis got underway. The executive told the police officer that he didn't know how fast he was going because the speedometer cable (which also operates the odometer) was disconnected.[3] When it was learned that Chrysler had systematically disconnected odometers on cars used by executives for testing and model purposes and then reconnected them before being sold, consumers reacted with outrage. Investors were right behind them. By the summer of 1987, a federal jury had indicted Chrysler for mail and wire fraud as well as conspiracy.

At issue was the fact that the company had routinely provided vehicles for assembly plant managers to test-drive, but many kept them for days or weeks at a time, with the odometers having been disconnected. When the vehicles were sold months later, customers assumed the cars were new, although as many as forty of them had been involved in minor accidents.

With investor confidence low, and institutional investors concerned over an erosion of value in stock price, chairman Iacocca went public in a series of hard-hitting press conferences and advertisements. He was well respected as an effective and personable communicator. This attribute, coupled with the fact that he was perceived by many as a credible manager, enhanced Iacocca's public persona. His message was emphatic: "America, we apologize.... Testing cars is a good idea. Disconnecting odometers is a lousy idea. That's a mistake we won't make again at Chrysler. Period."[4] (Despite the candor, however, questions remain unanswered about Chrysler's alleged unwillingness to release all pertinent data on the case.[5])

Chrysler is hardly the only auto manufacturer that has seen investors react to a crisis. As you will read, other leading auto manufacturers, including General Motors, have also experienced strained relations with stockholders.

Lee Iacocca of Chrysler, responding to reporters' questions. He has served as a credible spokesperson during at least two embarrassments since his tenure as chairperson.

Ralph Nader Challenges Industry Giant GM

One of the most famous examples of stockholders protesting corporate policy occurred in 1970 when consumer activist Ralph Nader, who owned only twelve shares of stock in General Motors, began his "Project on Corporate Responsibility." One of Nader's first projects was "Campaign GM," aimed at demanding that GM address social issues. Specifically, he argued that the company should include three consumers on GM's Board of Directors. He also presented the company a plan that would institute stronger air and water pollution standards as well as require GM to pledge to manufacture safer cars in the future.

GM and Nader separately courted stockholders on these proposals. As a result, the news media flocked to the annual meeting because the debate promised to be colorful and substantive. And the company received an unusually high number of requests to attend its annual meeting where Nader's proposal would be debated. In the end, a capacity crowd of 3,500 investors saw General Motors make a series of concessions, albeit small ones, to the growing consumer movement led by Nader.

National press attention was now squarely focused on Nader's "David versus Goliath" battle, and GM spent millions of dollars on consultants, documentary films, letters to shareholders, and public relations to discredit Nader's arguments.

Ralph Nader openly challenged the corporate policies of General Motors in 1970, causing the auto maker to quickly rally support from nervous investors.

(A more recent episode of one person challenging GM was reflected in the 1990 motion picture *Roger and Me*.) Some people who believe the corporation failed to act in a socially responsible manner have widely criticized GM's actions (and failure to act) during its battles with Nader.

Crisis managers need to be prepared to defend themselves, especially when the opponent is a highly regarded activist such as Nader who can achieve widespread publicity. In the case of General Motors, it is difficult to attribute any major drop in stock value to Nader's campaign, but public relations damage was clearly inflicted on the auto giant. Had GM ignored Nader and his evidence, the confidence of consumers and the financial community might have lessened, reducing the overall value of the company.

AT&T Courts NCR Acquisition

The attempt by American Telephone and Telegraph (AT&T) to seize control of computer giant National Cash Register (NCR) in early 1991 created an incipient crisis for a variety of publics, including employees and investors of both companies.

When AT&T publicly announced that it was interested in acquiring NCR and that it would pay as much as $90 a share in the company, both companies faced a potential crisis. AT&T was criticized for its interest in the computer industry, given its lackluster success in the past in that arena. And NCR employees and management were seriously concerned that in the event of a sale, they could lose their jobs. (In the end, it was actually AT&T employees who suffered the most: between 5,000 and 6,000 workers in the computer operations division lost their positions.)

Naturally, NCR shareholders had varying attitudes toward AT&T's takeover bid. For those who had purchased shares in NCR years earlier at $40 a share or less, the prospect of more than doubling their investment seemed welcome news.

NCR faced two sorts of crises. First, for those who had worked for many years to make NCR a leading computer entity, the entire "culture" of the company could soon be wiped out by the telecommunications giant. Second, NCR needed to convince shareholders who stood to reap huge profits from the sale of their stock that it was still in their best interest *not* to sign a proxy mailed to them by AT&T.

In reaction to the barrage of commentary on the deal in the news media, in investment newsletters, on Wall Street and elsewhere, both companies chose a highly visible communications strategy. Both AT&T and NCR wrote directly to all shareholders of record. Both purchased full-page advertisements in leading newspapers arguing for or against the acquisition of NCR. Both companies made available to talk shows and news programs a pool of articulate media spokespersons who could advance *their* organization's arguments while criticizing their opponent's statements. Correspondence between the chief executive officers of the two corporate giants reflects the magnitude of the crisis that they were facing. See Exhibit 4-1 for excerpts from those letters.

EXHIBIT 4-1   Correspondence Between the Chairmen of NCR and AT&T

AT&T, NCR Engaged in War of Words

A flurry of correspondence between NCR Chairman Charles E. Exley, Jr., and AT&T Chairman Robert E. Allen in 1990 escalated into a heated war of words over the merits of such a merger. What follows are excerpts from that correspondence:

Dear Bob:

... The board of directors of NCR has unanimously determined to reject AT&T's proposal to purchase NCR for $85 per share in AT&T stock as not in the best interests of the shareholders and other stakeholders of NCR.

... We at NCR are disappointed that, despite our having shared with you our most candid and careful evaluation of your proposal and the attendant risks for everyone affected by it, you have continued in your efforts to acquire NCR.

... If AT&T is prepared to offer a price which more accurately reflects what you characterized to our board as the substantial prospects of NCR's business plan.... NCR is prepared to enter into private discussions.

—Exley to Allen, Nov. 30

Dear Chuck:

... I had hoped by now we would be jointly announcing the successful negotiation of the merger. Unfortunately, this is not the case....

... To our surprise, your advisers promptly dismissed our higher proposal and stated that NCR would not share any information, meet with us or our advisers or even look at a draft of the merger agreement until we further increased our price to an unstated amount that you consider to be "preemptive."

... AT&T and its board of directors are committed to the combination of our two companies....

—Allen to Exley, Dec. 2

Dear Bob:

I am puzzled and dismayed by the misleading characterizations of the events to date both in your latest letter and AT&T's Dec. 2 press release. The press release could only have been written by someone with no knowledge of the facts.

... I want to set the record straight. You came to us with an unsolicited proposal to acquire NCR in an $85 stock-for-stock transaction, which threatened a hostile takeover.... We have never participated in negotiations with AT&T relating to any potential business combination.

... The combination of AT&T and NCR makes no sense from a business or strategic view.... Already the process of destroying [AT&T] shareholder value ... is under way.

—Exley to Allen, Dec. 3

Dear Bob:

... NCR is prepared to commence negotiations *if* AT&T offers to pay not less than $125 per NCR share.

... You have still given us no reason whatsoever to change our view that the transaction you propose makes no business sense, and so it must be a desperate attempt to salvage AT&T's disastrous foray into the computer business.

—Exley to Allen, Dec. 5

Dear Chuck:

I'm sorry to tell you that AT&T feels it now has no choice but to go ahead tomorrow and commence its cash tender offer for NCR at $90 per share.... We intend to continue our computer business under the NCR name and the leadership of NCR's senior management....

Second, we do not intend, in any way, that NCR's people be diverted from dedicating all their energies and resources toward NCR's existing programs and customers.... We do not understand how you can maintain ... that a merger at $125 in AT&T stock would work ... but a merger at $90 would be a strategic disaster. Chuck, all we have is a difference of opinion on price.

—Allen to Exley, Dec. 5

Source: Copyright 1990 by CW Publishing, Inc., Framingham, Massachusetts. Reprinted from *Computerworld*, p. 6.

On May 7, 1991, the two companies, after five months of costly and at times acrimonious exchanges of words, announced that they had settled their differences and that the acquisition was complete. AT&T had acquired NCR for $110 per share in a deal that is valued at more than $7.4 billion. Executives of NCR, who clearly had reservations about their company being gobbled by the mammoth AT&T, recognized that the gains to be accrued from the acquisition were in the best interests of all parties, given the alternative of a protracted and probably unsuccessful defense against the telecommunications giant.

TACTICAL MANEUVERS BEFORE AND DURING A FINANCIAL CRISIS

Whether a company uses an in-house investment communication specialist or an outside consultant, the options open to a company in the midst of an investment crisis include

1. Sending letters or faxes, or making phone calls to major investors of record.

2. Calling for a special informational meeting before a vote on a merger, sale, acquisition, or other major corporate action.

3. Calling for a news conference to announce a company's response to a particular crisis.

4. Creating a video news release in which a company executive articulates the response of an organization to the investment crisis. (The video may include helpful graphics to illustrate management's objectives.)

5. Issuing a news release to reputable news wire services such as the Associated Press, Reuters, Dow Jones, or others

6. If the content of news stories about the company is believed to be incomplete, inaccurate, or hostile, purchasing advertising space to explain the actions of the organization. (In many cases an 800 number is included so that investor questions can be addressed in a more personal fashion.)

Even though the number of leveraged buyouts has dwindled drastically in the 1990s, publicly traded companies still face a barrage of crises that could affect the value of their stock; recalls, product defects, and mergers are a few that have already been mentioned. Such companies should be prepared with

1. Regularly updated, preaddressed envelopes ready for mailing to stockholders so that any emergency message or brochure can rapidly communicate news of the company to investors.

2. Press kits that include stock photos of company managers, products, and headquarters building and fact sheets that give pertinent information on the company's history, growth, and product line. (When crisis hits, only the

last-minute news release or information update needs to be added for immediate distribution.)

3. A telecommunications plan so that an 800 number can be launched quickly to field questions from investors and consumers.

4. A frequently updated list of home phone numbers and cellular numbers of the executive staff so that investor relations managers can promptly address any emergency-related questions from regulators or major shareholders.

PRODUCT INVESTIGATIONS IN THE PUBLIC INTEREST

Over the years, the process of monitoring product safety has taken several forms. In Washington, D.C., the Consumer Product Safety Commission (CPSC) routinely tests a variety of products, from toys to hand mixers to ladders, to determine their strength, durability, and safety. The Food and Drug Administration (FDA) shares similar responsibilities for all storebought food and prescription and over-the-counter medicines intended for human consumption. The Consumers Union of the United States (based in Yonkers, New York) was founded in 1936 and publishes *Consumer Reports*, a highly regarded magazine that accepts no advertising and rates hundreds of products and services each year for their value and safety. Underwriters' Laboratories (UL) tests the safety of thousands of electric and telecommunications products each year. These and many other private and quasi-governmental agencies work vigilantly to protect the buying public.

Yet despite the best efforts of quality control managers, unannounced plant inspections and other safety checks, product defects or tampering occur all to often. For example, snack manufacturers have recalled popular candy bars because of the presence of rodent hairs and droppings. And almost every major automobile manufacturer has at one time or another found itself recalling tens of thousands of vehicles for a technical defect, mechanical failure, or potential safety threat. Toy manufacturers both here and abroad sometimes find their products being confiscated in foreign trade zones and on shipping piers once a state or federal agency announces that it is halting sales because of a threat to the lives of infants and children. In recent years, several notable pharmaceutical companies, including those already discussed (such as Johnson & Johnson and Burroughs Wellcome) have become victims of product tampering and were forced to recall entire lines of over-the-counter medicines.

PRODUCT DEFECTS AND RECALLS

Although most organizations work diligently to ensure that a safe and effective product is delivered to consumers, recalls can be triggered by an order of a federal agency after an intensive review, if product tampering is suspected, if new tests identify a threat to life not previously identified, or if consumer complaints are found to be legitimate. According to *The Communicator* (December 1990), more than 500,000 product liability lawsuits are now filed against manufacturers and distributors each year, compared with only 30,000 in 1960. And if you read just one page of the April 1991 issue of *Consumer Reports*, you would have found that these products were among some of those targeted for recall during the preceding month:[6]

- '89–'90 Jeep Cherokee and Comanche
- Little Levi's red leather girls' belts
- '88–'90 Eagle Premier, '90 Dodge Monaco
- Petrus umbrella strollers
- '91 Jeep Cherokee
- Bib to Bowl pacifiers
- B. F. Goodrich, Liberator, Parkway, Spartan, and Stratton tires
- '88–'90 Holiday Rambler motor homes
- '91 BMW M5
- Superior aloe vera drinks

To err is human, and recalls are often the result. Whether a product defect occurs because of machine misfunctions or human error, any defect inevitably poses a tremendous problem to an organization. In the life of every organization, it is commonplace to find "slips" in the normal process of production and distribution. Occasionally customers are told the wrong information about price or durability of a product, or hundreds of boxes of cereal are shipped without the free prize that is usually dropped in from a conveyer belt. These are hardly major crises and, although serious from a customer service viewpoint, have little bearing on crisis management.

Product defects become serious when there is a direct threat to the safety of the end user or when the reputation of the organization could be seriously tarnished. In these cases, swift, decisive, and socially responsible action is essential. In order to determine appropriate action in a recall situation, the FDA has established the guidelines shown on page 83.

Although the public is familiar with product recalls, the process of deciding when to issue a formal recall and how to manage and influence public opinion during this phase has not been well studied. For a young company whose managers have been working feverishly to gain market share, a recall is a crisis. A single recall can damage reputation and impair future sales. Even for a mature organization, a recall can lead to questions about the safety of other products or services the company offers. Almost every sector of the economy—food and beverages, drugs, electronic equipment, appliances, components, transportation, and others—have

---

CLASSIFICATIONS OF A RECALL

The Food, Drug, and Cosmetics Act divides recalls into three categories:

Class 1: Such recalls involve a threat to life. The FDA will demand a comprehensive consumer recall and meaningful and complete public announcements to ensure that the public is made aware of the threatening situation.

Class 2: In these potentially hazardous (but not life-threatening) cases, the FDA will usually insist on a recall but not require that the manufacturer comply with a 100 percent effectiveness check. Some kind of public announcement may be required by the government.

Class 3: Although there is no serious hazard to life or property, there is a limited recall of a product in certain regions or areas; no public announcements are deemed necessary.

---

all been faced with product recalls because of defects or tampering. Several notable examples merit brief review.

Consumer Reports and Chrysler

Consumer Reports discusses product safety, reliability, and price competitiveness in detail, but some corporate executives admit privately that they loathe the publication because the threat always exists that their products could be negatively mentioned. The magazine has chided the makers of the Suzuki Samurai, the Audi 5000, and hundreds of other products. In the summer of 1978, Consumer Reports carried a negative story about steering inconsistencies in the Plymouth Horizon/Dodge Omni line, and sales of the autos dropped dramatically.

In February 1991, Consumer Reports told its readers that the Chrysler Ultradrive transmission was a mechanical nightmare. This was a significant blow for Chrysler, whose Dodge Caravan and Plymouth Voyager vans had proven immensely popular with car buyers over the years. As a result of *Consumer Reports'* article and consumer outrage over the Ultradrive system, the company finally agreed to telephone all 1.1 million owners of vehicles that had that transmission to check on customer satisfaction.[7] One has to wonder whether Chrysler would have taken such a drastic (and expensive) step had it not been for such consumer guardians publicly demanding that companies produce safer and more reliable products.

Over the years we have witnessed a barrage of recalls or criticisms of products that ultimately lead to product redesign or discontinuance. One of the most notable recalls was the Ford Pinto, which received widespread negative publicity after numerous consumer publications and "60 Minutes" challenged the safety of the car's fuel tank design. Although two million units had been sold, car sales dwindled by 1978, and the model was eventually shelved.

The Tylenol Recall

On September 28, 1982, Johnson & Johnson's Tylenol commanded over 35 percent of the over-the-counter pain reliever market and was the envy of its competition. The product was widely respected by consumers, physicians, and hospitals for its effectiveness, and it generated about $400 million in annual sales. Then, between September 29 and October 1, 1982, seven people died after taking Extra-Strength Tylenol capsules.

Over these two days, as reports spread that cyanide had been placed in some capsules, sales dropped by 87 percent and public confidence waned. The company reacted swiftly and decisively: 22 million bottles were recalled and destroyed, at a cost exceeding $100 million.[8] In addition, an 800 telephone number system was quickly launched so that customers, law enforcement agencies, and others could ask questions of J&J officials.

The company received more than 2,500 media inquiries, resulting in over 125,000 press clippings. Astonishingly, the Tylenol scare received the most press coverage of any news story since the assassination of President John F. Kennedy in 1963.[9] In some ways, the story that evolved was not just one of consumers who had been victimized, but of the remarkably polished and professional public relations coup that J&J managers were executing. One press observer noted,

> A major factor in the public's willingness to buy Tylenol again was the public relations offensive developed by a seven-member J&J strategy group. The group met twice daily in Chairman Burke's office during the first six weeks of the crisis. The offensive included appearances by the chairman on major national television programs such as the "Phil Donahue Show," allowing Mike Wallace and a "60 Minutes" crew to film a strategy session, and a 30-city teleconference to reintroduce triple-sealed Tylenol capsules.[10]

Although one telephone survey in the aftermath of the recall showed that 45 percent of those questioned said they would not take Tylenol again because of the tampering, J&J's managerial response dramatically changed public perception of the safety and efficacy of the product.[11] In the end, Tylenol came out in tamper-resistant packages and reclaimed its market share. J&J has been widely praised for its superb handling of the crisis and the remarkable marketing rebound that was to follow. Harold Burson, chairman of Burson-Marsteller Public Relations and a consultant to J&J on the Tylenol crisis, wrote in *Management Review* that "By taking the offensive and addressing the concerns, real and imagined, of key audiences, a company is more likely to be viewed as a responsible and responsive citizen rather than a recalcitrant or indifferent monolith."[12] Bravo.

In addition to the tragic loss of life of those poisoned, the crisis can also be looked at in terms of Johnson & Johnson's financial loss. On May 13, 1991, the day that jury selection was set to begin in a suit against J&J by the families of the victims, the company settled the matter out of court for an undisclosed sum. The company also incurred a $100 million pretax charge for the 1982 recall of its product. Totaling the costs associated with the recall, advertising messages to customers during and after the poisoning crisis, pretax charges, and related costs, we can reasonably assume that Johnson & Johnson incurred about $500 million in costs due to the Tylenol crises. Moreover, Mark Mitchell, a professor at the University of Chicago, has researched the issue of recognizability of Tylenol and estimates that the loss in brand value has been about $1 billion since the first crisis occurred.[13]

Nevertheless, despite the tremendous cost to Johnson & Johnson in terms of image and profit, there is no question that their management's superb handling of the incident is the standard against which most other major incidents have been measured.

Rely Tampons: When Market Leaders Receive the Greatest Scrutiny

Rely Tampons, produced by Procter & Gamble, were embroiled in a massive public relations nightmare in June 1980 when the U.S. Centers for Disease Control (CDC) reported a possible link between toxic shock syndrome (TSS) and tampon use. Rely, a clear leader in terms of industry sales, received the brunt of consumer and regulatory scrutiny even though the CDC did not at first target a specific brand of tampon that might be lethal or harmful. By September of that year, the CDC had announced that Rely Tampons were more frequently associated with TSS than other tampons studied; twenty-five deaths from TSS were reported, although not all of these were due to use of Rely tampons. P&G lost over $55 million in terms of lost sales and legal and recall fees.

Speculation abounded in women's magazines and lifestyle pages of daily newspapers over whether tampon use was safe, whether "super absorbent" products placed the user at particularly high risk, and whether some manufacturers had been aware of potential dangers. After substantial study of tampons by independent testing laboratories and product makers, tampons were relabeled to warn consumers about the potential risks of TSS. However, irreparable harm had been done to the good name of Rely.

Sudafed: Was Burroughs Sleeping During the Tylenol Crisis?

Almost a decade after the Tylenol and Rely Tampon crises, in March 1991, Burroughs Wellcome was widely criticized for failing to swiftly inform the public that at least one instance of poisoned Sudafed capsules had surfaced. Reportedly, the company waited about a week to announce that poisoning may have been linked to its product. Company executives then ordered their 600 sales representatives to contact 18,000 pharmacies and other stores and retrieve Sudafed, a process that took about three days.

When analysts and reporters compared Johnson & Johnson's aggressive management and public actions in the Tylenol poisonings with Burroughs's reportedly sluggish response, a dichotomy was evident. The *Wall Street Journal* noted,

Burroughs Wellcome followed the textbook crisis management forged by Johnson & Johnson—but only up to a point . . . customers have been left largely in the dark regarding what comes next. The company set up a toll-free number to answer questions, for example, but never advertised it. It suggested in its first, March 3, news release that customers return all Sudafed 12-hour capsules, but didn't back that up with widespread information on refunds or exchanges.[14]

As the Sudafed story unfolded, regulators and others began to question why Burroughs Wellcome reportedly waited almost a full month after product tampering was first suspected to announce foul play, even though the first case was not *fatal* to the victim. And despite the best efforts of the sales representatives in recovering capsules from store shelves, Sudafed was still sold in some cities. The Associated Press quoted FDA spokesperson Susan Hutchcroft, in reporting that some capsules were still on shelves after the recall: "I don't know how stores have missed the news, but some apparently have."[15]

Perrier: Managing a Recall Across the Atlantic*

By January 1990, sales of Perrier bottled water had reached an all-time high. The French-based company commanded a tremendous market share lead over its competitors, as shown in Exhibit 4-2.

Then a crisis took its toll. In February 1990, the Perrier Group of Greenwich, Connecticut, voluntarily recalled 70 million bottles of Perrier water in the United States after traces of the chemical benzene were found in samples produced over a previous seven-month period. First introduced to U.S. consumers in 1977, Perrier became the world's best-known sparkling mineral water. As the premiere product within its category, Perrier had flourished during the 1980s as a fashionable drink for the wealthy and health conscious.

For almost forty years, Perrier has been produced by extracting its natural CO_2 gas and spring water separately from the same ground formation; the water and

EXHIBIT 4-2   Estimated 1989 Wholesale Revenue of Major U.S. Bottled-Water Companies

Perrier Group of America	**$640 million**
McKesson (Sparkletts)	225 million
Anjou (Hinckley & Schmitt)	125 million
Suntory (Kentwood)	100 million
Clorox (Deer Park)	50 million
Evian	50 million

Source: The Perrier Group of America, Inc.

---

*Portions of the Perrier discussion previously appeared in Laurence Barton's article "A Case in Crisis Management: The Perrier Recall," *Industrial Management and Data Systems* 7(1991).

gas are then combined in a bottling plant. The process has been reviewed by regulators in both France and the United States and found to be safe. Exhibit 4-3 shows how Perrier produces and distributes its product.

With news that abnormal traces of benzene, which occur naturally in this process, had been found in Perrier, company managers acted quickly. They arranged to have an 800 number promoted so that consumer concerns could be addressed, even though there was no apparent health risk. Company executives, who had wisely hired a crisis management firm a year earlier to advise it on precisely such a calamity, went to work. Their first pledge was to work to maintain the trust of the consuming public and to cooperate with FDA investigators.

Despite conflicting statements and press reports on the source of the benzene (a Paris press conference by the company on February 14 was called "raucous" by the *Wall Street Journal*), the company later determined that a faulty filtering process was to blame. When alterations to that process were completed, shipments of the product from France resumed within three months. The reintroduced Perrier water now carried a label marked New Production.

In the end, the *Wall Street Journal* estimated (February 12, 1990) that the recall cost Perrier some $40 million in lost sales. Earlier in this chapter, we discussed how stock prices of companies in the midst of a crisis can nose-dive, and Perrier was no exception. In one day alone—February 12, 1990—the recall caused Perrier's stock to tumble 202 French francs ($35.65) to close at 1,490 francs ($263). At one point that day, there were so many sell orders that the Paris market suspended further trading in Perrier stock.

EXHIBIT   4-3   The Perrier Pipeline from France to Major U.S. Distribution Points

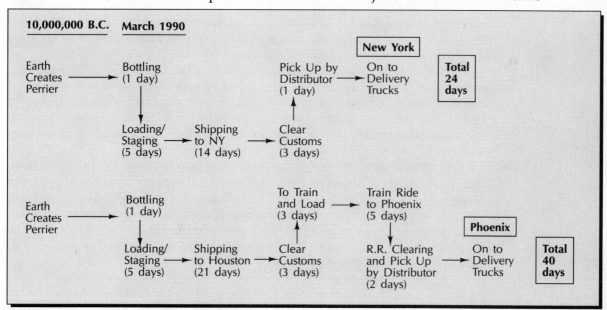

Source: The Perrier Group of America, Inc..

In the United States, Perrier is delivered to consumers through two primary distribution sites in New York and Phoenix. As Exhibit 4-3 indicates, the process of shipping to these cities varies considerably. On a piece of paper, list all the crises, both small and large, that could occur in either "pipeline" and that you believe company executives should consider in preparing Perrier's crisis management plan. Examine the chart carefully, and consider the possibility of industrial accidents, natural disasters, transportation disorders, and other crises mentioned thus far. ✳

Perrier had serious concern over public reaction to the reintroduced product. Their management contracted with the public relations firm of Burson-Marsteller to measure public attitudes toward the company in its primary markets, namely France, the United States, the United Kingdom, and Canada. In reintroducing the product, Perrier aggressively promoted the return of the popular drink by placing major advertisements in leading newspapers offering free bottles as a means of thanking customers for their loyalty and understanding. The marketing and promotion effort aimed at reintroducing the product to the consuming public cost Perrier some $25 million. One of several advertisements showing Perrier's response to its crisis is shown in Exhibit 4-4.

Perrier's crisis was especially intense because the product was considered to be the most upscale—and theoretically the most desirable—bottled water. Notions of a recall can linger with consumers for months and even years; several competitors of Perrier, sensing that the company was in chaos, increased their own advertising budgets in the days after the benzene incident was first reported. They were obviously attempting to lure away customers who had been loyal to Perrier.

In some circles, including industry trade publications and public relations professional associations, Perrier's response to the benzene crisis was praised for its effectiveness because management promptly recalled the product and cooperated with regulators. But the company was also criticized for having too many spokespersons offering different stories on the nature and resolution of the benzene crisis.

The International Bottled Water Association, an industry trade group, notes that while no case of illness in the United States has ever been attributed to bottled water, that is not true with tap water. The Centers for Disease Control in Atlanta, Georgia, reports that over 110,000 cases of illness have been caused by contaminated tap water in recent years. Perrier is tested for nearly 300 individual contaminants; 60 of these are tested on a daily basis. Yet, although the product may now be safer than ever before, concerns linger.

A single crisis such as this can create lingering effects for a product such as Perrier. For example, *Business Week* reported on June 25, 1990, that "several of the nation's swankiest restaurants" had dropped the beverage because of questions

EXHIBIT 4-4 The Perrier Promise

The Promise.

The problem has been fixed.

It was never a health or safety problem. But for a product known for purity, it was definitely a mistake.

It has been identified and corrected.

The spring water itself was never at issue. It's still as pure as it has been for thousands of years.

But to insure the good name of Perrier, we have recalled all of the product currently in the market. Future bottles will carry the "nouvelle production" labels pictured below. This will be your assurance of quality.

Unfortunately for all of our loyal customers we have created a bigger problem. We won't be able to totally resupply the country for some time. In some areas, maybe even several months.

But we make you this promise: we'll be back as soon as we possibly can. If you have any questions, call us toll-free at 1-800-937-2002.

The Proof.

The Perrier you've always loved. Same pure spring water. Same green bottle. Coming soon to the same restaurants, hotels and grocery stores you've always found us in before.

Perrier. Worth waiting for.

Source: The Perrier Group of America, Inc.

about the product; they included Spago in West Hollywood, California, Jean-Louis in Washington, D.C., and Chez Panisse in Berkeley, California. Since a third of Perrier's $140 million annual U.S. sales is generated by restaurant sales, the company's efforts to retain public trust in the coming years will need to be extremely effective. Fortunately, the company has a full stable of brands under its control that should be able to compensate for any losses caused by the benzene incident; Perrier also owns other popular bottled water brands, such as Poland Springs, Calistoga, and Arrowhead.

Recall Readiness and Aftermath

Any manufacturer that has not established a detailed product recall plan is facing serious legal jeopardy in today's litigious society. An excellent checklist appears in Exhibit 4-5. Such a plan should address, to name but a few tasks, which agencies would need to be contacted in the event of a recall, how complaints and calls will be documented, how wholesalers and retailers can be contacted in rapid fashion to protect the public, the role of public information, and communications with insurance carriers. One of the very best means for management to gauge its ability to sustain a product recall is to design and launch a role-playing scenario, as detailed in Chapter 7.

Customers tend to lose faith in recalled products not only immediately after a crisis but often for years after the recall. Exhibit 4-6 illustrates well that a company's handling of a recall and its aftermath can have a profound impact on long-term market share.

EXHIBIT 4-5 Checklist for Evaluation of a Product Recall Program

Yes	No	
		1. Regulatory Agency
☐	☐	• Is the product regulated by any regulatory agency?
		Name: _____
		2. Product Traceability
☐	☐	• Are critical parts identified by the design department?
☐	☐	• Are traceability records of raw materials and component parts maintained by lot/batch numbers, serial numbers, suppliers?
☐	☐	• Are traceability records of serial numbers, date/batch/lot codes, etc., recorded on sales, shipping, and billing documents?
☐	☐	• Are the markings on the product or package/container easily identifiable by the customer?
☐	☐	• Are the customer records maintained and updated?

continued

EXHIBIT 4-5

Yes No

3. Record Retention

☐ ☐   • Is there a formal document control and retention policy?

• Record retention period: _____ years

4. Field Monitoring

☐ ☐   • Is there an adequate program for field monitoring and feedback for product experience?

☐ ☐   • Is it capable of quickly identifying and isolating the problem by batch, plant, process, shift, etc.?

5. Recall Program

☐ ☐   • Is there a written recall plan?

☐ ☐   • Is the responsibility and authority for recall/retrofit decision assigned?

Title: _____

☐ ☐   • Is the responsibility and authority for the program coordination assigned?

Title: _____

☐ ☐   • Is the responsibility for reporting the recall to an appropriate regulatory agency assigned?

Title: _____

☐ ☐   • Is everyone familiar with the recall plan and procedures?

☐ ☐   • Is there a checklist for various steps/actions required before/during/after a recall?

• Do the procedures address specific details of

☐ ☐   Suspension of production/sales/distribution of recalled products?

☐ ☐   Recall publicity?

☐ ☐   Notification to customers, dealers, retailers, etc.?

☐ ☐   Collection of recalled products?

☐ ☐   Repair/retrofit/refunds for recalled product?

☐ ☐   Disposal of recalled products?

☐ ☐   • Is the recall plan tested by dry run/mock recall?

☐ ☐   • Was there any recall campaign in the past?

☐ ☐   • Effectiveness of recall: _____%

Source: Reprinted from "Product Recalls," *Professional Safety* (August 1988), official publication of the American Society of Safety Engineers.

The researchers Weinberger and Romeo concluded after an exhaustive study in 1989 that products receiving negative attention suffer from short- and long-term effects. In cases involving the Ford Pinto and Plymouth Horizon-Dodge Omni lines, a drop in market share of between 20 and 29 percent was experienced in the first month, as shown in the preceding exhibit. In the longer term, this drop became more pronounced, up to 33 percent after six months for the Pinto. The authors concluded that Ford was never able to put the negative public image of the Pinto to rest, while

EXHIBIT 4-6 Summary of Percentage Changes in Usage and Preference Patterns for Several Products

	Time Since Crisis			
	Immediate Effects (up to one year)	T_1 1–2 Years	T_2 2–3 Years	T_3 3–4 Years
Pinto (percentage of market share)[a]	–33.1 (six months)	–49.9	–59.6	
Horizon-Omni (percentage of unit sales)[b]	–11.7 (six months)	–7.1	–35.0	
Horizon-Omni (percentage of purchase intentions)[c]	–10.3 (three weeks)			
Tampons (percentage using)[d]		–12.7	–14.0	–12.2
Tylenol Label (percentage of dollar share)[e]	–35.9 (two months)	–18.9	–5.4	
Extra-Strength Tylenol (percentage using)[f]	–11	–2.8	+12.0	
Regular Tylenol (percentage using)[g]	–16.5	–14.0	–6.6	

[a] Based on changes from precrisis market share percentage (derived from *Automotive News*).

[b] Based on percentage losses of competitive market shares from precrisis levels (derived from R. L. Polk figures, 1978 Passenger Car Action Report).

[c] Based on percentage changes in experimental studies of purchase intentions averaged over T_1, T_2, and T_3 treatments and for the student group and adult group averaged.

[d] Based on changes from precrisis percentages of adults using the products (derived from Simmons, 1979–1985, Volume P-28, p. 28).

[e] Figures derived from *Advertising Age*, December 1982, October 1983, February 1986.

[f] Based on changes from precrisis percentage of adults using the products (derived from Simmons, 1979–1985, Volume P-28, p. 28).

[g] Based on changes from precrisis percentages of adults using the products (derived from Simmons, 1979–1985, Volume P-28, p. 28).

Source: Reprinted from Weinberger and Romeo, "The Impact of Negative Product News," *Business Horizons*, Jan.–Feb. 1989, p. 49. Copyright 1989 by the Foundation for the School of Business at Indiana University. Used with permission.

the Chrysler-Dodge strategists did meet this challenge. Procter & Gamble's prompt recall of Rely Tampons eased the pain for the manufacturer: after three years, tampon use decreased only 8 percent. After two years, the Tylenol brand had recaptured market share, due to effective marketing and crisis management.

PRODUCT BOYCOTTS

Product boycotts are becoming a serious problem for U.S. management. In recent years, organized boycotts of whole companies or certain products have met with varying degrees of success. For example, throughout the mid 1980s boycotts by religious fundamentalist groups of products advertised on programs they believed displayed overtly violent or sexually promiscuous behavior succeeded in getting some major corporations to withdraw advertising during such programs. The fear of being named in the newsletters of such organizations as "targeted" for a boycott obviously contributed to these decisions.

Another example is General Electric (GE), which for years has been targeted by opponents of nuclear weapons research. After years of being unable to reach a wider audience to join the boycott, activists turned up the heat on GE in June 1991. That month, Infact, a nonprofit organization dedicated to a halt in nuclear weapons production, distributed a 30-minute documentary, "Deadly Deception: General Electric, Nuclear Weapons and Our Environment," which the Associated Press called "slick." Infact stated that it intended to show the film to as many as 50 million viewers to alert the public to GE's unresponsiveness to social responsibility on the nuclear issue. Included in the documentary are interviews with residents who lived near a nuclear station formerly operated by GE and interviews with former workers at the Knolls Atomic Power Laboratory in New York.

The movie has received press attention in most major daily newspapers, and brief excerpts have been aired on the four major television networks. It is too early to assess whether or not Infact's campaign of persuasion has generated sympathy or active support among consumers. GE has issued public statements denouncing the tape, arguing that it contains incomplete and potentially misleading statements of fact. Despite GE's denunciation, "Deadly Deception" received the 1992 Oscar® for Best Short Documentary.

Another example: Sometimes something about a product itself rather than a company's policies or practices leads to consumer protests. Such an event occurred in 1988 when General Mills' Count Chocula cereal was introduced, in the midst of the fad in which young children were becoming increasingly fascinated with monsters. The producers of the cereal received protests from Jewish organizations that felt that a shape on Count Chocula's chest resembled the Star of David. The barrage of letters and phone calls prompted the manufacturer to promptly change the packaging.

AVERTING DISASTER: TAKING CHARGE OF A RECALL

Obviously some products are more susceptible to recall than others; food, drugs, toys, appliances, and automotive products are among those most commonly recalled. Organizations need to train their managers, especially those in the areas of public affairs, customer service, and public relations, to be especially sensitive to the role of complaints received, precisely because these signals represent the first indications that a crisis may be in the offing.[16]

Several suggestions may help avert disaster for a company that suspects it one day may face a recall or incident involving product tampering. First, take steps in advance to minimize risk. The double- or triple-sealing of products consumed by the public is now commonplace; a simple single wrapper is often no longer considered sufficient, given the severity of cases reported. Similarly, wrappers and cartons surrounding products should offer multiple warnings about potential hazards (electrical shock, tampering, leaving a motor running too long, not exposing a piece of equipment near an area where children play, and so on).[17]

Presenting such warnings in several languages is also becoming commonplace. Spanish, for example, has assumed new prominence in the United States. Illiteracy is also a problem, so graphically explicit warnings about potential product hazards should accompany the text. Even more important, organizations need to make sure their quality control procedures are not simply written on paper: they must be put into practice in the plants where products are made.[18] Regular, unannounced inspections and testing can save lives and spare embarrassment later. Inspections and regular testing can also help in the legal defense of an organization if managers have to respond to lawsuits from victims of poorly designed or mismanufactured products.

As shown in Chapter 8, the written crisis management plan in every organization should envision and be prepared to respond to an unexpected product recall. A company manager should be designated to routinely monitor the telephone and mail complaints received from customers, Better Business Bureaus, state departments of public safety, and others. Procedures must allow those who read the mail and answer phones to track the type of complaints received, the geographic region of the source,[19] and any similarities to other inquires recently received. When patterns begin to emerge, senior management must get involved immediately.

Company managers should know in advance how their telecommunications carrier (AT&T, MCI, Sprint, and so on) can provide an 800 line for customers on a moment's notice. The costs of operating such a system, and sample scripts of what employees would say, should also be readied within the organization's CMP.

A media program to handle a product recall should be developed. The crisis management team needs to answer the following questions, in advance if possible:

1. Who will speak for our company depending on what type of crisis occurs?
2. Where should a press conference be held?
3. What kind of press materials should be already in packets, ready for distribution?
4. Which advertising agency could be used on short notice to tape radio and television commercials to update consumers on the crisis?
5. How long would production of such messages take, and how long would it take to secure advertising space in the print and broadcast media?
6. Would federal regulators have to review the content of any such message, as required in the pharmaceutical industry and several others?
7. What kinds of human resource actions are necessary in a product recall? (e.g., reprimands)

8. If production is halted or suspended, how easy will it be to transfer duties from plant workers on one side of the company to the other?

9. How should workers be compensated if they are sent home for days or months at a time?

Both consumers and manufacturers can be victims of a recall. Johnson & Johnson did not intentionally poison its Tylenol customers, yet it was forced to spend millions of dollars to recoup public confidence in its organization because of a crisis it did not cause.[20] Simply because a product is recalled does not mean that the manufacturer has other defective products, or poor management, or a lackluster track record of satisfying its customers. A manufacturer seeks to ensure that the recall message comes through in a clear and effective manner precisely because it shows clear-headed management. Thus crisis management planning is especially imperative for companies whose products are even slightly at risk for a recall, now or in the future.

In addition to being prepared for a potential product recall or boycott, managers must also know how to deal with damaging rumors.

THESE RUMORS ARE WORTH LISTENING TO

As noted early in this book, an essential dimension of crisis is the element of surprise. And possibly no surprise can be as challenging as a rumor that is spread about your company, a key person in it, or your products. Rumors are as old as civilization itself, and they can be terribly disabling, costly, and time consuming for organizations. In some cases, they may be started by an innocent or unknowing person.

The *Wall Street Journal* is often a good source of rumors that are "making the rounds" of the U.S. business community. For example, on August 12, 1991, this newspaper prominently featured two stories involving rumors. On page one, the lead story reported that, at the request of Procter & Gamble, Ohio state prosecutors were issuing subpoenas of Cincinnati Bell Inc. telephone records. Procter & Gamble was concerned that current or former employees of the company were disclosing confidential and proprietary information to reporters, especially those at the *Wall Street Journal's* Pittsburgh bureau. The involvement of law enforcement officials led to rumors throughout the company as to who may have been providing news leaks to the press.

The same day the *Journal* reported that half-way across the globe, in Hong Kong, completely unfounded rumors about the insolvency of Citibank led to a major run on the bank over a two-day period. In the wake of a major international scandal involving the Bank of Credit and Commerce International (BCCI), rumors spread that Citibank was in an unsafe financial position. An unknown party sent hundreds of faxes warning people that Citibank would collapse. In addition, a Hong Kong official reported that there was an "orchestrated campaign" there to

CHALLENGE

Blockbuster Entertainment Corporation is the world's largest video rental chain. Its success has been hailed by *CFO Magazine* as "one of the great franchise success stories of the 1980's" (*CFO* stands for chief financial officer). In mid-1991, Blockbuster faced the greatest possible corporate crisis when false rumors spread throughout the financial community that the company was deeply troubled. Pam Weingarten, a California money manager, was quoted as calling Blockbuster a "casket case" in a nationally syndicated column written by analyst Dan Dorfman. *CFO Magazine* reports that she predicted that Blockbuster's stock value would drop from $9.62 per share to zero by 1994.[21] As a result of this and other forecasts, the financial press began scrutinizing Blockbuster.

For the video company's Chief Financial Officer, Steven Berrard, Weingarten's comments were merely the prelude to a prolonged crisis of confidence in his company. Over a three-week period, the company's stock declined 30 percent, even though the company had been profitable for the preceding eighteen quarters! Berrard faced a tremendous problem because some short sellers, described in the same *CFO Magazine* article as "traders who profit when a high-flying stock suffers a setback," were manipulating the future of a credible company that boasted over 2,000 stores and $633 million in 1990 revenues.

Berrard believes that such false rumors can destroy the core of confidence in an organization that management has worked so hard to build. Therefore, Berrard has decided to hire a national public relations agency; he is eager to take his case on the road by speaking to financial reporters in the trade, business, and electronic media. Your task is to design a detailed agenda of major issues that Berrard must emphasize in these presentations and interviews if he is to successfully and skillfully restore investor confidence in Blockbuster. ✳

Note: An excellent article on this case is "Blockbuster Battles the Shorts," by Stephen J. Govoni, *CFO Magazine*, December 1991, pp. 18–24.

destabilize the banking system. Meanwhile, Citibank officials faxed messages to branch managers throughout the world, aimed at assuring employees and depositors that the bank was sound.*

In recent years, corporations targeted by vicious rumors have found that such rumors sometimes originate from people who have an ax to grind, motivated by a personal, political, or social agenda they are carrying out. When your organization has worked for decades to cultivate and maintain a positive public image, a nasty rumor can undermine public confidence, injure sales, and potentially cripple your credibility. Just ask McDonald's, Procter & Gamble, Equitable Life Insurance, R. H. Macy & Company, or Continental Airlines.

Management cannot act on every rumor. Yet when a rumor contains patently false information that could undermine public confidence in a product or organi-

---

*Note to Readers: See "Hong Kong Officials Move To Restore Confidence After Runs on Two Banks," *Wall Street Journal* (August 12, 1991), p. A8.

zation and is being spread by many people with a potential far-reaching audience, swift and professional management intervention is clearly necessary.

For example, Procter & Gamble won a 1990 judgment against two people who had purposely spread false rumors that the company logo reflected an interest in Satan-worshipping. To undertake that prosecution, the company hired investigators and specialists to track down the source of the original rumor. The false information had made its way into a number of church bulletins, protests, newspaper articles, and radio talk shows around the country. Because some people believed the rumors and boycotted Procter & Gamble products for years as a result, the company knew it had to follow through on prosecution if it were to send a clear message to other potential "terrorists by word." Rumors can be lethal.

THE POWER OF RUMORS

Rumors about fast food chains, manufacturing giants, insurance companies, and other concerns have been rampant for years. Procter & Gamble was able to survive being a target of rumors because it had both financial prowess and truth on its side. But the mammoth financial house Drexel Burnham Lambert was not so lucky; just as it was trying to reorganize its finances (due to the mammoth junk bond excess of the mid-1980s), rumors spread throughout Wall Street that the firm was insolvent. *Business Week* reported that the company "crumbled in a matter of days once word got out that it couldn't pay its IOUs." Similar rumors struck the prominent New York retailer R. H. Macy, which went so far as to purchase a full-page ad in *Women's Wear Daily* to dispel rumors that it would file for bankruptcy.[22] Eventually it did file, but rumors hurt the company's sales a full year before reorganization.

In some cases, notably with Procter & Gamble, Drexel, and Macy, public relations consultants who specialize in rumor control helped advise the firms on the most appropriate strategy to inform the public about the fact that the company was being victimized by false rumors. Professor Irv Schenkler of New York University's Stern School of Business has designed a formal program that may help a company curtail rumors. He argues that company executives should publicly deny all falsehoods and reassure employees, consumers, and the competition that it remains a viable organization untainted by any attack made.

Although the rumor mill may not seem to be a classic case of management dilemma, the impact of rumors can cause a long-term, sustained crisis for any target. The mere fact that people are talking about your company negatively can lead to ramifications that are not fully identifiable at the outset. Therefore, many companies assess damage incrementally and decide to intervene only after contracts from clients have been canceled, or top recruits have rejected a firm's offer, or sales in a particular city or region have drastically dwindled. Clearly, consumer affairs departments, public relations executives, and senior management all need to be sensitive to "the word on the street."

VIOLENT CRIMES ON COMPANY PROPERTY: THE STORY OF ESL

Concurrent with the increase in destructive rumors in recent years, more companies have had to withstand extreme acts of violence on their premises. On February 16, 1988, a Sunnyvale, California, defense firm named ESL found itself the victim of a horrible crime. By that evening, the day's events had become the number one news story in North America, and stayed in that position over the next two days. The act of one former employee, in a horrifying six hours, had catapulted the rather obscure organization into unfortunate prominence. At 3 P.M. that day, Richard Farley, who had strapped a hundred rounds of ammunition around his body, forced his way into ESL's M5 building. By the end of his rampage, he had killed 7 employees, wounded 5 others, and left the remaining 2,500 employees in a state of shock.[23]

Chances are that you are familiar with similar unpredictable outrages by current or former employees. Almost all major U.S. cities and many small communities have been touched by such crimes, which have taken place at U.S. post offices, brokerage firms, shopping malls, and elsewhere.

What makes such crises so difficult to analyze is that they are not systematically related to any particular product, contract, or employee. This type of criminal behavior is difficult to anticipate because it is spontaneous, and it can strike any organization. The perpetrators of these crimes are difficult to identify in advance simply because companies find it difficult to conduct exhaustive and ongoing psychological profiles on every worker they employ. And even if such profiles could be performed, they may not be accurate. What is more important, the motivations behind such shootings may not even be related to work. Family or marital pressure, financial difficulties, sexual dysfunctions—these and other motives can all factor into such crimes.

In the case of ESL, crisis management was coordinated by company president Robert Kohler, who served as spokesperson for the organization during the six-hour siege and its aftermath. The company's senior communication specialist, Lynn Fisher, managed to field the myriad of inquiries that instantaneously reached ESL from all over the country. Problems associated with the killings and hostage crisis were multiple. Some employees were unable to get to their vehicles because of police barricades. Family members of employees who had heard of the hostage-shooting situation drove to the company's offices to check on the status of their loved ones, but their presence merely complicated the logistics of the situation. News media from around the country tried to reach ESL officials, although ESL wisely designated only one line for such calls, to reduce the chance of contradictory information being disseminated.

The morning following the tragedy, Kohler sent a memo to each employee summarizing the course of events; succeeding messages and bulletins updated employees on memorial services, the status of those injured, memorial funds that

CHALLENGE

On October 16, 1991, a depressed, out-of-work Texan drove his pickup truck through the front wall of a busy Luby's Cafeteria in Killeen, Texas. It was a lunch hour no one can forget. In a matter of minutes, he shot and killed some twenty-four men, women, and children. Scores of others were wounded. It was one of the worst mass killings in U.S. history.

At the same time that this crisis was unfolding, the company's board of directors was meeting to prepare for the company's upcoming special meeting of stockholders. The San Antonio, Texas-based company was completing plans to open a new restaurant in Independence, Missouri, the next week. With 151 restaurants in nine states, Luby's was a successful, high-profile publicly owned chain. For the year end-

ing August 31, 1991, the company reported sales of $328 million, compared with $311 million the year before. Even in the middle of a national recession, Luby's emerged from a highly competitive market as a winner.

Let's assume that you are Ralph "Pete" Erben, President and CEO of Luby's Cafeterias, Inc. You are in the middle of your October 16 meeting when word arrives that an internationally publicized disaster has just struck one of your restaurants. What steps should you take? What sources of information are at your disposal? How should you respond to the thousands of inquiries that are pouring into your office from news organizations, stockholders, brokerage firms, clients, your restaurants, and others? ✳

had been launched, and other facets of the crisis. ESL immediately engaged a counseling firm that it had successfully used for five years for its Employee Assistance Program. They brought trained counselors directly to the company to meet with grieving workers, some of whom remained in shock for days or weeks after the shootings.

Communications specialist Fisher launched a postcrisis assessment of how well the company had performed in the eyes of its employees during the crisis. This rarely used but important management tool distinguishes differences in the way ESL coped with crisis from the ways in which its many counterparts have coped with such crises.

For instance, 1,174 people, representing 47 percent of ESL's employee base, responded to a survey designed by Fisher and Dr. William Briggs of San Jose State University. Analyzing the company's performance, they wrote, "A total of 86 percent of the 1,174 employees who responded indicated that they were either satisfied (37 percent) or very satisfied (49 percent) with the company's employee communication following the tragedy." In addition, more than 90 percent of respondents indicated that the company had provided a great deal or an adequate amount of information.[24]

The interview with Pete Erben (see pages 100–102) focuses on another case of the crisis management—that executed by Luby's during one of the worst mass murders in U.S. history.

INTERVIEW

Ralph "Pete" Erben
Guiding a Corporation Through Tragedy

Ralph "Pete" Erben is CEO of Luby's Cafeterias Inc., a 151-outlet restaurant chain. One of the company's restaurants was targeted by a mass killer in October 1991.

Q *Mr. Erben, how have you grown as a result of this tragedy? What have you learned and experienced that really changed your career?*

A I think that, personally, I am more acutely aware of what's occurring around us and I must say it's made me more sensitive to today's society—predominantly people, good and bad. I have grown a great deal in just the realization that we're blessed that the majority of people are passionate, concerned, and interested in one another. We witnessed tremendous support for Luby's under circumstances that were deplorable, and people rallied to support the victims. In some ways, I think we are considered one of those victims.

Q *How did you learn of the incident?*

A We were taking a lunch break from our board of directors meeting. Someone came in and said they had just had a phone call and there was a shooting in our Killeen cafeteria, but they didn't know the extent of the problem. With that, we immediately made the determination that two corporate officers, Herbert

Knight and Jimmy Woliver, should drive immediately to Killeen and stop in Austin to call for an update. We then reconvened the meeting, and a subsequent updated news bulletin came in. Now word was that several people were killed. The board meeting adjourned, and I quickly arranged to get to Killeen as soon as possible. Our immediate response was to activate our public relations people, and one of them accompanied me to Killeen. One of our board members graciously offered us the use of his corporate plane and crew. We went directly to the plane, still not knowing any more than what we had initially heard, that there were several deaths. On the plane we monitored the news. It was worse with each successive message.

Q *Was your reaction shock, disbelief, numbness?*

A It was shock, coupled with concern for our people. I felt that it was awfully important that we make the right move by getting there and evaluating the condition of our people and customers. I just felt compelled to be there.

Q *Then you were on site within only a few hours?*

A Within two hours I was at the Killeen location. When we landed, we understood this was now a national story; many news helicopters hovered around. We were intercepted by the press, but we just didn't have much to tell them other than why we were there and that we had very limited information. But our mere presence gave a strong corporate message of concern.

Q *Where did you coordinate Luby's response?*

A We went immediately to the cafeteria, but all access had been restricted. However, we were permitted in to see our management team.

Q *Did you meet those people at that time?*

A No, everybody—the whole community—was still in a very severe state of shock and our managers were obviously shaken. We visited several employees and made sure the rest were accounted for. But one employee was missing. After visiting with management, we went to the chief of police, who was in charge of security and the overall investigation. We wanted as many facts as were available. Now we were told that twenty-two people were dead and some others were in critical shape. Nearly all the bodies were still in place in the restaurant; evidence was being collected. We got as much factual information regarding the victims as possible.

Q *How were you informed about your employees?*

A We knew one was injured, and we were just amazed and very thankful that there weren't more. She was later released, but we still had one missing person and no one knew where he was; that concerned us. We dealt with his family and continued to check the records of a local hospital.

Q *Was he later found?*

A Yes—of all things, and that was ironic, he had hidden in our big dishwashing machine and was not found until the next morning. There was a lot of consternation during that evening about him. He was obviously traumatized, but that puzzle was resolved.

Q *Where was your crisis control center? Was it the corporate office in San Antonio?*

A Our corporate office was the primary control center. John Lahourcade, our Chairman of the Board; Jim Hale, our legal counsel and corporate secretary; Jim Dublin, a partner of our public relations firm; John Curtis, our Chief Financial Officer; Vernon Schrader, our Vice President for Marketing; Jerry Ferris, our insurance coordinator; and a number of other volunteers who wanted to help were all at the corporate office helping us coordinate information and assisting in the many decisions being made. We established a Killeen communication center at a local La Quinta motel. We wanted to be sure that all the information we gave out was accurate. Our corporate office was receiving hundreds of phone calls, and we immediately had to set various objectives.

Q *What were they?*

A Fortunately, someone loaned us a cellular telephone. That saved the day, for the simple reason that local lines were jammed because calls were coming in from all over the world. If we had not had the cellular phone, we couldn't have called out. Subsequently, we went to the motel and used their fax machine to review statements, updates, and other written documents.

Q *Obviously you were concerned for employees in Killeen as well as employees at your other 150 restaurants. But there is a wider audience—stockholders, press, government officials. How was that handled?*

A Our public relations people identified those groups and assisted us a great deal. Our legal representative contacted the New York Stock Exchange and halted trading of our stock because of the severity of the crisis. We called our insurance representative who in turn had to call many other insurance companies. Our San Antonio staff contacted our board members for updates, and our corporate office kept our other 150 units up-to-date about events as we knew them. We avoided speculation.

Q *How did you respond to the media?*

A We limited our accessibility to the media at first because we didn't have anything to tell them other than we were full of concern and empathy. Our Vice President for Marketing in San Antonio provided basic corporate data to the press. The press asked us if the gunman had any relationship to us. Was he a current employee? Past one? Frequent customer? We had managers review personnel records, but this took much time. There was no indication that he was ever employed by Luby's. Even today, a month later, we know of no connection the gunman had with our company.

Q *You had no crisis plan?*

A We actually have a crisis plan that establishes headquarters as our crisis center. I did not refer to it because we all knew our responsibilities. All our people wanted to help, and nearly all volunteered to work into the night to assist in communicating what was going on to our units and to inquiring public and media. I don't think you would typically consider us or any restaurant high risk, at least for this type of crisis. Years ago, we organized a kind of mock crisis to test our response. I think the essence of our response was communication. You don't want to avoid the media. Be truthful to them, just tell what you know, don't speculate, and don't hesitate to talk about your mission.

Q *When you're running a corporation as geographically diverse as Luby's, how did you notify your other 150 restaurants?*

A Information was faxed to them from our San Antonio office. Each one has their own fax machine, which is important. We suspected there might be negative ramifications on business at our other units, that people might be hesitant to eat there. We told our managers to react to any threats they received and to call local police departments immediately. We urged them to secure armed protection at every facility that was threatened until further notice in case someone else tried to duplicate Killeen. Expense and economies of scale are not the dominant factor; the security of our people is the primary concern. Of course, when the threat of a second wave happened, we did worry. You know, there are nuts out there; there are strange people.

Q *At some point did your empathy and concern turn to anger?*

A You wonder about that. I don't think with the leadership responsibilities that I have that I can wallow in too much self-pity. I probably was more emotional than most people because I show my emotions, but they were directed at people more than events. There's a lot of soul-searching afterward, but you feel a tremendous responsibility to bring relief to many people.

Q *How did you communicate with those who witnessed this tragedy?*

A We visited with our employees the very next day at the motel and tried to assure them that we had to go forward and concern ourselves with the first priority, which was getting them to be emotionally well. We met at the La Quinta the following morning at 9 A.M. and shared our feelings as a group and individually. We vowed to attend to any immediate needs that they might have. We wanted to assure them that their incomes would not be affected and that if they needed any kind of assistance, we would provide it. We conferred with Dr. Rynearson of Scott and White Clinic in Temple, who is in charge of the psychiatric department. He provided some of the best information we'd ever had. I told him about the impending meeting with our people and told him my concern was that they might need professional help. He gave me some sound advice. He said that we needed to rally our staff with each other and be each other's support system. You can't rely on counselors as a crutch because it can multiply. If we had problems, he offered to assist. He didn't want them to depend on psychiatrists. When we met the next morning, it was astounding. I saw traumatized, blank faces. Yet within thirty minutes, we had transformed the group. Some were laughing and talking about some of the unusual aspects of what happened. There was nothing funny about the tragedy, but they had to release their emotions in an open session. They were helping each other. We prayed with them and did everything we thought was appropriate. This interaction was the greatest transformation of any group of people I have ever seen.

Q *During these hours, was there concern for the security of your Killeen site?*

A Yes. We hired security for our facility because police didn't remove bodies until nine and a half hours after the crisis. We didn't want any of your people having to go back in there, so we contacted a security agent. Actually, the police department had graciously arranged for two armed people to be on guard for twenty-four hours a day to secure the facility. It was a hectic, difficult catastrophe, but in hindsight we all gave it our best, and we never lost focus of the importance of our people.

CHRONOLOGY OF A CRISIS RESPONSE

How Luby's Cafeterias Inc. reacted to the October 16 mass shootings at its restaurant in Killeen, Texas.

Wednesday, October 16

12:40 P.M.: Belton resident George Hennard drives his truck through a front window of the Luby's Cafeteria in Killeen and opens fire on lunch-hour customers, killing twenty-three people and himself.

1 P.M.: From its headquarters in San Antonio, Luby's sends senior vice president Herbert Knight and vice president Jim Woliver, by car, to Killeen.

1:30–2 P.M.: On hearing of fatalities, Luby's president, Ralph "Pete" Erben, and public relations consultant Judy McCarter prepare to fly to Killeen.

2:30 P.M.: Luby's stock halts trading on the New York Stock Exchange.

3 P.M.: Erben and McCarter arrive at the scene in Killeen and begin visits with police and restaurant managers. They contact Luby's headquarters and arrange for a $100,000 contribution starting a relief fund for victims, families of victims, and employees.

Late afternoon, evening: Luby's officials contact employees to determine their whereabouts, injuries. No serious injuries are reported, but one employee is missing. They check injury and fatality lists at local hospitals, run computer checks to determine any links between the gunman and Luby's employees, and prepare for an employee meeting and a news conference the next day.

Thursday, October 17

7 A.M.: Mark Mathews, age 19, the missing Luby's employee, is found alive by a cafeteria manager, still hiding in a dish-washing machine in the restaurant.

9 A.M.: A meeting of cafeteria employees and their families is held in a meeting room at the La Quinta Motor Inn in Killeen.

10 A.M.: Erben holds the company's first news conference in a parking lot, outside the La Quinta.

Tuesday, December 3

11 A.M.: Luby's officials, Killeen city officials, victims, and families of victims gather for a news conference in Killeen to announce plans to remodel and reopen the restaurant. Reopening is expected in February or March.

Source: Luby's Cafeterias Inc. Reprinted with permission of the *Dallas Morning News*.

NEIGHBORS AND CRISIS: THE NIMBY SYNDROME

Organizations, like families, have to learn to live with their neighbors. That realization is one of the significant new areas of inquiry in the field of crisis management over the past decade.

Consider the issue of neighbors with regard to our hypothetical corporation, Arlington Plastics (AP). You will recall that company managers had grappled with how their organization would react in the event of certain crises. Now let's focus on those arising from a company's relationship with the surrounding community.

If AP managers wished, for example, to expand their manufacturing plant, there would be many new concerns in addition to the traditional ones of construction costs per square foot, equipment and overhead, and space design. When AP's current facility was built forty years ago, it was constructed in an area that had relatively few homes, few school buses, no crosswalks, and little traffic. No one noticed eighteen-wheel delivery trucks coming and going all day long. Pollution could spew from the plant with little notice; there was no local conservation commission or regional office of the Environmental Protection Agency (EPA).

By the 1990s, such a situation has become a rarity in the United States. Increased scrutiny of corporate plans to expand or relocate facilities, to build a shopping mall, or to secure zoning permits to launch new housing subdivisions— all this and more is under attack by citizen and neighborhood groups who often protest such plans in the streets or in the courtroom to protect their interests.

This pattern of protest is called the NIMBY syndrome—"Not In My Back Yard." And NIMBY has caused multiple crises for both small and large companies across the country.

Earlier, community relations would not have been regularly included in discussions regarding crisis. Yet in many recent cases, neighborhood and activist groups have taken action that is so sophisticated and so well orchestrated that their actions have indeed caused crises for a variety of organizations. Many antidevelopment, antiexpansion campaigns launched by such groups are well financed and garner positive publicity for their organizers, with corporate management often on the defensive. This lack of preparedness has indeed led to crises that are costly and embarrassing. Today, an increasing number of organizations designate at least one senior manager as community affairs director to cultivate local goodwill. This person usually works to avoid a crisis with neighbors in the future.

In surveying multiple cases where corporations have faced an embarrassing crisis because of the NIMBY syndrome, the *New York Times* asserted:

> NIMBYs are noisy. NIMBYs are powerful. NIMBYs are everywhere. NIMBYs are people who live near enough to corporate or government projects—and are upset enough about them—to work to stop, stall or shrink them. NIMBYs organize, march, sue and petition to block the developers they think are threatening them. They twist the arms of politicians and they learn how to influence legislators. They fight fiercely and then, win or lose, they vanish.[25]

The question for managers, of course, is, What can be done to prevent such fierce opposition? If residents do not want a nuclear waste dump in their community, if no one wants a new hospital that might generate traffic and ambulance sirens late at night, if residents do not want a new housing development in their district, where can progress be made? In the same *Times* article, Tufts University urban affairs professor Kent Portney claimed that nationwide, cities and towns are losing these and other kinds of developments faster than they are being replaced. The conclusion, he said, was, "We're rapidly getting to the point where we're going to be a crisis in many of those areas."

In a front-page article in November 1991, the *Wall Street Journal* reported that even houses of worship are increasingly facing bitter opposition when they seek to construct a new church or synagogue in a residential area. In many cases they have been forced to scale down plans, reduce the size of statues or crosses, redesign architecture to "conform" to the area, or add expensive parking facilities to reduce the "burden" on the neighborhood. For most of our country's history, churches were viewed as the cornerstone of community life—an important, valued resource. Sadly, in some areas of the United States today they are perceived by "community leaders" as nuisances.

NOT SO NEIGHBORLY?

Consider just a few cases of neighbors versus corporations. For example, some residents of Orange and Osceola counties in Florida have long contended that the Walt Disney Corporation has been a poor neighbor. Disney claims it pays more than its share for services (more than $17 million a year in property taxes), but it has avoided paying developer impact fees, much to the anger of competing builders. *Business Week* asserted, "Disney hasn't paid a cent to Orange County for its shopping center, the studio tour, or its new hotels. It cites the $100,000 it spent as 'goodwill' to fix up a nearby intersection, technically the county's job. That's not enough, say some county officials, who want Disney to help pay for the growth its development spurs."[26] In fact, at least fifty cities around the nation (including Fort Collins, Colorado; Fresno, California; and Atlanta, Georgia) have begun to demand that developers pay "impact" fees to help local governments cope with the added burdens that corporate expansion may place on local schools or emergency services.

Another example is comedian Bob Hope, who throughout 1990 faced widespread criticism from Santa Monica, California, residents for selling undeveloped and scenic land for the construction of homes and golf courses. Environmental activists were hoping he would donate or sell the land to the National Park Service, and they called talk shows, wrote letters to the editor, and otherwise tried diligently to put the issue on the public agenda. But Hope contended that he had made many contributions to the state and country throughout his life and that his actions were not extreme nor unreasonable.[27] Given his track record of philanthropy, he makes a compelling point.

There are many other examples. The sixteenth wealthiest U.S. citizen, Californian Donald Bren, controls the Irvine Company, a real estate conglomerate that owns nearly one-sixth of all the land in Orange County, California, and has many

Phyllis Sterling of Famett, Texas was profiled in a *New York Times* article as a typical American homeowner, here shown protesting real estate overdevelopment under a "Not in My Back Yard" homeowner's banner.

successful real estate projects to his credit. But community relations eventually hit a rough spot in late 1989, and Bren's Laguna Beach home was picketed by protesters who feared his 400-acre subdivision in a rural canyon would contribute to pollution and traffic.[28]

When groups around the country have tried to construct homes for mentally handicapped adults in residential neighborhoods, they have often been greeted by picket signs, protest letters, and cases of arson. Similarly, neighbors have opposed homes for the homeless, hospice centers for AIDS victims, prisons, and even foster homes.[29] Fortunately, common sense often prevails, and, after initial hysteria, these plans are sometimes approved.

Just who opposes development plans, and how can executives try to predict the next NIMBY crisis that may hit their company? Cerrell Associates, a leading consulting firm, prepared an exhaustive study for the California Waste Management Board that concluded the northeastern and western areas of the United States were most likely to produce NIMBY crises, and that young and middle-aged liberals who were registered Democrats were most likely to resist new projects.[30]

In facing a NIMBY-related crisis, managers should consider taking the following actions:

1. Meet with leaders of neighborhood associations before public meetings with all residents. This helps gauge the questions and problems that will surface when the press later attends public sessions.

2. Mail a periodic newsletter to neighbors that keeps them abreast of the organization's mission. Include question-and-answer columns and invite neighbors to selected open houses and special events. Such personal interaction can help break an impasse between individuals whose only previous contact has been by telephone, for example.

3. Meet with the local zoning director and community planning director to ascertain what changes in local building laws may be contemplated. Managers also need to inform local officials of their building plans early enough so that potential opposition can be addressed.

4. Join the local chamber of commerce or board of trade as well as other local groups, such as the Rotary or League of Women Voters. The organization should designate a manager to serve as liaison. Read the newsletters of these groups and budget a yearly contribution to support meaningful programs.

5. Hire a clipping service that scans all area newspapers and business magazines. These services, listed in the Yellow Pages, will send you copies of each article that mentions your organization or a topic you may be interested in. Often this survey serves as an early warning system for potential controversies in the community.

6. Occasionally issue news releases to the local press that update the community on your organization. Especially important are your promotions or new hires of community residents, special recognition or awards you give residents, and certainly any new product or service that might benefit local interests. Meet with the editor of the local newspaper and build a rapport with him or her.

7. Urge the organization to become active locally; maintaining positive relations with residents can only help when and if a crisis later occurs. Your group may wish to offer a speaker's bureau, making managers available to address local charitable groups; to hire summer interns from area high schools and colleges; and to ask for volunteers to serve on a community advisory board that meets quarterly and shares concerns with company officials.

8. Be sure that publications on your organization are available on request to any residents who ask for them. Many companies and institutions now publish periodic economic impact reports that tell the citizenry in simple numbers and words how many residents are employed; the value of the organization's expenditures for salaries, benefits, and goods and services

in the community; the amount of state and local taxes you add to public coffers; and other important data. When such benefits are totaled, they often represent a sizable sum that impresses local officials and others.

9. Some companies have established political action committees (PACs), which earmark funds specifically to advance candidates who understand those companies' interests. PACs have been the subject of both wide support and critical protests from many interests. Before an organization begins to earmark funds to support local candidates, legal counsel should refer to all appropriate laws, and the ramifications of such actions need to be seriously weighed.

10. If your company is considering major expansion of its facilities, a master plan may be requested by local officials and neighborhood leaders. Such plans are often developed in concert with architects, transportation and traffic planners, attorneys, arborists, and others. The purpose is to give local interests a picture of what a corporate headquarters or office complex may look like in two, five, and ten years from now. Sometimes these plans help avoid multiple crises for a company because managers have taken the time to tell the public up front what it is contemplating for the future.

11. Nonprofit institutions such as hospitals, museums, colleges, and art institutes have been asked by some cities such as Los Angeles, Boston, and San Francisco to make a "payment in lieu of taxes," or PILOT, since they cannot be required by law to pay property taxes. Some have agreed to make a contribution to help pay for police and fire protection services they receive. Others believe that because they serve the public interest and are nonprofit that they should not be financially obligated to the same degree as private corporations who have a greater capacity to pay.

These measures of cultivating support through an integrated and personalized community relations program work for many organizations, but not necessarily for all.

YOU MIGHT GET "SLAPPED"

A number of companies and institutions have found that the best means of combating the NIMBY syndrome is simply to bring litigation against those who oppose corporate plans. Two researchers at the University of Denver, George Pring and Penelope Canan, have studied 100 cases where individuals and advocacy groups were sued for their actions. Some corporations can and do enter court asserting that neighbor or activist suits are frivolous, without basis, or libelous. If the first attempt at an injunction order fails, they may personally sue the neighborhood leaders. Reviewing the aggressive attitude of many such corporations, *California Magazine* notes,

The message isn't limited to activists, town blowhards and the local branch of the Revolutionary League USA either: a housewife living near Santa Cruz writes a letter to her local paper complaining about a proposed development and is slapped with a $3 million libel suit by the developer; the League of Women Voters in Beverly Hills writes critical letters about a condominium project to its local newspaper and gets nailed with a $63 million suit from the developers; a West Virginia blueberry farmer tells authorities that operators of a coal mine are polluting a local river, and the miners sock him with a suit for $200,000. While these suits failed in court, they succeeded in another, more insidious way: they saddled their targets with the burden of mounting a defense and with considerable anxiety. They also had a chilling effect on activists.[31]

In July 1991, in response to the increasing number of such "SLAPPS"—strategic lawsuits against public participation—Ralph Nader's consumer coalition offered free defense to any individual or community group that finds itself thus intimidated by a corporation. Nader's effort should be applauded. In an era when underfunded, grassroots organizations already face an expensive, uphill battle in encouraging debate about potentially negative projects, any defense on their behalf is logical.

Unfortunately, many meetings with community residents are adversarial in nature. Thus the choice of words that managers use in these meetings is especially important. (See Exhibits 4-7 and 4-8.)

In conclusion, there are really two sides to the management plan to confront the NIMBY syndrome. The first rationale for a community relations plan is political—if there is an explosion at a local plant, or neighbors decide to bring placards and stage a protest at your front door over rumors that you are going to lay off 1,500 workers, you will want a reservoir of goodwill already established with community members. The second rationale is that an ongoing program of community relations can tangibly demonstrate that a company or institution cares about its host community. Each of these issues, by itself, justifies such an investment.

In preparing for crisis, corporate managers need to factor in the potential that one day the organization may be at odds with its neighbors. By proactively laying the foundation for goodwill through some of the measures just identified, it is less likely that the debate between corporation and community will be raucous. In many cases where the measures noted in Exhibits 4-7 and 4-8 were applied in working with community organizations, disagreements slowly edged away from finger pointing and accusations to a more reasoned discussion that was focused and almost always manageable. If management earnestly takes steps before a crisis to become an active contributor to its community, it may find itself with more empathy at a moment when it needs all the friends it can muster.

STRIKE ONE!

The role and importance of organized labor in the United States is largely a shadow of itself compared to just four decades ago. Many factors contributed to

EXHIBIT   4-7   Ten Things to ALWAYS Say to a Community Group

1. **"I understand your position."** Note the difference between this phrase and "I agree with your position." Understanding implies empathy and methodical judgment but not agreement. It also allow you to build a rapport with the more moderate element of the audience, which could otherwise prejudge you as belligerent or one-sided.

2. **"Let me restate your position."** It's not enough to nod your head in understanding. As succinctly as possible, restate the two or three significant points made by the opposing side. This guarantees to these individuals that you have listened and understood their main points and that you have listened actively, not passively. Remember to restate, but not give agreement.

3. **"We are willing to listen."** Community meetings can and often do become needless shouting matches. An excellent diffusing tactic is to let the dissent and vocal opposition run its course. At first they may seem to have seized the momentum, but actually they will have lost the chance to make key points during a debate, because those points will already have been aired.

4. **"We will continue to work on this issue."** Whether the topic is traffic congestion near a plant, an industrial accident, or a major layoff, problems are rarely solved overnight. Reinforce your message that you are willing and eager to maintain dialogue and to work toward a mutually agreeable solution.

5. **"I know who you are."** Individuals like to be stroked in different ways. When you confront a community group of strangers, an "us versus them" atmosphere immediately sets up in the room. Yet if you can begin with "It's a pleasure to see Joe Harrington—we serve in the Rotary Club together" or "Thank you, Mrs. O'Neill, for attending—I know you have been busy with the work of the League of Women Voters" you can break barriers and remind the audience about your community outreach efforts.

6. **"There are areas of difference."** Admitting that there *is* an opposing side doesn't weaken your position with the media—it actually enhances it. Let the opposing side appear myopic—*you* need to acknowledge that there are two sides to this story.

7. **"We care about our host community."** Your company may continually express its concern for the community, but many people may not be aware of your concern or may forget. Remind them through philanthropic contributions, loans of equipment, or other perks, that your company is hardly a stranger to the community.

8. **"We have common interests."** Make common interests explicit: "We employ 16 percent of community residents. We are taxpayers, like you. We care about the quality of our streets and utilities, as you do. We have a vested interest in the city's future, as you do."

9. **"This dialogue benefits all of us."** You will show yourself to be both humble and gracious if you acknowledge that community meetings and forums enhance communication between residents and organizations.

10. **"You will hear from us."** And keep your promise. Have someone on your staff actively solicit names and addresses for a mailing list, and work to communicate with neighbors at least once each quarter via a newsletter, open house, or other management tool.

Source: Adapted from Laurence Barton, "Community Relations Handbook" (NYNEX Properties Company, 60 State Street, Boston, MA 02109). Joseph Zukowski, editor. Copyright 1989.

EXHIBIT   4-8   Six Statements to Religiously AVOID Making to a Community Group

1. **"I agree with you."** If you agree with the opposition, throw in the towel and begin your job search. Senior management will not be pleased when it is reported in tomorrow's newspaper than "An executive from XVG Chemical Corporation agreed with neighborhood residents last night that a gas leak inside the plant could cause a catastrophe leading to injury and deaths."

2. **"You don't understand."** Sometimes in the heat of an exchange, managers will inadvertently turn up the heat of a debate by making an innocent but loaded statement. It is much better to say, "We have information that suggests otherwise," than to make the offensive remark "You don't understand."

3. **"We need more time."** Unfortunately, you probably do need more time, but this statement will likely be reported by both residents and the press as a stalling tactic or sign of managerial weakness. Pledge to meet again in one week or ten days, and indicate that this is so that senior management can review all contingencies, but avoid this statement at all costs.

4. **"They're wrong."** On many occasions executives have made this statement at public hearings, and later been chastised by local officials, who will stand by their electorate rather than local executives. It is not your place to state who is right or wrong; that question will ultimately be decided by consumers, regulators, or the courts.

5. **"The media has distorted this problem."** You may be right, but any attack on the news media will alienate a critical and influential audience that can cause you damage at a very sensitive time. There are other ways to express your displeasure with the press, such as not returning phone calls or ceasing all advertising, but even these are decisions that should only be made as a last resort. Most reporters are doing their job in an honest and fair manner. If you find that is not the case, you should seek a meeting with that reporter's editor immediately to set the record straight. Bring a tape recorder, but not your attorney.

6. **"This is a one-time request (or problem)."** This statement will be long remembered, and you may live to eat these words, damaging your credibility and the reputation of your organization. Always avoid such statements.

Source: Adapted from Laurence Barton, "Community Relations Handbook" (NYNEX Properties Company, 60 State Street, Boston, MA 02109). Joseph Zukowski, editor. Copyright 1989.

this situation, including

- Deregulation of certain industries
- Major racketeering cases against certain corrupt union leaders
- Negative publicity about union use of its members' pension funds
- Increased sophistication on the part of management in offering better benefits before a union is organized
- A series of steps at the federal level to reduce the power of unions, such as President Reagan's decision to fire hundreds of air traffic controllers who struck during the first months of his administration. This was viewed by some as a warning to other major unions contemplating such action.

All these events have reduced union power. Yet labor is an important, even essential part of management in some sectors of the U.S. economy; unions have made a number of notable contributions to the welfare and economic progress of workers, especially those who are poor and working in communities where heavy manufacturing and mining is concentrated. When negotiations between union representatives and management meet a standstill, however, the process leading to a strike can be a painful and occasionally costly crisis for both sides.

In recent years, companies such as Greyhound and Hormel, and institutions such as Harvard University, have faced strikes that have become malicious, even violent. In almost all cases, it has been impossible for management to prove that the destruction of corporate property, including damage to machinery, software programs, or managers' vehicles, was deliberately orchestrated by union organizers or members. Therein lies a great quagmire associated with strikes—in the absence of conclusive evidence about worker wrongdoing, the prosecution of guilty parties is extremely difficult.

This scenario complicates an already difficult situation for management, which may now find that it is being characterized in the local and national news media as unfair, exploitative, and manipulative. In some cases, to be sure, management deserves all three accusations, but not always. Regardless of the cause of a strike, there is no question that the unrest and violence that sometimes is associated with a work action can create a significant crisis for management.

THE UNITED AIRLINES STRIKE

Although some strikes occur with little advance warning, management is almost always forewarned that disagreement over principal issues such as salaries or benefits could lead to a walkout. A case in point is United Airlines. Traditionally one of the strongest air carriers in the nation, by the 1980s United boasted some of the most strategic and profitable routing systems, coupled with strong upper management. However, labor costs throughout the organization were excessive in comparison to rivals, particularly American Airlines.

Union activity at United has always been particularly strong, culminating in May 1985 when several unions attempted to buy United's parent company, UAL, without success. A major strike by employees disrupted operations and seriously impaired United's operational abilities. Customers were unsure if employee discontent could lead to canceled flights. Management tried to keep the media abreast of its negotiations. Each side, employees and management, took to the radio and television talk shows to explain how the other side was being cruel, greedy, or manipulative.

Parent company UAL pushed on; it purchased luxury hotels and Hertz Rent-A-Car in an attempt to become an integrated travel organization, but these decisions loaded the company with debt. In 1989, new management infused the company with strong hopes and, more importantly, cash. But the machinists' and pilots' unions earnestly believed that employee ownership was the best medicine for UAL. They vowed not to retreat from their intention to purchase the carrier.

The unions offered UAL wage and benefit concessions totaling more than $2 billion, and several major banks agreed to lend the unions the funds necessary to purchase the airline. Management now found itself in a crisis that did not share the characteristics of most others described in this book. This was not a sudden and immediate turn of events, but an incremental problem that kept growing in scope. With each new announcement, news conference, or bargaining session, the volatility of the debate grew. Management and employees were locked in a ruthless struggle over the future of UAL.

With the Iraqi invasion of Kuwait in August 1990, United, like most other major international carriers, found itself in the midst of a global economic panic. Stock markets nose-dived, and an agreement between UAL and the unions collapsed. United survived as a major carrier, though now it had no union employees.

For a variety of reasons—some tactical, some simply bad timing—the very unions that attempted to buy UAL actually helped United eliminate union activities and the high costs associated with such activities. Pickets, protests, union meetings, and news conferences by the pilots' and machinists' representatives simply did not work in the long run, although they did generate publicity, albeit temporarily. United suffered significant, negative publicity—to be sure, much of it deserved.

In the early stages of negotiation with union officers, UAL should have anticipated in its strategic planning that the entire debate could be affected by external factors such as war. If it had done so, it might have been able to anticipate the enormous additional costs associated with that burden and to present this consideration to union officials in negotiations. Although it is unknown whether union officials would have responded to that contingency with concessions, that question is important in evaluating UAL's strategy for crisis contingency.

For some reasons within its control (unwillingness to bend on certain issues) and others beyond its control (Hussein invaded Kuwait), UAL found itself criticized by a variety of parties from Wall Street to the editorial pages. Although UAL survived this prolonged strike, many of its loyal employees were not as fortunate. By striking against the carrier, many lost their jobs or had their careers impaired. If there is a lesson to be learned from the UAL case, it is that not all crises subside in twenty-four or forty-eight hours; many can and do linger for months or even years.

MUST-DO'S WHEN PREPARING FOR A STRIKE

When a strike appears imminent, management should move quickly to assemble a task force whose responsibilities will include:

- Releasing press statements from company managers that set the record straight on any untrue accusations made by a union group.
- Assessing the vulnerability of the corporation to any breaches of sensitive or classified information, including computer hardware and software that could be manipulated and destroyed. Information shared on this topic should be selectively distributed, as it is not uncommon for unions that expect

a long strike to identify "insiders" who may leak information that could help complicate corporate operations.

■ Protecting the physical resources of the company, including its plant, corporate headquarters, vehicles, machinery, and other tangible assets both in the immediate location and those in other cities.

■ Assessing external factors in the national economy or international arena that could impact negotiations.

■ Coordinating all company responses necessary to interested publics—including stockholders, police and fire personnel, the news media, neighbors, and others—from a central control room where a phone and bank of fax machines has been established.

As with most crises, in a strike preparedness is invaluable.

Charles F. Vance, a former Secret Service agent and now president of a professional security firm, Vance International, Inc., has written in *Security Management* magazine that managers facing a strike should also consider

■ Examining lighting around the property so that vital fixtures such as transformers cannot be shot and destroyed.

■ Educating all workers who are not striking about the possibility that nails could be thrown on roadways leading to the site, and that windows may be broken or tires slashed. Security firms must aggressively patrol the area in advance before workers report for the day.

■ Arranging private security, if needed, at the homes of senior managers, especially after dark.

■ Equipping a control room that includes riot shields, Mace, helmets, and even bullet-resistant vests.[32]

As dramatic as these suggestions may sound, hundreds of strikes occur in the United States each year. Many are settled amiably in a matter of hours or days. Many others, however, become ugly and bloody. They can be harmful to both the strikers as well as the corporation, school district, hospital, or other entity that has been targeted for a job stoppage. As with almost all aspects of crisis management, preparing a crisis management plan in advance of any acrimony between management and labor may be the best defense, one that could avert disaster at the main gate.

SERVICE DISRUPTION

Corporations, especially utilities, need to assess their vulnerability in terms of potential financial losses that their customers may incur if there is a widespread disruption of service. For example, in June 1988, local businesses filed a series of

lawsuits against Illinois Bell Telephone Co. after the worst service disaster in the company's history, caused by a major fire. Water used to fight the fire destroyed fiber optic equipment, and tens of thousands of residential and business customers were forced to wait from three to as many as thirty days for resumption of service. Typical of the many suits filed against the phone company was a $100,000 claim by a leading catering company that depended on phone orders, and a travel agency that claimed it lost nearly $250,000 in billings due to the outage. While Illinois Bell was covered for its property losses in the fire, few if any of its customers (including business customers) were covered for losses incurred by a utility failure.

Another notable case of service disruption caused havoc for the Northwestern National Bank (now Norwest Bank) of Minneapolis, whose seventeen-story headquarters building was destroyed by a five-alarm fire on Thanksgiving Day, 1982. Reportedly, two youths playing at a construction site next to the structure ignited the fire; a $70 million claim was later filed against the neighboring contractor. In addition, the bank received a $74 million insurance settlement for assets lost in the blaze. The manner in which the bank coped with the ultimate corporate crisis (*nothing* was left except safety deposit boxes—Minnesota did not allow branch banking at the time) has been widely praised as a model for crisis management.

Just six months earlier, executive vice president Virgil Dissmeyer had completed one of the first crisis management plans ever written for a bank. The document, hundreds of pages long and more than two inches thick, discussed operations for a crisis center, how vendors and employees would be contacted, how operations could be temporarily located in other sites, and how the news media could be accommodated, among many other items. Recovery of computer data operations were addressed in a separate crisis plan.

The existence of that CMP proved fortuitous. Within hours after the fire, a crisis center was established in a small conference room across the street; for the next three months, the bank president and members of his executive team directed all operations from that room. Some 1,500 employees of the bank were told to stay at home until otherwise instructed. Within days, the bank had established temporary locations in an abandoned clothing store and vacant warehouses. In an extraordinary move, the U.S. Controller of the Currency gave approval for other banks in Minneapolis to accept Northwestern's deposits and withdrawals for up to ninety days. Meanwhile, 200 essential employees reported to work in a room adjacent to the crisis center. Other employees were paid full salary and benefits until they were needed, and many did not return for several weeks.*

Officials of Northwestern National Bank told *Business Insurance* (February 13, 1989) that even with a disaster recovery plan, they had never contemplated that a fire would destroy all of their headquarters facilities. Richard Klovstad, Northwestern vice president, told the magazine: "We never thought that a fire would

---

*Note to readers: For more information on service disruptions as a crisis for business, see Meg Fletcher, "Illinois Bell Sued Over Service Disruptions," *Business Insurance*, June 13, 1988, p. 35.

destroy as much as it did, and we learned that you have to think of the worst-case scenario and plan for it."

INTERVIEW

Virgil Dissmeyer
What Do You Mean, My Bank
No Longer Exists?

Now a retired consultant in financial crisis management, Virgil Dissmeyer has worked for a variety of clients, including First Interstate Bank and two other institutions that suffered damage as a result of the 1989 California earthquake that struck the San Francisco Bay Area. He notes, "Ten years ago, we had no material to work with, no data to rely upon. We made it all up. Today, the government requires a crisis plan for all banks, but there was no such requirement at the time. We spent weeks trying to identify everywhere we were vulnerable. Most of our assumptions and contingency plans were correct, and this was invaluable in retaining the public's trust."

Q *You developed a crisis management plan for Northwestern National Bank* several months prior to the catastrophe. What motivated you to act?

A Two things. First, in the fall of 1981 we had two tremendous snowstorms in Minnesota that forced us to close down the bank. What a mess! Second, we had started installation of the now popular personal com-

puters. We started discussing the status of our contingency plan, which really didn't exist. I was then given the assignment to draft one.

Q *Is it true that at that time the state of Minnesota did not allow banks to have branches? Didn't that contribute to the problems associated with any kind of calamity?*

A That's true, because all of our operations were concentrated in one location. The only secondary site we had was an operating center for computer and data processing equipment that was housed several blocks away. The computer center was not damaged by our subsequent fire, which saved us.

Q *How did you learn of the fire?*

A In the contingency plan I had written, we had key people leave contact numbers with our security department so that if we needed to contact them for any reason, they could get a hold of us. Now remember, it was Thanksgiving and people were scattered. I was in Nebraska when the head of security pulled out that contact list and started calling people (or, if no answer, he called their children to relay the message). Some of our executives had to charter an airplane to fly back from Florida. I drove all night and was back at the bank Friday morning.

Q *At that point, was the bank destroyed?*

A Yes. Completely. We established a command center in a downtown office building across the street. We had identified it in advance, so key executives knew where to report. Our bank president met the team, pulled out our contingency plan, and began executing the steps he had identified. That room held between six and eight people, and it really became the nerve center, if you will, of a multimillion-dollar operation. It remained so for roughly three months. There were no fax machines then, so we relied on telephone and two-way radios as our means of communication. We had to quickly identify alternate banking sites. We identified what bank departments needed how much space. We contacted several building owners and determined we needed 300,000 square feet of space in twelve different locations.

Q *How was public relations coordinated?*

A Certainly people with safety deposit boxes were panicking. People with money in the bank assumed it was documented, but they too were concerned. One of the key persons in the command center was our director of public relations. That individual went public with a statement emphasizing that no lives were lost, that records were safe in our data center, and we were fully insured. We didn't tell people that all paper records were gone. The purpose was to keep the public calm. We further stated that we would update the community by radio and television media as we learned about the status of the bank and how we would continue to serve them.

Q *What was the most important attribute of your own public relations people?*

A We resolved in our plan that only one person would speak for the bank—our director of public relations. Thus we had a common voice with an established working relationship with the media. He would level with them and tell them as much as he could when it became available. As things calmed down, we assigned separate rooms, one for the print press, one for radio, and one for television. Our CEO and public relations director would circulate to each room and update them.

Q *For the next three months your bank was operating in multiple sites, often under rather unaesthetic conditions. How loyal were employees and customers?*

A Employees were paid full salary even though some did not come to work for several days or weeks. Over 1,500 workers were displaced! There was a real attempt to keep family units together and not to put employees in jeopardy. We also decided to rent replacement equipment and not lease because we wanted to make sure we could later replace what we lost with compatible equipment after insurance matters were settled. Then we had to make a judgment as to how long it would take to rebuild the bank. We assumed it would take us three years to repair it, five years to rebuild. So we entered into lease agreements for at least three years. Employees were loyal—they knew we were going to hang in there. Most customers were loyal.

Q *How did you arrange for the regulators to allow you a ninety-day reprieve to have more than one location?*

A Because of the crisis, they gave us ninety days' breathing room to establish temporary sites. Several of our competitors agreed to take our deposits. In a disaster you'll find that associates in your industry will rally because it's not to anyone's benefit for one member of a group to fail to serve the public. Our major competitors, First National Bank and Twin City Federal, made their facilities available to some of our key staff. Isn't that amazing? Certainly something you don't see every day.

Q *How long did it actually take to rebuild that structure?*

A The old building was torn down, and the new bank was occupied in early 1988—a total of over five years. During that period there was no significant loss in customers or deposits. In fact, some customers rallied tremendously because they too understood the difficulty the bank was operating under. We did suffer a loss of business accounts, probably because we couldn't compete effectively in bidding for new business. We fought like mad to retain corporate clients, but some split their business with our competitors. The bank and holding company affiliates later changed their name from variations of Northwestern National Bank to Norwest Bank of Minnesota N.A., to project a common identity. The affiliates were active in seven states.

Q *What was total dollar damage?*

A The lawsuit and insurance settlement came to

approximately $140 million, settled in 1983. The safety deposit boxes in the basement worried us because of possible water damage. About a week after the fire, we pumped the water out, reinforced the walls, and entered those vaults. We found that the construction from back in the 1930s was so good that water was kept out except for maybe an inch in the bottom. All was safe. The fire had raged from Thanksgiving Day (Thursday) until Monday morning.

Q *You obviously coordinated one of (if not the) major banking crises up until that time. Could you tell me about your work today?*

A While still with the bank, I received numerous inquiries for copies of our plan and speeches. With my retirement in 1984, it was just logical for me to use my experiences as kind of an avocation. I established a consulting firm and now counsel others, primarily financial institutions—banks, savings and loans, and credit unions.

Q *Can you cite a sample case?*

A In California I have two major clients, one in the securities sector and one in the financial services industry. I developed a plan that was used by them in the San Francisco earthquake of 1989. I went back afterward to conduct a post-crisis audit to see what should be changed or enhanced. I'm convinced that just as important as advance planning is post-crisis evaluation. We did that at Norwest Bank, and I urge every organization to assess its crisis responsiveness after the fact. ❑

CASE STUDY: THESE MAGICANS WEREN'T SO MAGICAL

Coca-Cola is one of the icons of U.S. industry. In 1886, John Styth Pemberton, an Atlanta pharmacist, concocted a soft drink formula that has since become the undisputed leader among all beverages. In the ensuing years, Coca-Cola has become a multinational powerhouse whose products have often been copied but never duplicated. The company prides itself on a quality core product, imaginative and often-changing marketing strategies, and a driven, talented sales force.

When Coca-Cola faces a crisis, many parties—investors, competitors, financial analysts, and consumers—take notice. In some cases, the company's creative executive team has been able to turn a crisis into an opportunity, such as the April 23, 1985, decision to drop the original Coke formula in favor of a "new" Coke. Although the new formula proved popular in test markets, the reformulated Coke faced a barrage of criticism from customers loyal to the original formula. It also provided its rival Pepsi-Cola an opportunity to publicly challenge whether Coca-Cola understood its customers. By July 3, the company decided that Coke Classic would return alongside its new companion. On July 22, 1985, *Newsweek* noted that "Coke has given its customers the rare satisfaction of forcing a giant corporation to do an about-face."

In June 1990, Coca-Cola officials eagerly awaited the debut of Coke in newly developed MagiCans—aluminum containers that looked, weighed and felt like a typical can of soda. When opened, a small percentage of cans would pop forward with cash or certificates for prizes. Three weeks into the promotion, Coca-Cola faced a slew of problems with the multimillion-dollar campaign: Test markets in Iowa and Illinois reported that some cans were filled only with water (not even soda!) when they were supposed to contain a prize. A flight attendant on a United Airlines flight from Chicago to San Francisco was bothered when nothing came out of her just-opened Coke can. Fearing that the can might have been tampered with, she contacted a ground crew. When the plane landed, the local bomb squad was called and experts carefully pried open the potential explosive—only to find a $10 bill inside.

Some seventy complaints about faulty cans were reported to Coca-Cola. Although Coke says that less than 1 percent of all MagiCans were defective, it yanked the promotion and launched an 800 number that would respond to MagiCan questions and complaints. The *Wall Street Journal*, in its June 5, 1990, report on the MagiCan, summarized the case best: "Coke's adventure with MagiCans—the malfunctions, the bomb scare, the big launch and the quick retreat—may serve well as a promotional primer, illustrating both marketing mastery and missteps."

Let's assume that you are assistant vice president for Coca-Cola's promotion division. A group of institutional investors who own major blocks of Coca-Cola stock will be meeting in your Atlanta, Georgia, headquarters in two days for their annual update. Your vice president has asked that you pre-empt any negative questions or concerns that might be voiced by preparing a presentation on how Coca-Cola plans to respond to this crisis. In this presentation, specify what steps the company plans to take, and in what order, regarding the MagiCan crisis. Keep in mind that the ingredients of any such campaign might include the following:

- Production and schedule problems—machinery currently incorporates a certain number of MagiCan prizes in each lot
- Competition—what statements or actions may they take during this embarrassing period
- Role of major stockholders who will be concerned about financial and nonfinancial costs of this fiasco
- Advertising agencies and other creative personnel
- Regulators concerned about public health and welfare
- Retailers and distributors of Coke products
- Industry press and the general news media
- Specific marketing themes that may accompany a new promotion
- Improvement of test marketing for such promotions

We know that Coca-Cola has a reputation for turning strategic mistakes into marketing miracles. How will you approach this crisis that involves marketing, strategic planning, and communications? ❏

Source: This case is based on Michael J. McCarthy, "How Coca-Cola Stumbled: MagiCan'ts," *Wall Street Journal*, June 4, 1990, p. B1.

ENDNOTES

1. Otis Baskin and Craig Aronoff, *Public Relations: The Profession and the Practice,* 2d ed. (Dubuque, IA: Brown, 1988), p. 308.
2. Ibid., p. 309.
3. Thomas G. Donlan, "Still a Lousy Idea: The Odometer Imbroglio Haunts Chrysler," *Barron's* (March 6, 1990): 24.
4. Ibid.
5. Ibid.
6. "Chrysler Transmission Woes," *Consumer Reports* (April 1991): 47.
7. Ibid.
8. "Chicago's Poisoned Tylenol Scare, 1982," *Wall Street Journal* (November 29, 1989): B1.
9. Marion K. Pinsdorf, *Communicating When Your Company Is Under Siege* (Lexington, MA: Lexington Books, 1987), p. 49.
10. Mitchell, Leon, "Tylenol Fights Back," *Public Relations Journal* (March 1983): 12.
11. Weinberger and Romeo, "The Impact of Negative Product News," *Business Horizons* (Jan–Feb. 1989): 49.
12. Harold Burson, *Management Review* 72 (August 1990): 2.
13. Paul H. Rubin, "Sudafed's the Last Thing To Be Afraid of," *Wall Street Journal* (March 13, 1991): 16.
14. Joanne Lipman, "Sudafed Maker Faulted for Failing to Follow Through after Recall," *Wall Street Journal,* (March 11, 1991): B6.
15. "Timing of Sudafed Alerts Probed," *Las Vegas Review-Journal* (March 5, 1991): 8A.
16. "Terrorism on High Street," *Management Today* (January 1990): 56.
17. Ibid., p. 58.
18. Carl L. Swanson, "The New and Growing Management Problem of Terrorism," *IM,* (May–June 1987): 2.
19. George McKinley, "Terrorism: Growing Factor in Location Decisions," *Site Selection Handbook* (August 1986): 952.
20. "Business Copes with Terrorism," *Fortune,* (January 6, 1986): 55.
21. "Hong Kong Officials Move To Restore Confidence after Runs on Two Banks," *Wall Street Journal,* (August 12, 1991): A8.
22. "Killing a Rumor Before It Kills A Company," *Business Week* (December 24, 1990): 23.
23. Lynn Fisher and William Briggs, "Communicating with Employees During a Time of Tragedy," *IABC Communications World* 6 (February 1989): 32.
24. Ibid.
25. William Glaberson, "Coping in the Age of NIMBY," *New York Times* (June 19, 1988): 25.
26. "A Sweet Deal for Disney Is Souring Its Neighbors," *Business Week,* (August 8, 1988): 49.
27. "Hope Deflects Pleas to Sell or Donate Land," *Las Vegas Sun* (February 26, 1990): 26.
28. "Donald Trump, Move Over," *Newsweek* (February 5, 1990): 43.
29. "Not in My Backyard, You Don't," *Time* (June 27, 1988): 44.
30. Glaberson.
31. Eve Pell, "The HIGH Cost of Speaking Out," *California Magazine* (November 1988): 142.
32. Charles F. Vance, "When Trouble Comes," *Security Management* (January 1988): 27.

5

Communication as a Management Tool

There are shared experiences, like elections, or emergencies of the order of the Persian Gulf Crisis; there are profoundly devastating national tragedies, like the assassinations of John F. Kennedy, Robert Kennedy and Martin Luther King, Jr. Like contemporary neighborhoods, we may be most passionately linked to one another by dramatic crises, which by their very nature are unpredictable, thus especially frightening. Indeed, it may well be that crisis, with its myriad faces and names, will become our communal rallying-point of the 1990s. The rituals attending them will be media-generated, media-ordained. Tocqueville's insight of the mid-1800s—that the media make associations—is true now in a way he could have never anticipated. ❏

Joyce Carol Oates, *Fortune* magazine (1991)

Effective communication is essential to the success of every organization. Without staff meetings, telephones, fax machines, public relations functions, memoranda, and face-to-face communication, it would simply be impossible for executives to manage people and projects. That being the case, it is no surprise that identifying and carrying out a series of communication strategies in the midst of crisis is difficult. Sometimes there is no time for an overall "strategy"—managers simply make choices as best they can in a limited amount of time, deciding if they will speak with the press, issue a photograph, or call for a press conference. In other crises, however, the choices are more strategically planned, often developed in consort with attorneys and consultants. Knowing in advance which communication options are available helps managers in deciding how to effectively reach many different publics in the event of a crisis.

Although there are many dimensions to the term communication, such as "interpersonal," "group," "broadcast," and "international," this chapter focuses on the role of public relations as a communication strategy during crises. As already noted, which communication tools managers use to tackle their objectives can often significantly influence their ultimate success. When managers choose a news conference rather than a printed news release, for example, they should do so only after having evaluated the consequences of their choice. They may be praised for that selection, or they could be criticized on the editorial page of tomorrow's newspaper—there is rarely an in-between.

COMMUNICATION *IS* STRATEGY

Business communication is more than effective speaking and writing. It is a crucial strategy employed by every organization during times of both crisis and calm. Churches publish newsletters and magazines to maintain interest in and support for their causes; political parties call press conferences and announce party platforms to generate awareness and interest; and corporations routinely produce reports, direct mail promotions, and advertising campaigns to stimulate consumer demand.

If you attended Harvard Business School, one of the first courses you would be required to take covers management communication. In that course, students are taught that, to be successful, virtually every piece of communication they will compose in their careers demands that they consider the following elements:

- Audience
- Goal
- Message
- Source
- Support and information
- Feedback

These are the building blocks of communication strategy.

Audience

In a crisis, managers must know their audience. This knowledge is essential to the job of returning an organization to normalcy. The challenge for every manager, of course, is to identify his or her audience before crisis. But this is no easy task.

If you know before a crisis whom you should be concerned about, you can design a crisis management plan that is audience specific. This means that the information you share with major stockholders may differ from that which you issue to a federal regulatory commission, which in turn may differ from the information you share with protesters outside your corporate headquarters. The reason for this is not to deceive or mislead these parties. Rather, effective management requires that you consider all audiences in advance. For example, which regulators are important to your organization, and who should speak to them if you experience a crisis? Which neighborhood activists really matter, and who within your company has a good rapport with these people? This type of *audience segmentation* is common in corporate America today. It is a shrewd strategy combining marketing, organizational behavior, and public relations.

Certainly you do not want to learn about audience segmentation *after* a crisis has taken place, when you may find you have the wrong company spokespeople speaking to the wrong audience. In such cases, your colleagues may be offending the audience segment they are addressing because they are not sensitive to their concerns. Worse yet, corporate officers may contradict each other or mislead audiences simply because some are not as well informed as others in the organization.

Audience segments vary greatly by size and complexity. If you own a small chemical company in Memphis, Tennessee, that distributes products used solely by air-conditioning manufacturers, your audience might consist of only four or five large distributors who buy your product. You would likely have little concern for communicating with end users, because you never deal with them directly. But that is not the case if you are manager of food quality at General Mills. Now your audience is larger, more complex, and far more difficult to judge in advance. You must be concerned with millions of consumers, hundreds of thousands of stockholders, hundreds of federal and state food regulators, numerous distributors and public interest groups, and thousands of supermarket managers.

Therefore, before crisis occurs—whether a recall or industrial accident—managers need to evaluate audiences to identify those parties that are *now* concerned about their company and those additional parties that may be *later* interested in their company if a crisis were to occur. In preparing this audience analysis, consider the following questions:

1. Where are these audiences located?
2. Can you reach them by calling a meeting of interested parties in your company auditorium, or will you use the mass media? Would a mailing or telegram suffice?

3. Would a press conference reach the intended audiences, or would it bypass those who have a specific interest in this crisis?

4. Could you communicate with interested individuals in one day, or would a crisis communications program take several days or longer? (Recalling a product, for instance, requires drafting a letter that must be reviewed by senior management, corporate attorneys, and possibly major stockholders in your organization. Consulting with regulators may not be required but is usually a good idea, and the entire process can take several days or more.)

5. Do you have accurate information on the correct names and addresses of individuals who are vital to implementing this plan? It has been estimated that one quarter of all 260 million Americans move every year. Given that statistic, how can a company maintain an up-to-date list of its publics? (Some mailing houses promise a list that is 90 percent accurate. In other cases, companies that use stock brokerage houses for all mailings of annual reports and proxies would use them also for special announcements because these firms usually maintain excellent data bases of customers who own shares in the companies they service. For a private concern, however, the matter is considerably more complicated).

6. Can you make any judgments about the demographic composition of your audience? (For instance, if you are writing to notify customers about a recall, you will need to inform consumers who have a third-grade education as well as those with advanced degrees. Thus the choice of language to communicate with your intended audience is important—you do not want to confuse some people with eight-syllable words, nor do you want to insult the intelligence of others with simplistic wording).

Given these points, consider Arlington Plastics (AP), our fictitious company. Let's say an AP manager has begun to identify the various audiences with whom management should communicate should a crisis occur, and the goals of communication with each audience. One of AP's concerns is its plastic catheters, a potentially defective product used in hospitals. Think about the many issues and challenges associated with a product recall for AP catheters and then complete the audience-goal analysis on the next page, which already has a few ideas written in to get you started.

Goal

To be effective, your communication during a crisis should have a clearly articulated goal for each audience (for example, for stockholders you'll want to maintain price of stock; for consumers, you'll want to avoid a lasting negative image of the product).

Let's say you believe that the first goal in a product recall is to inform receivers of the recall and the circumstances surrounding it. You should also make clear *why* you are communicating with them ("Because you use our product, we care about

AUDIENCES	GOALS
Stockholders	*Retain confidence*
Regulators	*Avoid fine, penalty*

you and want to retain your trust") and *how* you are working to alleviate the crisis and retain their trust ("We have recalled three million bottles of Pergo, and product shipments will stop until we are assured that the problem has been fully corrected").

In developing your communication during a crisis, consider these questions:

1. Do you know what you want to say, or are you merely communicating because it seems like the right thing to do? Will your communication help bring the crisis closer to closure, or could it complicate the problem?

2. How can you prevent misunderstandings? Should you merely clarify existing information?

3. Is someone spreading misinformation about your organization? How can you counter that? In this case, your goal may be not only to inform your customers, but to warn those who might take advantage of your misfortune: If they spread lies or rumors that are unfounded, you will take whatever actions are necessary to protect your reputation and market share.

4. Is your communication goal to calm people, or is it to alert them to potential harm? Should you even attempt to soothe the public if there is a distinct possibility that further damage, deaths, or injuries could still occur? In this situation, be especially careful that you do not promise that your product will be back on the shelf in a few weeks if that is not yet a certainty—consumers will appreciate it when a company works doubly hard to ensure that

its reintroduced product is clear of defects and problems and is completely safe.

5. Do you seek to delay public scrutiny of your organization, or do you welcome inspections and tours at this time? For example, in the days immediately following the Bhopal, India, tragedy, in which more than 2,400 people died of toxic poisoning, Union Carbide faced thousands of inquiries about the safety of plants that produced similar chemicals in the United States. The company agreed to allow members of Congress, regulators, and neighbors of plants to tour facilities (some wore gas masks) as a means of overcoming any notion that the company had something to hide.

Message

In preparing any message, whether to colleagues down the hall or to reporters, you will want to consider three major variables:

- Tone (Should you be upbeat, conciliatory, concerned, angry, or a mixture of these and others?)
- Content (Do you need to communicate fact, opinion, speculation, or a combination of these?)
- Receiver (How much does the receiver know about you? about your company? about the problem you face? about your ability and that of your organization to fix the problem? about your sincerity and skill?)

These variables are different in each crisis and for each organization. Messages need to be tailored to enhance your goal.

Source

Who is the source of information to be conveyed? Could that person be a technical expert with poor communcative skills, or an otherwise articulate spokesperson who may be unable to adequately address highly technical questions? The selection of a spokesperson who has high credibility with the target audience is vital. Second, how well acquainted will receivers of your information be with your spokesperson? with his or her background and their responsibilities? How can the organization provide this information if necessary?

In many cases, the decision of who will speak for your organization is especially important. Quite often a CEO of a company will insist that he or she must assume responsibility for a crisis and will want to play a prominent role in recouping public trust. However, a situation may be so embarrassing and painful that highlighting your most prominent spokesperson during a crisis could later require years of effort and millions of dollars to refocus positive attention on your company. For example, negative press stories about the business associates of chicken magnate Frank Perdue certainly injured the reputation of this popular business owner and celebrity in the late 1980s. In the wake of widespread unflattering press reports, the Perdue organization switched the focus of its marketing campaign away from Frank Perdue as company spokesperson to other messages.

In considering your message, these points should guide the strategy and composition of your communication:

1. Will your message be brief, or does the complexity of the crisis require a carefully composed and organized, detailed message?

2. Should the message be delivered in person or by way of videoconference or other channel? What assumptions will people make about your organization given the channel you select?

3. Should the crisis invite further dialogue between the parties? Should the message have a tone that indicates that the crisis has been or is about to be solved, thus discouraging future communication?

Review your audience and goal statements regarding a recall. Now consider what *specific* messages the AP team may want to send to these audiences in the midst of that crisis. See how many more you can add to the following box:

MESSAGES

First recall at APix 6 years

2,200 hospitals use our products

_____

_____

_____

Support and Information

In the box on the next page, list other resources of support and information (internal and external) that AP executives would want to turn to for advice and credible assistance in managing a product recall.

Feedback

In the aftermath of chaos, members of the management team should launch an analysis (possibly conducted by an objective third party) on its effectiveness in communicating with targeted publics. How did people first learn of your problem?

```
┌─────────────────────────────────────────────────────────────┐
│              SOURCES OF SUPPORT AND INFORMATION               │
│        Internal                          External             │
│                                                               │
│   Corporate counsel              FDA                          │
│   _____            _____          │
│   Director of product safety                                  │
│   _____            _____          │
│                                                               │
│   _____            _____          │
│                                                               │
│   _____            _____          │
│                                                               │
│   _____            _____          │
└─────────────────────────────────────────────────────────────┘
```

How effective was your response? Did you convey the correct series of messages? Whom did you offend, isolate, or fail to reach? If you were frequently asked to correct mistakes or provide amplification, why was this the case? Which messages were most effective in mitigating the problem, and which were least successful? How can you maintain an ongoing dialogue with especially important audience members? These questions are important for many reasons, the most important of which are the lessons learned that may help prevent future disasters.

COMMUNICATING IN A CRISIS

U.S. corporations spend millions of dollars on a daily basis to project a positive image with the consuming public. By placing corporate spokespeople on talk shows, mailing press kits, participating in trade shows, and making charitable donations, organizations hope to build and maintain an image that will enhance their overall performance. During a crisis, a variety of public relations tools are used to help weather the storm that is brewing.

Press Releases

During a crisis, organizations often issue press releases (also called news releases) to keep the news media informed of situations and decisions that may have widespread impact. A press release about a crisis is a printed statement (ideally one page in length) that identifies how an organization is responding to the crisis and who is at the helm of the management team, and it often outlines goals for resolving the problem. During a prolonged crisis, such as a product recall, as many as half a dozen different releases could be issued as news of the event reaches the general press, trade journals, financial cable networks, and other media.

First developed by public relations practitioners at the turn of the century, press releases serve a legitimate function in that they provide a definitive statement from a company that can be quoted by reporters. Sometimes, however, releases are used as a shield when executives feel they do not want to speak personally with reporters, arguing that their press release "says all there is to say." Most corporate public relations professionals would agree that press releases should only rarely serve as the sole statement from an organization during a crisis; rather, they can help amplify the problem and provide detailed technical information. Exhibit 5-1 is the news release issued by the Perrier Group during its well-publicized product recall.

Press Kits

A press kit is one of the most commonly used tools of public relations. Inside a printed envelope or kit, the news media will find several press releases from a company whose crisis is newsworthy. In addition, the company customarily includes black-and-white photographs of key company executives, a fact sheet with essential background data on the company's history, and occasionally a list of phone numbers for spokespeople.

The preparation time involved in the generation of a press kit can be considerable, so many leading companies keep a "boilerplate" press kit with essential corporate data that is already packaged and ready in boxes for distribution in the case of emergency. In the event of a crisis, the last ingredient included is a specific press release related to the immediate events. This strategy is wise and appropriate, because in a crisis the public relations staff could be tied up with hundreds of phone calls, important meetings, news conferences, and other duties.

A number of firms assist corporations that have multinational operations and that need a vehicle for rapid communication with their publics. One such firm, Investor Relations Service Bureau of New York, charges clients a flat fee of $8,500. For this fee, clients' news releases are sent to major print media and to television and radio stations worldwide.

News Conferences

Few companies experiencing a major crisis can escape arranging for a news conference. To ensure that the news media receive a consistent message from a responsible spokesperson, and because it would be impossible for a corporate executive to speak with hundreds of reporters individually, news conferences can be effective vehicles for disseminating corporate reactions to crises.

News conferences should be arranged and managed by people who have experience in press relations. As mentioned previously, corporate public relations staff members are often former reporters who know the needs of the press; they use that past experience to their advantage in arranging news conferences. Today, with satellites able to transmit executive comments and responses live to thousands of radio, television, and cable stations, the need for adequately preparing those who will speak at a news conference has never been greater.

EXHIBIT 5-1   Perrier Recall Press Release

---

perrier®

The Perrier Group
777 WEST PUTNAM AVENUE • P.O. BOX 2313 • GREENWICH, CT 06836

━━━━━━◖◦◗━━━━━━

FOR IMMEDIATE RELEASE   CONTACT Jane Lazgin
                                                (203) 531-4100
                                                (203) 863-6240

(GREENWICH, CT, February 10, 1990) — The Perrier Group
of America, Inc. is voluntarily recalling all Perrier
Sparkling Water (regular and flavored) in the United
States. Testing by the federal Food and Drug Administration and the State of North Carolina showed the
presence of the chemical benzene at levels above
proposed federal standards in isolated samples of
product produced between June 1989 and January 1990.

      "While the federal Food & Drug Administration
advises us that the levels reported do not pose a
significant health risk, we're acting aggressively and
responsibly in the interests of the public," said
Ronald V. Davis, President of the Perrier Group of
America.

      Perrier Sparkling Water is drawn from a natural
underground mineral spring in Vergeze, France, and is
bottled only at the source. No benzene has been
discovered in the source during regular testing by
Perrier and by the French government.

                        (more)

continued

EXHIBIT 5-1

PAGE TWO

The search for a possible cause of the chemical intrusion is focusing on the packaging and distribution process. In the meantime, the company has stopped all shipment of Perrier into the United States.

FDA officials have told the company that the level of benzene found in 13 product samples (12 to 19 parts per billion) does not pose a significant short-term health risk.

An FDA spokesperson was quoted today as saying that even if one drank 16 fluid ounces of Perrier per day containing the levels of benzene found in the isolated samples over the course of their lifetime, the probable increase of health risk would be only one in one million.

Perrier is cooperating fully with the FDA and the State of North Carolina, and has set up a toll-free 800 number beginning Sunday, February 11, 12:00 noon EST to handle consumer questions: 800-937-2002.

###

Source: The Perrier Group of America, Inc.

It is especially important to emphasize that reporters are skilled at identifying real news stories. In crises, an organization should not even consider calling a news conference unless it has an important, timely statement to offer.

Meet the Press: Preparation Is the Key

Many studies suggest that public speaking is the number one fear of most people. Certainly speaking to the largest possible audience—namely a massive television audience, including a global one—magnifies such fears for many executives.

Meeting the press in a public forum allows an immediate response to potentially hundreds of reporters who may be individually attempting to speak to corporate officers, so a press conference can be an efficient and time-saving device. It allows for one statement, one consistent message, and one forum during an otherwise unsettled, possibly chaotic, period. Yet the decision to opt for a press conference should be made carefully and after consultation with an accredited public relations professional. Among the questions that should be asked are

1. What will be achieved?
2. What alternatives to a press conference exist?
3. Will providing answers to reporters' questions help mitigate a problem, or could they add to further confusion?
4. What responsibility does the organization have to the public to address its record in this incident, or its plans for mitigation or other response?
5. Would providing a prepared statement at the beginning of the press conference help in clarifying complicated issues?

In addition to answering these questions, the following suggestions are offered for managers who may find themselves being asked to speak to the press.

Rehearsal Is Vital. When President John F. Kennedy became the first president to conduct live press conferences, he spent hours rehearsing with his press secretary, Pierre Salinger. Role-playing a reporter, Salinger would prepare hundreds of potential questions that reporters might ask the president. President Kennedy would give his answer, and then Salinger and other White House advisers would help Kennedy refine and improve his responses so that they were understandable to the popular audience. Similarly, corporate CEOs rarely venture before cameras without an intensive rehearsal with corporate public relations experts.*

Selecting the most effective spokesperson is important. Public relations professionals trained in media relations may be asked to respond, but many reporters

---

*Note to Readers: An excellent video on rehearsing for news conferences is "Thank You, Mr. President," by Worldvision Video, 1987.

EXHIBIT   5-2   Meeting with the Press During a Crisis

A MEDIA EXPERT GIVES ADVICE

Ammerman Enterprises Inc. of Stafford, Texas, provides training to managers in need of exposure to press relations during and after crisis situations. In his work on crisis communication, chairman and CEO Dan Ammerman offers this excellent advice in the area of media training:

What the media does not understand, they view negatively. That which they view negatively, they express with outrage. You have to make sure they understand. It is your responsibility to be understood, not their responsibility to understand. If you expect the media to get a quick Master's Degree in your business in order to understand what you are saying, you have already failed. In a crisis, we want you to know what you are saying and we want the media to understand....

Some of us have a language picked up in our field over a lifetime that most people do not understand ... technical words and phases. The military speaks in acronyms. Some corporations do as well. Speak to the tenth grade level of understanding. Eliminate technical jargon whenever possible. If you must use it, explain what it means.

The easiest way to get into quicksand is to respond with personal opinions. No one can fault a person who responds when asked for a personal opinion on something about which everyone is talking. However, you must remember that you are the company. You cannot publicly separate yourself from the company image. You are being interviewed mainly because of who you are in a company context, not who you are privately. When you offer a personal opinion that differs from the company's opinion, you appear to contradict yourself, creating a negative perception which is difficult to overcome....

For example, Police Chief Daryl Gates of the Los Angeles Police Department responded to a media barrage because a police suspect was killed while being subdued with a choke hold. The inquiry should have centered on the question of excessive force. Chief Gates, in his attempt to explain why a choke hold would kill a black suspect easier than a white one, said that blacks are built differently than normal people. That unfortunate comment became the story that spread nationally. The media lost interest in the original story.

Source: Excerpted from *The Ammerman Experience.* Available from Ammerman Enterprises, 4800 Sugar Grove Blvd., Stafford, Texas. Reprinted with permission.

prefer to speak directly with the CEO. Exhibit 5-2 gives some suggestions for corporate spokespeople who must face the press.

Introduce Yourself and Your Company. The purpose of a news conference is not to lecture the press and the public on the steps the organization is contemplating but to give a brief overview. Reporters are often eager to get beyond "canned" news to the more spontaneous question-and-answer session in a news conference, so brevity is crucial. In many cases, the public relations staff includes a copy of the introductory remarks in press kits that are distributed at the end of the news conference so that facts and figures needed by reporters will be accurate.

Remove the Company's Logo. Remove from the staging area where the news conference will be held any visible association of the company with you when you are speaking, including the company's name, logo, or banners. The reason for this is that when a television report is aired, or a photograph of the executive appears in the next day's newspaper, the intensity of public association with the company is reduced, even if only temporarily.

Call a News Conference as Soon as Practical. The timing of news conferences is especially important. They should not be conducted *so* early in the crisis that little or no credible information can be provided. Company executives usually agree to a news conference only after they have been given enough information by their own staff, regulators, emergency crews, or technical specialists that they have a credible grasp of how the organization is responding. In prolonged crises, such as a product-tampering case, several news conferences may be required.

Press conferences are ideally scheduled for early afternoon hours so that executives can spend the morning refining their information and so that reporters still have several hours to prepare their reports for the evening news or a newspaper's deadline for the next day's edition. To inform the press that the organization is calling a news conference, the public relations staff may telephone or fax an announcement to the city desk of area newspapers and the news directors of area radio and television stations. The news media appreciate at least three to four hours' notice so that reporters and camera crews can be assigned to the story.

Engage Technical Experts. In many cases, a company or organization directly assists the press by introducing an internal or external expert. That person may want to distribute technical information that has been carefully reviewed for accuracy, to explain both the causes of the crisis and the steps taken toward its resolution.

In addition to an overview of the crisis given by the responsible executive, a specialist who works for the company may be asked to provide more expert and detailed background. Thus, a geologist may discuss damage to a utility line from an earthquake, or a management information specialist may discuss how someone invaded a company's computer system and destroyed sensitive data. Because no executive can address all details of every crisis with precision, including at least one technical expert at a press conference can reflect management's concern that ideas be accurately and completely presented.

Maintain a Sense of Calm. Regardless of who is selected to speak for an organization, that person needs to be reminded that remaining calm under pressure can only benefit an organization that is facing a crisis. After having received the negative news associated with a crisis, managers may feel frustrated, but they should speak with concern, not anger, to the news media.

Reporters do not want to report incorrect information, and they do not seek to malign the character of management. If they believe that management is hiding something, however, or that managers have been evasive or misleading in their statements, serious questions could be raised about the credibility of the organization. For these reasons, considerable care should be invested to ensure that those speaking for the company do so with candid and complete statements.

Managers are well advised to avoid "off the record" remarks. In the days of Franklin D. Roosevelt, the president could turn to a trusted cadre of reporters and share details and confidential findings, knowing that reporters respected his position and authority. Today, "off the record" remarks should never be offered, first, because they place a reporter in an unfair and awkward position, and second, because no one can be absolutely assured that his or her remarks will indeed remain private. When speaking with a reporter, assume that everything you say could be quoted, verbatim.

A reporter is generally trained, either in a school of journalism or through internship training or both, to report a news event with as much objectivity and balance as is possible. Managers are usually advised by their public relations staff or consultants to be candid and thorough in responding to a reporter's questions. If a manager feels that his or her statements or actions were not reported correctly by a reporter, a prompt inquiry should be made to the reporter's editor. Most news organizations have a policy to correct only factual errors, however—not impressions that the subject feels were negative.

Monitor Press Reports. When a company faces a crisis and holds a news conference, it will want to be sure that its message reaches the intended audience. For this reason, a news clipping service should be engaged, if one is not already on retainer. Such companies (for example, Burrell's and many others) can be found in the business sections of most telephone directories.

Clipping services are specialized companies that provide a useful resource function to corporations and other organizations. They scan thousands of newspapers, magazines, and trade publications and will send their clients copies of every story that mentions a particular company or product (or those of a competitor, for instance), usually for fees that range from a few hundred to several thousand dollars per month. In addition, video clip services tape local and network news and talk shows and also deliver copies of each story that mentions your company's crisis. Because the client is charged for each print or broadcast story (or "clip") sent, managers should be judicious about telling the service *exactly* which newspapers or stations they wish to be scanned.

The value of clipping services to management is multifold. Executives can later evaluate whether the organization reached the media and public effectively. Members of the crisis team will gain insight as to how editorials and opinion columns treated the company during a crisis. Because various regions show cultural, religious, and political differences, management may also use the service to gauge whether different areas of the country were more or less favorable in news reporting and editorials. All this information, and much more that can be extrapolated from a review of crisis news, can be invaluable in preparing for future crises that the organization could face.

Postcrisis Evaluation Is Crucial. Managers need to assess where they and their associates succeeded and failed, as is discussed in detail in Appendix A. Assessment and evaluation turns lessons into future successes. In addition, an expression of appreciation to employees for a job well done makes good business sense.

Video News Releases (VNRs)

In recent years, television news has changed so dramatically due to enhancements in technologies, particularly satellites, that adverse news about one company can easily reach beyond a local city and even beyond national borders. Because organizations are interested in enhancing their image in the aftermath of a crisis, technology plays an important role in repeating negative images associated with a corporate tragedy.

Because most people receive their news from television and not the print media, major corporations have experimented with a new variation of the traditional press release. In an attempt to give a more controlled and graphic "spin," or angle, to a story, an increasing number of companies now engage television production companies to produce video news releases (VNRs). Prepared on three-quarter-inch broadcast-ready videotapes, these tools of crisis communications are used by executives who may find themselves needing to explain their company's response to a crisis, but who do not wish to expose themselves to the impromptu give-and-take of a news conference. This excerpt from an *Entertainment Weekly* article explains the economic appeal of VNRs.

> At a crisis point in TV news—when longer programs and shrinking budgets have left station directors scrambling to fill an ever-expanding "news hole"—corporate-sponsored VNRs are infiltrating the airwaves. In the last five years, the number of independents producing their own morning news shows has virtually doubled.... But at the same time, budget cutbacks ranging from 20 percent at the stations in larger markets to 50 percent at smaller ones have hampered their ability to produce top-quality news.... The resulting squeeze has created an opening for VNRs, which provide professional quality footage at no cost.[1]

Exhibit 5-3 illustrates the technology used to distribute these messages.

Video news releases present an ethical dilemma for some television stations that may choose to air portions of the release when traditional news-gathering sources are not available. For instance, if a Pittsburgh television station does not have the resources to send its crew to Los Angeles for a pretrial hearing on Charles Keating (a former Lincoln Federal Savings and Loan president charged with multiple crimes), should it air portions of Keating's video news release, which seeks to exonerate him? On the tape, Keating may be interviewed by a well-dressed interviewer who looks and sounds like a legitimate news anchor, but who is actually a paid performer.

And here is a case from the Gulf War in 1991: What should a television network do when it seeks to show damage inflicted on civilian neighborhoods in Iraq from allied forces, but the only footage it can get its hands on is from Iraq-controlled

EXHIBIT   5-3   The Satellite Media Tour: How It Works

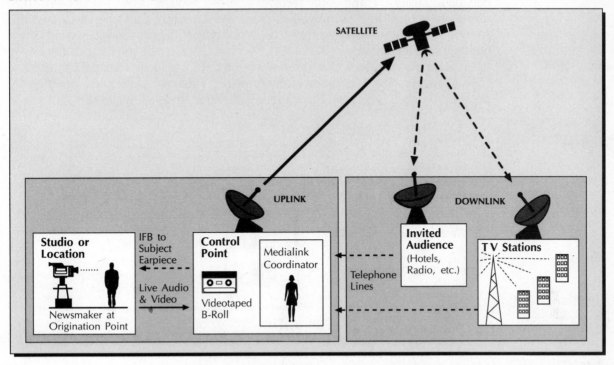

In a crisis situation, a corporate CEO or spokesperson often wishes to speak to the largest possible audience quickly and inexpensively. From a studio, that executive can speak to several thousand employees gathered at a hotel or other site (and many sites if desired with a downlink dish). In many cases, a company such as Medialink will place the executive on a satellite media tour so that hundreds of television stations can use the statement or news conference live or retained for later use in a newscast. Using this technology, individual stations can also have their anchorpersons interview the executive.

Source: Courtesy of Medialink (New York, Los Angeles). Used with permission.

government agencies? The tape could be accurate and portray actual conditions, or it could be exaggerated or even fabricated. The same is true of tapes released every week by terrorist groups that claim their videotape shows a victim admitting he or she was a spy. Was the person forced into making that statement in order to save his or her own life? Under such conditions, is the statement valid? What impact will that footage have on the victim's families?

Many news groups will not use VNRs unless necessary. For example, Houston's NBC affiliate, WPRC-TV, for example, will not air a VNR unless other video cannot be accessed by the station.[2] Yet 75 percent of the nearly 700 local television news programs now on the air in the United States use VNRs regularly.[3] Most VNRs cost less than $30,000 (averaging less than $10,000) to produce and distribute, and have been widely used by several key industries, including automobile, pharmaceutical, and entertainment interests. Several leading charitable organizations such as the American Red Cross, the American Cancer Society, and the American Diabetes Association also use VNRs.[4] The costs of producing a VNR are outlined in Exhibit 5-4.

If a corporation feels that the news media are not likely to treat it fairly in a crisis, managers may wish to carefully prepare a video news release so that there is no question about the position of the organization. In 1989, when the Wall Street

EXHIBIT   5-4   A Service and Fee List for VNR Production

Medialink Video Distribution Services

Rates Effective Jan. 1, 1992

New York: (212) 682-8300
Los Angeles: (213) 465-0111
Chicago: (312) 222-9850
Washington: (202) 628-3800

Satellite VNR Distribution:
USA Telefeed Plus:

Notification to all US television newsrooms (770 points incl. cable television outlets, foreign news bureaus and TV stations via the Medialink/AP express Newswire and targeted phone calls). Includes two separate C-band satellite transmissions in Medialink's daily New York-based satellite feed with additional wire notification, plus re-transmission of the VNR package only in Medialink's weekly "VNR Roundup." Usage monitoring included, comprised of video clipping services, Nielsen Media Research telephone surveys, phone calls, direct mail response and database searches.   **$5,900**

USA Telefeed:

Notification to all US television newsrooms as described above. Video is transmitted once via C-band satellite in Medialink's daily satellite feed with re-transmission in weekly VNR round-up. Monitoring included.   **$5,200**

USA Telefeed Guaranteed:

USA Telefeed or USA Telefeed Plus as above with an additional feature -- "guaranteed" airing in the weekly VNR newsmagazine "Newsworthy" airing weekly nationwide.   **add $1,400**

Combination Satellite and Cassette VNR Distribution Services
Sat Plus 50:

USA Telefeed as described above plus dubbing and express courier delivery of 50 3/4-inch cassettes to targeted television·newsrooms.   **$7,600**

Sat Plus 100:

USA Telefeed as described above plus dubbing and express courier delivery of 100 3/4-inch cassettes to targeted television newsrooms.   **$9,700**

European Distribution:

Cassette or satellite distribution to all major European broadcasters.   **Call for pricing**

In an era in which even remote areas of the world now routinely receive satellite transmissions, delivering a message to various audiences has become comparatively inexpensive. From the same studio, executives can reach every continent and speak with reporters or their own management teams on any continent. The video news release (VNR) has become a common tool of crisis communication, allowing a company to send a well-rehearsed, taped message over which it has complete control to thousands of broadcasters worldwide. The cost of such services averages less than $10,000 for one VNR.

Source: Courtesy of Medialink (New York, Los Angeles). Used with permission.

brokerage firm Drexel Burnham Lambert found itself charged with major federal securities law violations, it raced to produce a VNR that featured its chief executive officer responding to the controversy. Relayed by satellite to local television stations around the country, the VNR also reached an estimated 75 million viewers when the "CBS Evening News with Dan Rather" included footage from the tape on its program.[5]

Thus it is not surprising that major corporations and institutions are increasingly turning to VNRs as a vehicle to get their message across during an emergency. For instance, a television station in Phoenix, Arizona, probably could not afford to send its own crew to Alaska to cover the *Exxon Valdez* spill. So the news director of this and many other stations faced a dilemma: should they air some portion of an Exxon video news release on the story, giving the company's version of events without being able to properly balance them? Although companies in crisis have only begun to experiment with video news releases in recent years, VNR use is certain to proliferate as more organizations seek to influence the way they are treated during a disaster. Exhibit 5-5 describes the importance of understanding the legal ramifications of statements made, on a VNR or any other public forum, during a crisis.

EXHIBIT   5-5   The Legality of Crisis Communication

WHAT *NOT* TO SAY

A host of laws affect what should be said and what should be avoided in a crisis communication setting. Often in the heat of chaos, managers may be angry and thus eager to place blame. The following considerations should be reviewed by any manager who meets with the press in a crisis situation.

Libel is the *written* defamation of character; *slander* is the *oral* defamation. When an individual makes a statement about another party, in the case of libel that person could be sued for defamation of character if it can be proven that the statement (1) was published, including broadcast; (2) identified another party; and (3) defamed the other party. To avoid a defamation charge, managers need to be especially careful that what they say about another person or corporation is accurate and that they can substantiate all such comments. The failure to do so places them at substantial risk, as the defamed party can sue and claim substantial losses in terms of potential lost income and customers from irreparable damage to organizational reputation.

One of the nastier cases of business libel was reported by the *National Law Journal* on March 26, 1990. According to the journal, Nix Used Car Center of Columbia, South Carolina, was ordered by a jury to pay customer Tommy Carter $73,300 because the company libeled Carter when he complained about service. The customer, unhappy with repair service, drove his car repeatedly in front of the store with huge signs that read, "Nix Lemon." Someone at the dealership responded with a sign that read, "Tommy Carter is a faggot." So much for customer service.

A key element in libel is identification. The law explicitly states that a person does

continued

EXHIBIT   5-5

not need to be actually named in order to have been defamed, only that a reasonable person would conclude that the libelous reference relates to the plaintiff (*Gnapinsky v. Goldyn*, 23 N.J. 243, 128 A.2d 697 (1957). Thus, when someone states that "senior management at Madison Electric caused the death of those workers," that person could potentially face a suit from anyone in management at Madison Electric who is innocent and suffered in terms of employment or social status as a result.

WHAT *DO* WE SAY?

Here are some sample pairs of statements that show how to choose an appropriate form for your message:

Inappropriate: "The defective catheters were caused by a faulty substance provided to us by GY&K of Toledo. They designed that product for us in 1989, and it worked fine. But there's no question about it, the design of the process allowed for abnormal traces of zinc to get into the process, we fear."

Appropriate: "We are uncertain as to the causes of the accident. We prefer not to speculate as to what persons or systems contributed to the breakdown. Only after investigators check all factors can we say definitely what caused the problem."

Inappropriate: "The actions of Ms. Jensen are inexcusable. By signing the approval for the design of the catheter, she knew she was a party to fraud. The ultimate responsibility lies with Jensen and her colleagues, who routinely checked those records and had to have known that there was a problem."

Appropriate: "Questions have been raised as to whether or not any AP employees knew about the zinc. Those questions will be aggressively pursued by the investigators. If any of those parties are found to be guilty, we will pursue prosecution, but let me emphasize that the answers are not clear yet."

Inappropriate: "The videotape by Channel 8 is a lie. It doesn't show anything more than three workers shredding documents. Businesses shred documents every day. What does that show? What is Channel 8 trying to prove? You can make any video look like anything you want it to be if the voiceover leads you to believe it. Channel 8 is out to punish us, and thinks it has succeeded."

Appropriate: "The videotape is of questionable value. The district attorney's case against those workers will need to be based on an objective evaluation of what is shown and not shown on the tape, when it was taken, and what conditions surrounded the actions of those individuals. All evidence will need to be credible. A jury will decide if 16 seconds on such a tape is substantial and definitive enough to prosecute."

AP MANAGERS DISCUSS THEIR COMMUNICATION PROGRAM

Let's assume that Arlington Plastics (AP) believes it has adequately planned for the ramifications of a product recall and has trained its team members in avoiding the pitfalls illustrated in the preceding list of statements. Now the team must turn to other potential crises.

John, Arlington Plastic's CEO, asked operations vice president Marie, human resources vice president Roberto, director of advertising and public relations Laurie, director of tooling Donald, and director of orders Luis to look at potential crises the company could face. Let's take a look at how the issue of crisis communications was treated at their next meeting

John: You will recall that last week I asked that we begin to look at potential crises, and I'm especially interested in whether or not we are adequately prepared from a crisis perspective. I assume everyone has some ideas on this.

Laurie: Well, communications is my area, but before I give you some thoughts on planning, we should really prioritize the kinds of crisis we would consider especially important.

John: Good. Marie and I worked this week to develop the three most significant crises that could affect A.P. After plenty of discussion and research, we believe the worst possible scenario would be an industrial accident here at the plant, because of the obvious damage to our personnel, the facility, and our reputation. The second worst crisis would probably be if one of our products were recalled due to a safety or manufacturing malfunction. The third worst would be if a major customer canceled its contract. None of them would be good news, that's for sure.

Luis: Would you really put the loss of a major customer in the same category with a plant explosion?

Donald: Not the same category, but pretty close in terms of the impact it could have on us. I think that's a good list.

John: For now, let's act on this assumption—there are plenty of other crises we may have to face, but these are our "big three." OK, Laurie, tell us about communications.

Laurie: On the first issue of an industrial accident, there's no question that, from a communications angle, we are vulnerable. Our plant is manufacturing based, and we have chemicals on site, including plenty of flammables. We have intricate equipment. There is a major underground gas line near the parking lot. And we know from our trade journals that plant explosions at plastic-related firms *have* taken place.

From the media side, accidents or explosions make for "good copy" because they are crises everyone can see—smoke, fire, ambulances—they're very visible crises. The problem in planning for such a crisis is that we can't predict when it would occur, let alone if it might occur. The best we can do on this one is to have a policy regarding who would speak for the company, what agencies we would need to contact at the state and federal level, and how we could evacuate our employees safely.

Luis: You forgot something. Do we even *know* all the types of chemicals we have on site? And what antitoxins exist to prevent injury from them if they are inhaled?

Laurie: Good question. I know that we're supposed to because OSHA [Occupational Safety and Health Administration] wants us to, but I'm not sure—

Luis: Look, I'll admit it if no one else will: We don't.

John: OK, let's get that by Thursday afternoon—a complete inventory, Luis, of all chemicals on site, and a map as well as to where they are stored. Check with the directories to make sure nothing is stored where it's not supposed to be. Laurie, I assume you'll write a plan for that kind of crisis. Let's hear the second.

Laurie: A product recall could be more important because we manufacture goods that are used by millions of consumers. Plastic catheters are pretty intrusive. But we've never had a problem. Because we make molds used in other plants, the recall could possibly impact the safety of patients if defective. I don't want to downplay this. Hundreds could be hurt or killed in an explosion here, but thousands could be impaired with a product recall.

John: Good. What you're really saying is that an explosion or fire generates media attention because there's police, fire, ambulances. A recall is more dramatic, with the potential for more of a national story.

Laurie: That's true, and not comforting. Patient suits against us could be very costly. Communications for such crises are based more on planning, and that takes time. We need to think about the nature of the recall, how many molds are affected, what part of the country our products are more used in, and so on. We'd probably get negative national news media.

Marie: Fine, how about the third crisis, namely losing a major client?

Laurie: Now that could really be a complex problem for us. In this community, we are a major employer with over 400 people working here. We're the second biggest taxpayer in town. We give thousands of dollars to local charities every year. If we lose a major contract, we would probably have to make cutbacks in the work force, trim budgets, retrench—unless we had another client waiting in the wings. If all this happened during a recession, we could have a major problem. This kind of story tends not to be national news; it's much more restricted to the local and regional press. But we can't discount the fact that we are a well-known, large employer in these woods. If we lose a client or a contract, that would be a crisis. I'd expect that a press conference, press kits, maybe some statements from other satisfied clients—all of that may be necessary.

Marie: Wait a minute. You're saying that if we lost Johnson & Johnson as a client, for instance, that you might ask Ford Motor Company to talk to the press about what a great job we do? Doesn't that put Ford on the spot?

Laurie: It might, but when all the news is negative it makes sense from a media angle that we're going to get negative news. If we can have an outside party say something good about us, we can buffer the damage to the company.

John: Well, what I hear you saying is that with a plant explosion, we can prepare almost immediately with a plan of action—in fact, we're already jumping on that. In terms of a potential recall, we would probably not receive much bad publicity, but we can largely handle that ad hoc. On this one, are you actually suggesting that we come up with a list of clients we'd turn to for testimonials in the event we lost another client?

Laurie: If we lost a client, the media will expect us to take it on the chin and say something like "We regret the loss of this contract, but we've got a bright picture ahead of us." Sounds great but rarely gets heard by people—what they hear is that you've lost a round. I'd like to think in terms of contingency—whom could we turn to at other companies that we could fly in to talk to the media about the good work we do, the great products we make? It's better to have *them* support us at press conference than for me to speak in public relations, or John as CEO, or any of us at this table. We're seen as prejudiced sources of news. Other companies would not be seen that way.

After a hearty discussion, the AP senior management team decides that even though the third issue, losing a major client, is less significant than an accident or recall, it poses the most complex media dilemma. They have engaged you, a corporate communication consultant, to help the company on this issue. In fact, there is a distinct possibility that AP could lose a major client over the next six months, as that client has been extremely unhappy with the company recently. For AP, such a loss constitutes a true crisis because the news could come without warning.

As the communication consultant, consider these questions:

1. Would you agree with Laurie's suggestion to ask other clients that they speak on behalf of the company? Why or why not?

2. If John believes, from meetings with a key client, that the company could lose that organization's business in the next six months, what specific steps in terms of crisis management does he need to consider? What should he share with his senior management team? What information should he withhold? By giving such statements or information, will he be helping management or creating the possibility of rumors? How can John retain control over this potential, but not certain, loss of business?

3. Laurie's budget for advertising and public relations at AP is $140,000 for this year, not including salaries. Given the three crisis scenarios discussed earlier (plant accident or explosion, recall, and loss of client or contract), what budget needs should John and Laurie discuss that may need to be added to prepare for these situations? Currently the company has a press kit but few other media tools. The company spends most of the $140,000 on advertising in trade journals and for corporate brochures.

INTERVIEW

Phil Levy
A Television News Producer
on Crisis Communication

In a crisis, corporate managers often worry about how their company will be treated by the news media. In a television newsroom, several key actors help shape how the news is reported. In addition to the anchors, who often write some of the news stories as well as deliver them, a station relies on several reporters who go into the field each day to prepare stories. Overseeing the entire "package" of news is the program's news producer. This person is often a seasoned news pro who may have reporting and production expertise. His or her job is to assemble stories based on wire reports, police information, tips, and other sources, to help write the program format and content, and then to place the stories in a logical order for viewers.

Phil Levy is a former assignment editor and accomplished news producer who has been responsible for thousands of newscasts at WBZ-TV, WNAC-TV, and (since 1979) WCVB-TV in Boston, Massachusetts. WCVB is considered by many in the industry to be the nation's best station for local television news, with an army of Associated Press, United Press International, Peabody, and Emmy awards to its credit. In addition to a distinguished career in television news, Levy has taught journalism at Boston University and Emerson College. He was interviewed for this book regarding crisis communication and the role of the television newsroom.

A television news producer must rank stories based on their impact on various segments of the viewing audience. Levy says that corporate managers are often poorly trained in crisis communication skills.

Q *Phil, why should a corporate executive need to know what you do?*

A For the most part, corporate people probably don't think about how to deal with the media until they find they have to for one reason or another. Usually that happens when they find themselves in trouble and find their switchboards jammed with calls from media people.

This is probably the first time that they begin to wonder about reporters, producers, assignment editors, and so on.

Q *So you're saying that today's manager really should understand how the media operates.*

A Absolutely. In many newscasts, you will see someone who misunderstood how to react in a crisis situation, although people are learning. This applies not only to corporations, but also to individuals, sports teams, churches, government agencies, nonprofit organizations, and just about everyone. We in the media don't try to embarrass anyone. We just want to present the facts of a story and inform the public. We go out of our way to be fair by presenting both sides of all stories. However, problems often arise when an organization or person under fire doesn't want to talk to us to give their side of the story.

Q *What criteria do you use in selecting a story about a company in the midst of a crisis?*

A When deciding whether or not to do a story, an important thing for us to consider is: How does this story affect the public? We're dealing with masses of people, and we look for stories that impact them. Some stories affect only a few, but some have broader implications. Bear in mind, these decisions are subjective. In newsrooms all over the country, there are morning editorial meetings. Often they include the news director, the assistant news director, the executive producers, producers, assignment managers, and so on. These people look at the story possibilities for the day and decide which ones will be covered.

Often there are stories that these people feel are important, but are not covered for various reasons, such as lack of reporters or photographers, geographic location, and time restrictions. Often the prominence of the people involved in a story will dictate whether or not the story gets covered. There are no set rules. Every day is different. Every situation is different.

Q *You've been in the news business more than twenty-five years, and I'm sure you've seen more than your share of crises that were handled well and not so well by managers. Can you give us some insight as to how managers can be better prepared?*

A If a corporation plans a news conference, usually the first thing to do is notify the media. It is important to mail, fax, or call in the information well in advance of the event. This makes it easier for planning purposes. A follow-up call on the day of the event is helpful.

In such cases, timing is important. It is not our job to tell people when to have news conferences or plan events. However, it's common sense that to get the most out of an event, the earlier you plan it, the better. Radio stations are always looking for fresh stories for their newscasts. Early events can help. Many television stations have newscasts at noon. Therefore, it makes good sense to have the event early enough for your story to make that newscast. It also gives producers and reporters sufficient time to put together a good presentation for newscasts later in the day.

Also, planned news events should start on time. It is frustrating for media people to show up at an appointed time and then find the event is delayed. Often news crews go from one story to the next, and their time is budgeted.

On some occasions, we have been working on a legitimate story only to have the corporate spokespeople refuse to talk with us. They don't return calls, or they hang up, or they might threaten us with talk of a lawsuit. Lawyers often tell company public relations

people not to talk with us, which is not necessarily the best advice. When PR people are doing their job and getting favorable publicity for their companies, they are very hospitable to us. But, when the chips are down and, for example, someone has been indicted or their product has been recalled, or they're being investigated, it's a whole new ball game. They need to remember that it's a two-way street. Smart PR people know that regardless of the situation, they have to talk to us or they will look like the heavy in the story. Smart PR people also know that it is often possible to take a negative situation and turn it into a positive event.

Q *Can you give an example?*

A Several years ago, a major insurance carrier and one of Massachusetts's biggest employers was the focus of a story. We received a tip that some of their employees had been arrested for allegedly dealing drugs on company property. We also learned that the company had cooperated with the police in making the arrests.

We called the company public relations person and requested confirmation and an interview about what had happened. While waiting for them to call us back, we sent a news crew to their office building. When we didn't hear from the company, the crew began trying to interview employees. They were escorted off the property by company security. The public relations person, who had been a friend of mine, called and screamed at me for sending the crew to the building. He told me there would be no on-camera interviews with anyone from the company. He would come outside and deliver a printed statement to the crew, and they were to leave the premises immediately. I tried to convince him that this was not a good idea because it would make the company look bad. I even suggested that he should be pleased that the company had cooperated with the authorities in making the arrest. He disagreed. I called the crew and told them he would be walking out of the building shortly with the printed statement. I also suggested that the only video they might get is this PR person making the long walk from the door to the street, which is considerable.

This was a major story that would most likely lead the 6 o'clock newscast, and we obviously weren't dropping the story just because they wouldn't talk. It was unfortunate to have to quote their printed statement instead of having a spokesman for them to answer questions. What is sad is that they could have taken this story and made it into positive publicity for them. They could have said something like "When we learned it was happening, we cooperated fully in catching the alleged dealers." They also could have said that they didn't condone such things going on in their building, and they would do anything to prevent such things. They could have come off as heroes. Instead, they looked awkward.

Q *What about news conferences, video news releases, and press kits? Do you pay attention to any of them when a company faces a crisis?*

A As for VNRs, we sometimes use them. Sometimes they provide needed video to tell a story. Normally, we shoot our own stories or get video or sound from our affiliated network or from a program service to which we subscribe. Possibly small stations use them. We do so only in rare cases. More and more of them are being produced and sent by satellite to hundreds of stations. We get several calls a week from public relations people telling us their company has something on a satellite feed and they rattle off the coordinates. They call a few days later and ask us if we used the story. The answer is usually no.

News conferences are a fact of life, but are not the only way to tell a story. More and more, news organizations use them as a jumping-off point for a story. That is not to say that companies shouldn't have them. Just make sure they have a purpose. Sometimes they are important to everyone. Sometimes they are important to that firm or their employees, but not to the masses. If a company finds itself in a bad situation such as under attack for some particular reason, it is a good idea to go public and try to correct a problem or image. If companies are smart, they can often take a bad situation and use it to their advantage. The worst thing they can do is avoid the media and hope the problem will go away. It won't. An effort must be made to improve the situation.

Q *How do you treat a news conference?*

A We will carry a news conference live only if we feel it is necessary and if we feel it has information that cannot wait until the next scheduled newscast. In 1978, we experienced the worst blizzard in several decades. Some areas were buried in up to four feet or more or snow. Much of the state was paralyzed. You couldn't get out of your driveway, much less to a hospital, a police station, a food store. Michael Dukakis was governor at the time. He called several news conferences to discuss emergency preparedness and what the state was doing to open up key roads and airport runways. Here was a major crisis impacting millions of our viewers. We covered it live.

If there is a major disaster, or if a well-known figure is announcing a candidacy for or is resigning, we would consider going live. When Paul Tsongas revealed he had cancer and was resigning his Senate seat, we covered it live. In 1991 when he announced he would run for the Democratic nomination for president, he made the announcement in Lowell and we carried it live.

There are some people who schedule their news conferences at noon or at 6 P.M. in hopes we will do it live. Admittedly, we have been used this way before, but we have learned that it is usually better to tape the event and play it later in the newscast. This way, we can monitor what is being said and determine the news value.

Shortly after he was sworn into office in 1991, Governor William Weld wanted to be live on the three Boston network affiliate stations at noon to make what was billed as a "major" announcement about dealing with the state's fiscal problems. He scheduled his announcement from his office for 12:15 P.M.—right in the middle of those stations' noon newscasts. We elected to carry it live. As I recall, the others did not. In hindsight, we probably shouldn't have done it. His announcement contained no specifics as anticipated. We learned this only when his office distributed a copy of his speech earlier that morning, and we were already committed. I doubt that this will happen again. ❏

CASE STUDY: "THESE SODAS ARE BEING MANUFACTURED BY THE KU KLUX KLAN"

Brooklyn Bottling is a small, family-owned maker of gourmet and specialty soda that was first launched in 1937 and is now managed by the founder's grandson, Eric Miller. The company almost declared bankruptcy in 1987. Yet the introduction of a flavorful and inexpensive soda line called Tropical Fantasy boosted company sales by 50 percent to $12 million in annual earnings by 1990.

Priced at 49 cents for a 20-ounce bottle to undercut market share leaders Coca-Cola and Pepsi, Tropical Fantasy could be competitive because marketing and distribution was largely concentrated in poor, lower-class neighborhoods in Brooklyn and Harlem in New York City, near the company's headquarters. Overhead was less, advertising was restricted to mostly in-store promotions, and Miller believed that word of mouth would further propel the brand to new heights.

Then a vicious, untrue rumor spread like wildfire throughout the streets of New York. About three months after its successful introduction in December 1990, rumors began spreading that Tropical Fantasy was being secretly manufactured by the Ku Klux Klan in an attempt to sterilize black men. Soon fliers were being distributed in subways, on street corners, and in local supermarkets. "Attention!!! Attention!!! Attention!!!" the flyer began. "Did You See [TV Show] 20/20???"

In actuality, "20/20" never broadcast a single sentence about Tropical Fantasy. But the suggestion that the ABC television news program had somehow exposed the Klan's nonexistent interest in the drink nevertheless sparked a circle of hate and distrust that sent Tropical Fantasy sales nose-diving by 70 percent within of six months.

On May 10, 1991, Miller told the *Wall Street Journal*: "I made all the right moves. I was fair to my workers and my community. I offered a high-quality product at a proper price. This was a fantasy I shared with fellow New Yorkers—and then all of a sudden, someone put up a brick wall."[6] But who? And why?

New York State investigators began questioning whether Brooklyn Bottling had been targeted by Teamsters Local 812 because Miller's company is a nonunion shop and because Brooklyn Bottling and several other small bottlers had made successful market penetrations in an industry dominated by large corporations. Questions also surfaced in the press as to whether executives or distributors associated with the two market leaders, Coca-Cola and Pepsi, may have shared in complicity in the campaign to smear Tropical Fantasy. Even some truck drivers of the large-selling brands acknowledged that Tropical Fantasy was hurting their employers. One Pepsi driver told the *Wall Street Journal* that Pepsi sales were down 25 percent due to Tropical Fantasy's success, and a Coca-Cola driver was quoted in the paper as saying that the 49-cent sodas "cut in a hell of a lot."[7]

The phenomenal manner in which rumors can and do spread should not be underestimated. In the case of Tropical Fantasy, this was not an isolated and innocent case of wrong identity. Someone had produced and printed thousands of fliers libeling the brand, an act that could also be punishable as violations of restraint of trade laws. Many unknowing and earnest residents of Harlem and the South Bronx took the fliers and made copies, distributing or hanging them in stores, community centers, and on school bulletin boards. Finally, in an attempt to place some respectability behind the brand, New York Mayor David Dinkins, a leading member of the black community, went on New York television and agreed to drink the product to demonstrate its safety.

Let's assume that you are Eric Miller, owner of Brooklyn Bottling. It is May 1991, and sales of Tropical Fantasy have not responded to your marketing and public relations attempts to give the product an aura of respectability and safety. Although city and state law enforcement agencies have pledged to work with you, any prosecution of those who began this smear campaign could take years. In the meantime, you must try to regain your market share by taking on the following tasks:

1. Develop a comprehensive strategy that addresses as many possible issues as you can identify. Within that strategy, be sure to consider the many different publics that the bottler must identify.

2. Write a memo to your employees advising them of the situation and asking for their support, encouragement, and ideas during this ordeal.

3. Write a formal letter to the various owners of small supermarkets who are the largest distributors of Tropical Fantasy. Your goal is to retain their trust and to ask for their patience; remember that a number of customers are eager to have these store owners remove your product from the shelves because they have been led to believe you are part of a Ku Klux Klan conspiracy. How can you overcome that stigma?

4. You have engaged a management consultant who has recommended three options to you. The first is to change the name of the product altogether (but that may not eliminate a new set of rumors). The second is to move the company plant to a less volatile area (but competition will likely be situated wherever you move). The third is to place a note on every bottle that a percentage of sales will be contributed to black and minority causes, in an attempt to overcome the KKK connotation (but this could backfire because Coca-Cola and Pepsi could make donations of far greater value, given their size). On a piece of paper, evaluate the pros and cons associated with each of these three options. Then ask yourself whether or not the management consultant has effectively presented every option open for consideration. Can you think of others that are available to the owners of Brooklyn Bottling?

5. Your employee committee has recommended to you that Brooklyn Bottling take out full-page advertisements in neighborhood publications that bluntly informs readers of the crisis. They believe that a personalized letter from you will add credibility and candor to the campaign. Write that open letter to your customers that sets the record straight. ❏

Source: Based on "Rumor Turns Fantasy into Bad Dream," *Wall Street Journal,* May 10, 1991, p. B1. Used with permission of Dow Jones & Company, Inc.

ENDNOTES

1. *Entertainment Weekly*, May 17, 1991, p. 23.
2. "TV Vets Producing More VNRs That Are on Target," Special Study, *O'Dwyers PR Service Report*, April 1990, p. 3
3. "VNRs Are Elixir That May Request Government Regulation," Special Study, *O'Dwyers PR Service Report*, April 1990, p. 7.
4. Ibid.
5. Ibid.
6. "Rumor Turns Fantasy into Bad Dream," *Wall Street Journal*, May 10, 1991, p. B1.
7. Ibid.

CHAPTER 6

When the Crisis Has an Environmental Impact

According to *Fortune* magazine, consumers have responded to scores of reports regarding crises caused by environmental disasters; three out of four Americans now say a company's environmental reputation affects their buying decisions. ❏

Marshall Loeb, *Fortune* (1990)

In the past two decades, possibly no other issue has affected organizations as much as that associated with managing the impact of corporate operations on our environment. As shown in Exhibit 6-1, companies can be rated in terms of actions (or lack of them) that affect the environment.

Judging a company on its environmental commitment is in consort with the broader public mandate for social responsibility by large corporations. Managers are increasingly expected to adhere to socially accepted norms that meet the needs of society while continuing corporate activities. Today, many corporations actively embrace a program of social responsibility; some donate a percentage of their net profits to charitable causes (for example, Target Department Stores), while others such as Levi Strauss actively support causes such as AIDS education and prevention. Yet no other component of social responsibility (or *ir*responsibility) is arguably more alarming, more visible, and more quantifiable than concern with the environment. We have experienced the ozone crisis. The toxic gas crisis. The acid rain crisis. The rainforest crisis. And scores of others.

Clearly, the environment has no boundaries. Underneath the earth, hundreds of millions of pipelines carry natural gas and oil. Thousands of factories worldwide emit toxins (especially now in Third World countries, where fewer emission controls are in place). The threat of global warming continues. In addition, you may have read that the United States is quickly running out of room for the millions of pounds of waste it generates daily. Finally, your community may be one of hundreds that have faced, or will face shortly, acute water shortages.

A LEGACY OF NEGLECT LEADS TO POLICY RESPONSES

Business and industry, managed by people, is in some measure responsible for the many environmental crises that we face today. For decades, factories here and abroad polluted the earth's atmosphere with substances that had not been studied and evaluated for their potential damage to living things. Although Los Angeles instituted some air quality controls in the late 1970s, the skyline that envelops it is still pinkish brown. Many smaller communities, especially those with a heavy concentration of mining and factory interests, have been equally devastated. In several parts of the country, rates of tuberculosis, cancer, and birth defects are notably higher in areas where environmental damage has been extensive.

Although until the early 1970s business could plead ignorance about its role in managing and shaping environmental disasters, it can hardly do so today. The Environmental Protection Agency (EPA), created during the Nixon administration, began to systematically regulate the amount of environmental damage that could be caused by factories and, later, by utilities and others. In the years after the creation of the EPA, each state developed its own Department of Natural Resources or Department of Energy to ensure compliance with federal statutes and to implement its own additional safeguards. To provide the individual state assemblies with more control over pollution and intentional damage to the environment, many legislatures have enacted stern environmental protection acts.

EXHIBIT   6-1   How One Investment Firm Rates Twenty-Five Companies on the Environment

Industry	Company	Rating (1 = best, 5 = worst)	
Chemicals	H. B. Fuller	1.5	Environmental initiatives in HQ construction
	Monsanto	4.0	Pesticides, toxic dumps, offset by clean-air efforts
	W. R. Grace	5.0	Toxic dumps, several environmental lawsuits
Computers	Apple Computer	1.5	Recycles, lets environmental groups solicit on site
	IBM	3.5	High CFC emissions
Electric Utilities	Louisville Gas & Electric	2.0	Leader in installing smokestack scrubbers
	Southern	5.0	High SO_2 emissions contribute to acid rain
Environmental Services	Safety-Kleen	2.5	Leading recycler of solvents and motor oil
	Wellman	2.5	Leading recycler of plastic
	Browning-Ferris	5.0	Numerous landfill violations
	Waste Management	5.0	Numerous landfill violations
Forest Products	Jefferson Smurfit	2.5	Leading recycler of paper
	Louisiana-Pacific	4.0	Air and water pollution violations
Natural Gas	Consolidated Natural Gas	2.5	Promotes new, clean-burning techniques
	Panhandle Eastern	4.0	Substantial PCB pollution problems
Oil	Amoco	2.0	Strong waste minimization program
	Exxon	5.0	Poor response to Valdez oil spill
Photo Equipment	Polaroid	2.5	Strong waste minimization program
	Eastman Kodak	4.0	Substantial leaks in Rochester sites
Steel	Nucor	2.0	State-of-the-art mills, uses recycled metals
	Bethlehem Steel	4.0	Old mills with numerous environmental problems
Other	Wal-Mart Stores	2.0	Promotes environmental products, recycling
	Borden	4.0	Toxic dumps, air and water complaints
	General Electric	4.0	Major PCB cleanup problems
	General Motors	5.0	Toxic dumps, air and water problems

Franklin Research & Development of Boston, which calls itself a "socially responsible" investment firm and manages $200 million, bases these ratings on several factors. Each company starts with a score of 3, which then rises or falls based on corporate actions that harm or help the environment. Companies such as Franklin hope that publishing these ratings will encourage major industrial corporations to respond with more socially responsible environmental programs.

Source: Franklin Research & Development Corporation, Boston, Massachusetts. Used with permission.

These laws regulate the use of waterways, the transportation of hazardous chemicals over roadways, and the disposal of wastes and toxins that factories create.

How have society and business responded to environmental crises over the past decade? A few prominent examples follow.

Love Canal: A Neighborhood at the Nucleus of Crisis

Love Canal, New York, a suburb of Niagara Falls, represents one of the major environmental crises of twentieth-century America. Many lessons can be learned from Love Canal in terms of how individual "actors" in a single case responded to chaos. For years, the Hooker Chemical Company and others had dumped an estimated 21,000 tons of toxic wastes on a vacant piece of property. A public school was later constructed near the site.[1] Children were often found playing near what residents called a "lagoon" of black, oily substances that had risen to the surface.

Over a period of two years from 1977–1979, a group of concerned Love Canal housewives began to notice a pattern of illnesses emerging in their neighborhood: these included breast cancers, stillbirths, heart disease among middle-aged men, and leukemia in young children. The women launched a nonprofit organization and began to survey residents on their health disorders and then asked local and county officials to offer technical assistance in verifying that the patterns were related to Hooker's dumping of toxins in earlier years.

Little if any help was forthcoming. So the members of the Love Canal Homeowners Association began to map the location of homes where serious illnesses had been reported. Soon they had evidence that was compelling: there was a strong correlation between homes located near the Hooker Chemical dump site and people in them who were seriously ill, dying, or dead.

In presenting their data to local and state health authorities, the housewives were treated to a chain of bureaucratic delays. Some officials considered the women "neurotic." They were told that studies, formal scientific reviews, and investigations on Love Canal could take years. The group then contacted their congressional representatives and the White House. Both offered sympathy but feared taking any concrete action because of the precedent it would involve: thousands of other communities around the country may have experienced similar dumping of toxic wastes. There was great reluctance to act. By the time a 1980 EPA study reported significant abnormalities in the chromosomes in eleven of thirty-six children studied, hundreds of residents had already packed their belongings and abandoned their homes. Others, whose entire financial equity was tied up in their properties, simply *could not* leave.

At the height of their desperation over the authorities' inaction, the leaders of the Homeowners Association invited actress and activist Jane Fonda to visit the neighborhood. Fonda's public persona had been incrementally shaped not just by her film performances but also by her public criticism of U.S. involvement in the Vietnam War. Fonda accepted the invitation to visit Love Canal and toured the neighborhood with Lois Gibbs, president of the Homeowners Association, and a contingent of area residents. Then Fonda returned to the association headquarters to participate in a press conference. There, she grabbed a bullhorn and told residents (and the rest of a national viewing audience) that they should "Let yourself go, get mad as hell, and together, we can win this thing."

Now, with national publicity squarely focused on their dilemma, the neighborhood that was trying to deal with its crisis had created a crisis for the federal government. Frustrated because no federal monies were available for purchasing their homes and allowing them to relocate elsewhere, the homeowners took an unprecedented step. They held two EPA officials hostage in a private home for six hours while 250 residents protested outside. The national news media rushed to Love Canal. Neighborhood organizer Gibbs sent President Carter a telegram that read in part, "Don't let our people get lost in a sea of red tape as we watch our babies fighting sickness and growing up in an uncertain future." The White House called about the hostages and promised that the federal government would act; Gibbs ordered the members to release the hostages. As she later stated on an insightful television documentary called "Not in My Backyard," "We had taken people hostage. Now people all over the country were asking, If they took hostages, what could they possibly do next?"[2]

Eventually, the Carter administration provided loans and fiscal guarantees to the state of New York that led to the government's purchasing some homes. By April 1983, some 423 properties had been abandoned, scores of people had died, many had contracted serious illness, and the community of Love Canal had suffered a profound worldwide public relations stigma. As a result, some companies in the area relocated, others decided not to invest there, and yet others simply closed their doors permanently. For Hooker Chemical Company, Love Canal had become an environmental nightmare. In the end, the company became overwhelmed with multiple lawsuits, including a claim by the U.S. government for $124 million.[3]

WHO WILL REPORT YOU?

The Occupational Safety and Health Administration (OSHA) has launched a toll-free hotline so that any individual, including an employee of a firm, can report on the risks they have seen associated with toxic chemicals, hazards at the workplace, or unreported accidents. The number is 1-800-321-OSHA.

Asbestos: A Commonly Used Product Is Found to Cause Cancer

Asbestos, a substance widely used between 1946 and 1972 in the fireproofing and insulation trades, is at the heart of one of the most complex environmental crises in history. Companies that manufactured and distributed asbestos, such as the Johns Manville Company, were virtually crippled by the staggering sums demanded in lawsuits filed when residents of buildings containing asbestos contracted cancers of the lungs or throat, among other illnesses.

Many physicians suspected or knew that the product was causing harm to patients, but scientific studies were not acted on. Although the asbestos danger is difficult to visualize because of the absence of immediate death or even symptoms, the mismanagement of that product from the time it was first suspected to be injurious to human life remains one of the most outrageous environmental episodes of this century. At fault were a variety of manufacturers, distributors, and health officials, each of whom failed to act with the precision and determination necessary to resolve an evolving catastrophe.

By the late 1970s, studies on asbestos showed that the product was clearly hazardous. But removing the substance is no easy task: fibers can become airborne and actually do more damage that way than when lodged inside a ceiling or wall. Therefore, workers who remove the substance need special training. When stories emerged throughout the 1980s about widespread use of asbestos in buildings in numerous cities, trade unions began to ask for protection for workers, television documentaries raised questions about safety in schools and public places, and cruise ships were asked to document whether they had used asbestos in constructing guest cabins.

The asbestos revelations also raised one of the most complex issues in crisis management for many companies since the 1970s: managers in certain industries must now consider the possibility of unknown hazards—that is, whether in the future their product or its manufacturing by-products might be found to be harmful to humans (assuming that the technology or body of knowledge that could detect such danger is not currently available).

In some ways, the asbestos crisis was another Love Canal in that it was a management disaster for everyone involved. Only this time it was not hundreds at risk; rather *millions* were potentially exposed to asbestos in office buildings, hotels, restaurants, schools, malls, and homes.

To this day, efforts aimed at removing asbestos continue under a series of federal and state mandates. When the University of California at Berkeley found asbestos fibers in its campus buildings in 1988, it was shocked at the price tag required to remove the substance: $2 million for one building alone.[4] At the University of Virginia, an effort (spanning several years) to remove asbestos from campus facilities will cost $30 million, according to one estimate.[5] No one is certain of the total costs that asbestos removal has generated for private industry in the United States, but it is well above $1 billion since the early 1980s.

INFORMATION AS A CRISIS RESPONSE TOOL

In the wake of the Love Canal and asbestos crises, which all but destroyed the manufacturers associated with the products used, Congress enacted in 1988 the Community Right to Know amendment to the Superfund law of 1986. Under this law, industrial companies that make or use significant amounts of some three hundred chemicals must now notify local, state and federal authorities of the type and quantity of materials they release into the environment. With the passage of that legislation, some 30,000 companies around the country faced a crisis of information—they were now forced by federal law to disclose to their neighbors just what chemicals were on site and their potential dangers. Compliance with the law requires each community to develop a four-pronged approach to solving a potential environmental crisis:

- Emergency planning (for example, hospital personnel and EMT training)
- Emergency notification (contacting state and federal officials promptly about any disaster or industrial accident)
- Right-to-know reporting requirements (detailed lists of chemicals on site at any location must be filed and regularly updated)
- Toxic chemical reporting (informing the public of the known threat, if any, posed by chemicals on site)

After the law was passed, Theresa Pugh, environmental energy director for the National Association of Manufacturers, confided to *Business Week*, "Many companies have never explained their manufacturing processes to the public before." A few months later, after her organization stated in a letter to its 8,000 member companies that they could be fined up to $25,000 per day if they did not comply with the new law, Pugh told *Public Relations Journal* that her office received more than a thousand phone calls, some from executives expressing "surprise and dismay."[6]

U.S. industry has responded with varying degrees of success. Chemical maker Rohm & Haas Company announced that it releases one million pounds of chemicals into the air of Bristol, Pennsylvania, each year. Texaco Inc. said it releases 76,000 pounds of benzene, known to cause leukemia, into the air around Port Arthur, Texas, each year. (Although that amount sounds threatening, Texaco could inform the public that it is not a health risk—it translates into two parts per billion on average, well within federal limits.)[7]

In spite of the new openness, an impression was now forming among hundreds of citizen activist groups around the country that industrial damage to the environment required stiffer penalties. Since 1988, scores of new right-to-know laws (also called "sunshine" laws) have been passed that impose severe penalties for the intentional dumping of toxic chemicals. Moreover, some communities have tried to prevent the transport of hazardous chemicals across their borders, thus complicating delivery schedules for hundreds of manufacturers. For a small company with a limited chemical product line, this crisis of confidence can be costly.

Some companies have responded to the new federal requirements by launching an aggressive public relations campaign. Others have actually used the opportunity to increase public awareness about environmental threats and the potential for an industrial crisis. Dow Chemical, for example, has distributed brochures to both their employees and residents of local communities where it has plants. These publications discuss how waste is being reduced and how the company is meeting emissions standards at its plants. From its Midland, Michigan, plant the company has launched a computer data base that is accessible to the public and that identifies where chemicals are stored and used. The company has also sponsored seminars for managers of other companies on the new law and its impact.[8]

Dow's sophisticated hometown audience of Midland boasts the highest concentration of people with doctorates in the United States, and Dow has tried to develop a social contract with Midland that has received widespread positive publicity. Despite damage caused by the company over the years to the local air and water supply, Dow has worked aggressively to become a better neighbor and a more conscientious corporate citizen. Nearly a third of the city's 37,000 residents are employed by Dow, and contributions by the company to just about every environmental cause or other community charity have been impressive.

In anticipation of crisis, Dow's management has created an emergency response program (ERP). This written plan specifies that two to four experts are always on call, twenty-four hours a day, ready to travel to any company plant in the event of an accident or chemical leak. Dow has divided the U.S. into five regions, and teams in each region are designated far enough in advance so that each manager knows who would coordinate a disaster should such an event occur. In the process of developing these and many other preparedness measures, Dow has become a model organization that is now widely emulated by other companies throughout the United States.

IF YOU POLLUTE, YOU WILL PAY

A flurry of lawsuits on environmental pollution have caused both concern and major costs for a variety of businesses. In April 1991, the *Wall Street Journal* reported that the Superfund law has created costly litigation for many small businesses who never expected to be dragged into environmental crises. A case in point: the *Journal* noted that in Utica, New York, a pizza store owner, Doreen Merlino, was handed inch-thick papers of a lawsuit charging that she was liable for a certain portion of the hazardous waste in an area landfill. Who filed the suit against her? The answer is, two significantly larger area corporations that had been charged with violating pollution statutes, Special Metals Corporation and Chesebrough-Ponds.[9]

In agreeing to clean up a local landfill, these two companies decided to pursue other large and small entities that may have caused pollution in Utica. Ms. Merlino was told that her share of the cleanup was $3,000 (although $1,500 would be accepted if it were offered quickly).[10] But the two companies did not stop with Merlino; they went on to name some 602 other defendants, including an Elks lodge, a doughnut shop, an exercise gym, two nursing homes, and forty-four cities and towns.[11]

Is this the way the Superfund law was supposed to work? What if small businesses cannot pay the amounts levied by plaintiffs—should they be forced to close their doors? Small businesses and charities lack the corporate infrastructure of big business. They often have less access to professional organizations that warn major corporations of the hazards associated with trash or waste products. Yet nonprofit agencies and entrepreneurs share a problem with the Fortune 500—they must dispose of their waste. Now legislators face a thorny policy dilemma: although the chemicals and waste products disposed of years ago may not have been known to cause environmental damage, shouldn't the small polluters be now held as accountable as major ones? The answer may surprise you. As the Wall Street *Journal's* front page noted,

> Passed in 1980, the law was based on the principle that polluters, not taxpayers, should pay to clean up the worst toxic problems. For a time, the cleanup burden fell primarily on deep-pocket corporations. But now, some alleged corporate polluters are trying to spread the pain. Their primary weapon is garbage. Some corporations argue that they will have to treat tons of municipal solid waste to get to the hazardous material they are supposed to clean up. Others contend that even seemingly innocuous trash is laced with hazardous substances found in everyday products. Either way, they contend, any entity that generates, hauls or dumps garbage or—as some California municipalities have found—merely allows a trash hauler to do business within its boundaries, can be held liable for cleanup costs.[12]

Thus the environmental movement has succeeded in increasing awareness of the problems associated with waste management. The crisis has been an expensive lesson, for the homeowners at Love Canal, for small business owners, and for just about everyone else.

The largest settlement ever orchestrated by the EPA against a U.S. firm was a $15 million civil penalty assessed against Texas Eastern Company in 1987. The size of that settlement is unusually large compared to most EPA actions, which are typically well under $1 million—substantial nevertheless for a small to mid-sized firm. Another case in point is a $700,000 fine assessed by the agency against Coors Brewing Company in October 1991. The EPA charged that Coors contaminated soils and waters under its brewery from 1981 to 1984 and that Coors, knowing of the contamination, had failed to notify the agency as required by law. In a double whammy, the EPA fine came one day after the state of Colorado announced that it had fined Coors another $211,000 for a variety of violations of the firm's wastewater discharge permit.

In a nationally syndicated article on November 7, 1991, Knight-Ridder newspapers journalist John Woestendiek commented on the Coors wastewater crisis:

> Thousands of fish died after up to 300,000 gallons of beer were mistakenly fed into a plant sewage line. The beer was diluted and partially treated before it hit the creek, but that didn't stop it from wiping out aquatic life for a five mile stretch, nor did it stop late-night comedians from making jokes. Coors officials didn't laugh. For much of its recent history it has been the butt of jokes, an object of anger and the subject of boycotts. It has borne the wrath of racial minorities, organized labor, women, gays and students.

Countering those comments, Coors president Peter Coors said (in the same article), "We've got a terrific story to tell, but it gets overshadowed by one mishap that kills a bunch of trap fish in Clear Creek."[13] So much for sensitivity.

Chernobyl: A Complete Accounting Could Take a Century

The explosion that rocked the nuclear power plant at Chernobyl in the Ukraine on April 26, 1986, remains one of the great environmental crises in history. That evening (incredibly, during a safety exercise), the core of the reactor was exposed by incompetent managers, followed by a series of explosions that shattered the roof of the plant. When the roof exploded, some fifty tons of radioactive isotopes entered the atmosphere, triggering an environmental chain reaction, the extent of which may not be adequately measured for centuries. Sixteen other nuclear facilities in the former Soviet Union have a design configuration and operating system similar to the one that existed at Chernobyl.

Plant managers, fearing their lack of preparedness could land them in jail, insisted that the reactor was intact and working and that the glow over the plant was nothing to be concerned about. Throughout that evening, as the reactor core blazed, area residents fished in a cooling pond outside the Chernobyl plant, unaware that the world's worst nuclear accident was emanating radiation that would lead to their deaths. Even doctors in nearby Pripyat, who treated thousands of victims who soon flooded area hospitals and clinics complaining of headaches and burning sensations in their throats and lungs, were also poisoned: their patients were spreading radiation to every individual who came in contact with them.

Although the Soviet government steadfastly maintained that only 31 people died from the accident, in April 1991 *The Economist*, on the fifth anniversary of the accident, offered a major analysis on the crisis and its aftermath. The highly regarded newsweekly asserted that at least 7,000 died as a result of the Chernobyl disaster. Several Soviet organizations have claimed that under the shroud of secrecy, the number of dead was actually closer to 300,000.[14] More than 180,000 others were evacuated after radiation seeped into the atmosphere. After extensive research, the International Atomic Energy Agency (IAEA) in Vienna found an appalling lack of sophistication on the part of Soviet physicians who treated victims, leading to certain misdiagnoses. The credibility of the Soviet medical community was further eroded by a poll showing that 399 of 400 patients who were poisoned at Chernobyl and treated at the Center for Radiation Studies in Kiev did not believe what their doctors had told them.

The Economist's analysis of the Chernobyl crisis offers important insight into how one environmental crisis can create a snowball effect for other projects and plans being contemplated:

> All over the rest of the Soviet Union, the Chernobyl explosion was a powerful force in making people think about the environment. During the past two years work on seven nuclear power stations has been halted, two existing ones have been closed, and the planned construction of four more has been cancelled. Elsewhere in the neighborhood suspicions of nuclear power have grown just as strongly. Poland has stopped building the only atomic plant it had in mind. The Germans have shut down the remaining Chernobyl-style RBMK-1000 nuclear plants in the eastern part of their now united country. Nuclear nervousness predates Chernobyl; but what happened there greatly strengthened it.[15]

The former chief engineer of the Chernobyl plant, Grigori Medvedev, in his masterful work, *The Truth About Chernobyl* (Basic Books, 1991), argues that a "conspiracy of silence" contributed to the devastation caused by the plant crisis. The coverup by the Soviet government in the days and months following the disaster delayed international medical assistance, bona fide scientific inquiries that could help prevent a future catastrophe, and detailed investigations that could have brought those guilty of complicity to account for their actions.

Fortunately, the United States has never experienced a nuclear calamity even close to the catastrophe at Chernobyl. The Three Mile Island nuclear accident in Pennsylvania led to significant delays and the cancellation of several other nuclear projects being contemplated; it also spawned the creation of new activist groups that publicly questioned the safety of such plants in the first place. Yet one must question whether the many lessons of Chernobyl have been fully studied, and whether there has been enough public debate. If it is true that nuclear energy is an essential element of America's energy policy and that overwhelming reliance upon oil and natural gas could cripple our country and economy in the future, a robust review of the questions raised at Chernobyl is desperately needed.

REGULATORY ENFORCEMENTS MAY HELP AVERT CRISES

With all the problems associated with AIDS-infected medical waste, the ozone layer depletion, oil spills, pipeline explosions, and a proliferation of lawsuits, is there any hope? From a crisis perspective, the answer may actually be encouraging.

The EPA now offers a $10,000 reward for information leading to the conviction of anyone found violating Superfund statutes.[16] Between 1987 and 1990, there was a 170 percent increase in criminal prosecutions of environmental crimes.[17] In one year alone, 1989, the Department of Justice indicted 101 corporations and individuals, leading to seventy-two convictions resulting in a total of fifty-three years of prison time and $13 million in fines.[18] Today, the EPA has over two hundred enforcement officials on its full-time payroll, and the FBI now works in concert with the EPA in pursuing leads it believes concern serious potential damage to the environment.

Thus, the prevention of an environmental disaster requires a commitment by executive teams, an astute program of monitoring pollution levels by every organization, and a reasonably aggressive program of management education on the issue as well. For instance, the sheer volume of regulations being approved every year regarding environmental matters is staggering—in 1990 alone, over 10,000 pages of new regulations were written at the federal level.[19] Managers who are not actively participating in trade group educational programs, or interacting with citizen and advocacy groups, could find themselves one day having to pay dearly for their lack of initiative in monitoring both trends and the emerging body of law.

INITIATIVES TO ADDRESS ENVIRONMENTAL ABUSE

In the aftermath of these and many other environmental disasters, a number of companies have taken positive steps in recent years to avoid crises that could land them in trouble with the government and environmental groups. For example, since the construction of its plant in 1951, International Flavors & Fragrances (IFF) of Union Beach, New Jersey, has avoided public scrutiny of its operations because there were few local residents. The area's local economy was boosted primarily by summer tourists. But as the population of year-round residents grew throughout the 1980s, community awareness of odors emanating from the plant's waste treatment facility dramatically increased. The company responded in 1987 by constructing a massive polyester fabric dome, 330 by 140 feet in diameter, costing some $750,000.[20] In addition to constructing the dome, which was welcomed by state authorities but not required by them, IFF has since launched an aggressive community education program that includes annual training seminars for local officials on chemicals and storage procedures used at IFF, and emergency response drills to test both company and community responsiveness to simulated crises.[21]

McDonald's, one of the nation's largest producers of paper and plastic waste, has become an aggressive advocate of recycling and has pledged to become a leading source of public education on environmental issues. In recent years the company phased out the use of containers made of nonrecyclable material and has offered grants to environmental groups. McDonald's has been forced to change its operations as the environmental movement shifts gears. The company had curtailed use of paper products in 1976 because critics said it was destroying trees for cups, cartons, and bags. Now McDonald's has abandoned the very products that were supposed to replace those and returned to paper, albeit recycled, containers.

Few companies have surprised both activists and, apparently, themselves, as much as Du Pont has. After assuming his post as chief executive officer of the company in April 1989, Edgar Woolard traveled to London to give a speech titled "Corporate Environmentalism." On returning home, he declared that, "Avoiding environmental incidents remains the single greatest imperative facing industry today." [22] At his own choosing, Woolard meets monthly with environmental activists. In addition, he became one of the first leading CEOs to order suspension of the use of chlorofluorocarbons (CFCs). He has also taken dramatic, often expensive steps, to avoid an environmental disaster at Du Pont's manufacturing facilities. As both a good corporate citizen and a proactive crisis manager, Woolard has won accolades from business publications such as *Fortune, Business Week,* and numerous others.

A Boston public relations consultant who specializes in environmental strategies, David Stephenson, comments, "The grass-roots groups are concerned about the value of their homes and the health of their children. That means they are relentless. In general, unlike the mainstream environmental groups, they are not interested in mediation or compromise."[23] Moreover, the charges of environmental pollution being hurled at corporations in the United States are proliferating as the government continues to step up enforcement of existing regulations. The costs involved in meeting such a crisis head on—for attorneys, scientific consultants, media relations, and other factors—can be high. In May 1991, for example, New York pharmaceutical maker Pfizer agreed to pay $3.1 million for water pollution violations at a plant it formerly owned near the Delaware River, but that fine did not include all of the internal costs involved in preparing the company for its legal battle with the U.S. Justice Department and the Environmental Protection Agency.[24]

Similarly, it may take years for all the costs associated with the *Exxon Valdez* disaster to be fully assessed. In March 1991, Exxon and the U.S. Department of Justice reached agreement on a major settlement that called for Exxon to pay at least $900 million to settle civil suits. The company also pleaded guilty to four environmental crimes and agreed to pay an additional $100 million in fines. Exxon's chairman, Lawrence G. Rawl, who had been criticized by the press early in the *Valdez* crisis for a series of decisions perceived to be uncaring about damage caused by the spill, said that, "The settlement will have no noticeable effect on our financial results."[25] As *Business Week* noted, "Presumably, the chairman was seeking to reassure investors, but he wound up further infuriating the public with his apparent lack of remorse."[26]

Rawl's comments apparently found their way to Alaska. In a stunning rebuke, U.S. District Court Judge H. Russel Holland rejected the settlement, stating, "I am afraid that the fines send the wrong message, suggesting that spills are a cost of business that can be absorbed."[27] He ordered both parties back to the bargaining table to find a settlement that would propel Exxon from being a sympathetic party in an environmental crisis into becoming a model environmental citizen. The very same day that Judge Holland criticized the agreement, Exxon announced a first-quarter profit of $2.24 billion.

Thus Lawrence Rawl, an executive whose career was considered exemplary within the oil industry, found himself the target of scathing criticism—on radio and television talk shows, in editorials, in public protests, and in the halls of Congress. For an individual whose career had been so successful in terms of building partnerships, exploiting new markets, increasing productivity and profit—to name but a few achievements—the realization that his career will be best remembered for the *Valdez* disaster must be disturbing for Rawl.

AVOIDING DISASTERS: IS ECOTERRORISM THE ANSWER?

How can almost every organization avoid an environmental crisis? Even those companies with no activities related to chemicals or manufacturing certainly affect the environment; their employees drive to offices, they create garbage, and every facility in some way releases products into the local water and sewer systems. For that reason, industry at all levels needs to understand its role as a corporate citizen within the larger "community." Compounding the urgency of environmental awareness is the increasing influence of radical environmental groups.

Each year large timber-related companies such as Weyerhauser and Louisiana-Pacific, utilities, and other corporations suffer as much as $25 million in damages from ecoterrorists.[28] The mission of these groups is to destroy or disable machinery or technology they believe is damaging the earth's fragile environment. To damage logging equipment, ecoterrorists engage in "tree spiking," driving thousands of nails into tree trunks. In Oregon, environmentalists have engaged in "tree sitting," in which they remain some 80 feet in the air, moving from tree to tree with ropes, to delay equipment and tree-cutting operations.

In his book *Green Rage*, one of the leaders of the movement, Christopher Manes, quotes one stree-sitter as saying, "I figure I've done about a million dollars' worth of damage in the last two years. They can sue me—I don't care, I don't have the money!"[29] In Canada, ecoterrorists destroyed the $4.5 million British Columbia substation on Vancouver Island; in Australia, Thailand, Germany, and Norway, such individuals have used explosives and arson to destroy their targets.[30] Just how far the ecoterrorists wish to take their battle is unclear, yet their challenge to the status quo is real, sophisticated, and appealing to many.

Manes ends his book on ecoterrorism with an appeal:

> Dave Foreman (Earth First! founder) has called for a new warrior society to defend what remains of the Earth's beauty. For all its controversies and shortcomings, perhaps radical environmentalism is the spearhead of that society, and perhaps it will be able to put all of the rage of the times, that warrior spirit, to use in the best context—the defense of the integrity of life on this planet.[31]

Both extremes—ecoterrorism and environmental neglect by management—may miss the mark. However, the environmental movement has successfully raised our collective conscience that steps should be taken to protect the earth and its residents, both human and otherwise, from injury. Thus, to avoid a crisis that further damages the ecosystem, managers should consider taking the following steps:

1. Evaluate the chemicals or toxins that exist on site. This evaluation should detail where and how they are stored and what managers are responsible for their proper disposal. How can such toxins be reduced in number? What plan for their replacement can be instituted?

2. Ensure that the responsible managers receive frequent training from certified instructors in waste management and that the company maintains complete records on material storage.

3. Develop an evacuation plan for employees and customers in the event of an environmental disaster. Most buildings are governed by local zoning laws that dictate the number of fire exits, but organizations also need to create

Protests regarding the logging of old-growth redwood forests are often organized by peaceful, law-abiding activists such as those shown here. Ecoterrorists, on the other hand, have occasionally taken a more violent approach and destroyed corporate facilities or property.

traffic egress plans so that employees in one section of an office park exit through one driveway while others exit out an alternative driveway. In the event of a chemical spill, employees need to know such procedures.

4. At least annually, managers of plants where hazardous materials are stored or tested should meet with local fire, police, and evacuation authorities to review and update plans as appropriate.

5. Because local, state, and federal environmental laws are changing so rapidly and so dramatically, with fines and penalties being continually increased, managers should subscribe to trade publications in their field. They may also want to consider engaging an environmental consultant on retainer. The responsibilities of this consultant should be to ensure that the organization is kept adequately informed of all pertinent changes to environmental regulations. The consultant could also recommend new cost-saving devices or techniques that should be integrated into plant operations to reduce the risk of a chemical accident or spill.

The following interview explores the role of corporate responsibility with one of the nation's leading experts on environmental law, Zygmunt Plater. His insight is based on teaching law as well as on his involvement as consultant in scores of major suits brought against corporations.

INTERVIEW

Zygmunt J. B. Plater
Legal Landscape: The Environment
and the Law

In 1990, attorney and Boston College law professor Zygmunt J. B. Plater headed a team of legal consultants who visited the state of Alaska to recommend legislation aimed at preventing another environmental crisis such as the *Exxon Valdez* spill. He represented environmental activists in the now famous Tennessee Valley Authority Tellico Dam suit, in which citizens opposed construction of a major dam in order to protect a small fish called a snail darter from extinction. Plater believes that with forethought and careful planning, environmental crises can be averted.

Q *What is the ethic behind environmental law?*

A It's a recognition that ecological balances developed over several billion years have some moral claim on humankind. It's the world's accounting system. It says to the power elite of the corporate and governmental worlds, "You have been systematically ignoring things we can no longer afford to ignore."

Q *What are the main areas of concern?*

A There are three major global categories: population, destructive consumption of resources, and pollution. Population is the most threatening problem. We're around 6 billion now, and it's estimated that within the next generation there will be 10 billion peo-

ple on earth. That's frightening. We already have impossible constraints on the quality of human life in much of the world. How will we handle nearly twice as many people? Next is our pattern of essentially suicidal malconsumption. We destroy, burn, and waste resources at an unbelievable rate. We don't replenish them, we're incredibly wasteful, and our national energy policies have changed little since the 1950s. Then there's pollution. Our life-sustaining resources are finite. They cannot be treated as the ultimate dump sites for human waste. By ignoring their destruction and derogation, we are killing the systems of life support for ourselves and every other creature on earth.

Q *How effective is the law in dealing with these problems?*

A It's effective in inverse order. The law deals best with pollution because the sources of pollution can be identified and brought to justice. With consumption, the law can impose preservationist and management protocols, and force marketing constraints, if there's the political will to do so, which there isn't. Population is where the law has the least effect because the issue is physically, morally, and spiritually sensitive, incredibly so. But we're ostriches if we don't come to grips with the problem.

Q *What makes American environmental legislation special?*

A It exists, for one thing, which is rare. And virtually every federal environmental statute has a citizens' suit provision. There's a wonderfully pluralistic democracy in the American legal system. Environmental statutes specifically invite citizen enforcement. It's as if Congress was prompted to say, "We *know* the Department of Agriculture is often not going to enforce the pesticide regulations, so here's a provision in the law by which citizens can make the Secretary of Agriculture come into court and explain why nothing's being done." Such explicit provisions were unthinkable twenty-five years ago.

In this country, the gains for environmental law can usually be traced to efforts by non-governmental organizations—spontaneous neighborhood organizations like the Love Canal action group, or people like Ralph Nader—not bureaucracies. In fact, it's essentially an anti-bureaucratic movement, as were the civil rights and consumer protection movements.

Q *How has progress been made in the United States?*

A By fits and starts. By guerrilla action on the part of individual citizens. By occasional lurches in the right direction, sometimes by mistake. The National Environmental Policy Act of 1969, for example—a milestone piece of legislation imitated all over the world—was passed by mistake. It was supposed to be a nice, weightless collection of hortatory platitudes. But environmentalists slipped in a little passage requiring adequate environmental impact statements on any large project. That sentence was a snake in the grass, because impact statements have become the Achilles heel by which huge development projects are defeated.

Q *Where is the environmental movement going?*

A First of all, it is becoming increasingly sophisticated about publicity. You can make all the sensible arguments in the world, but unless you get on the evening news, and into the public consciousness, you don't exist.

The environmental movement also is constantly improving its ability to make the economic argument—"good ecology is good economics." Environmentalists can talk until they're blue in the face about the sacredness of the land, the wonder of life, the rights of all creatures, but to a congressional committee it's the bottom line that counts. The marketplace has no way of capturing invisible, intangible, or diffuse values. It's into short-term profits. Note that recycling did not become popular, if it can be called popular even now, until companies realized there was a market for those products. The clinching argument of the environmental movement will be an economic one showing corporate and political America that

there's money in being environmentally conscious. There's profit in it. There are healthy markets out there. It makes *business* sense.

Q *What do you think of radical environmental groups like Earth First?*

A I understand their frustration. I wish there were no need for groups like Earth First, but typically it takes something dramatic, riveting, disastrous, to make an institution notice. There's such a mismatch between insiders and outsiders, between those looking after long-term environmental values and those interested in short-term profit. Too many times environmentalists have gone to court, won an injunction against something, and watched as some senator with pork barrel on his mind attached a rider to an appropriations bill, overriding a court decision. That's when the radical groups put a spike in a tree, or blow up a bulldozer, or put sugar in gas tanks, or blow up dams. As a lawyer I find myself terribly dismayed by such activity. I've got to believe that human beings can take the long view. But I understand, all too well, how they feel. I can't be disgusted by someone trying to block a bulldozer that's illegally stripping a forest.

Q *What problems does the movement face in the future?*

A There are so many problems that need correcting. The easiest thing to do is shrug your shoulders and lament what will never return. But I'm optimistic. I see an immense increase in scientific information and technological response on environmental issues. I see many young people going into environmental law. I see the law getting more sophisticated, more imaginative, more comprehensive. I see intangible long-term values coming into legal debates. I see environmental consciousness slowly becoming conventional wisdom. We're so far ahead of where we were twenty years ago that it astonishes me. It amazes me. And the potential is endless. That's good. That's very good. ❏

Source: Reprinted with permission of *Boston College Magazine*.

CASE STUDY: WHEN AN EARTHQUAKE STRIKES

Safeway Stores is one of America's leading supermarket chains—the $13.6 billion-a-year firm boasts over 900 stores, most of them located in Western states. In 1989, the company did not have a crisis management plan. Its message to managers was a simple one: in the event of an emergency, work diligently to restore operations as rapidly as possible.

On October 17, that credo came in handy when many Safeway managers faced one of their most complex corporate crises. There were no terrorists, stock market crashes, or protestors causing the problem; rather, an earthquake centered in Santa Cruz County struck at 5:04 P.M. From that moment on, the lives of millions of Californians, and certainly the lives of many managers, would never be the same again.

The tremor lasted only 15 seconds, but the damage caused by the quake to homes, highways, and commercial interests was mammoth. About 140 of Safeway's 240 northern California stores suffered damage, some of it extensive structural damage. Moreover, after the earthquake, when many people had lost their food supply or could not return to their neighborhoods, customers needed quick access to a supermarket for essentials.

Frank Crivello serves as manager for one of Safeway's stores in Aptos, California. His store was an understandable mess after the quake: bottles of wine (some priced at more than $50) stained the floors, thousands of bottles of ketchup, peanut butter, and jelly were broken. Shelves were broken, refrigerator cases fell over, light fixtures had fallen to the ground. The local fire department ordered Crivello to keep customers out of the store.

Yet arriving at his store were scores of customers Crivello had known for years—many crying, others still in shock. They asked for water, milk, bread, batteries—whatever was available. Communicating with senior management was difficult because most phone lines were inoperative. When the quake struck, several key Safeway executives were at Candlestick Park, awaiting the start of the third game of the World Series. Within minutes, however, they were using their car phones, trying to call various stores to assess damage and coordinate matters of security and operations.

Crivello told *Fortune* magazine that his store was in ruins, and he could understand what his customers faced at home: "We think of ourselves as part of the community. It was an emergency. We couldn't sell anything, so we dug out batteries, bottled water, whatever we could find, and we stood there and gave the essentials away until they were all gone." Other Safeway managers faced the same challenges at their locations and tried to cope with multiple crises at once—injured employees, customers asking for essentials, senior management on the phone, and the potential of fires from broken gas pipes in and around store locations.

Let's assume that you are George Unti, an executive with the northern California division of Safeway. It is your responsibility to coordinate the multitude of details associated with this crisis. Safeway's CEO has called an emergency meeting of the executive team and asks you to lead that staff meeting. You will need to specifically identify what actions the company should take, what resources you will need to accomplish the job, and what timetables you feel are realistic to get your 140 damaged stores up and running once again. Although you may never have worked in a food store, let alone managed a chain of them, the principles of crisis management outlined thus far can be applied to this case. Begin with audience, goal, and message, and plan accordingly after that matrix is finished. Before you begin the staff meeting, consider these points:

1. Damage to many stores is severe, and product loss has been high. You need to find out from your warehouses how quickly essential products can be shipped and restocked. To do that, you need to identify which roads are open and when drivers can be contacted to begin shipment.

2. Which stores should you open first? Those in heavily populated areas will soon be visited by thousands of customers. Do you turn them away? Whom could you contact to coordinate emergency relief services? What plan of action would you recommend be implemented in cooperation with such agencies?

3. If you can retrieve some food items from store shelves, should they be sold at price, at discount, or given away? What is the impact of your decision, both pro and con?

4. How can you contact your clerks and delivery people who are off shift during this natural disaster, when most phone lines are not working? What contingency plan for staffing can you turn to?

5. How can you maintain contact with the managers of the 240 Safeway stores you oversee? What kind of communications center can you quickly establish? What resources will you need to keep the center operative for the next several days?

6. The news media have a justifiable interest in reporting how you are coping with crisis and how well you are responding to customer needs. Some are visiting local Safeways trying to interview managers and customers. In other locations, photographers are snapping pictures of Safeway aisles that are in disarray. Draft a press release that could be released to the electronic and print media about your response thus far and your expectations for the next few days.

7. In addition to your immediate concern over the safety of your employees and customers, you are concerned about other publics. Write letters that would be faxed or sent by Mail Gram to key stockholders of Safeway, insurance agents, and structural engineers and electrical crews who must be contracted with immediately. o

Source: This case is based on "How Safeway Coped with the Quake" by Gary Hector, *Fortune*, November 20, 1989, pp. 101–104. Used with permission.

ENDNOTES

1. M. Clark, M. Hager et al., "Fleeing the Love Canal," *Newsweek,* June 2, 1980, p. 56.
2. *Not in My Backyard,* film produced by Bullfrog Films, 1985.
3. Clark, Hager et al.
4. Denise K. Magner, "Huge Cost of Removing Asbestos Causing Concern on Campuses," *Chronicle of Higher Education*, December 7, 1988, p. A28.
5. Ibid.
6. David L. Schultz, "Toxic Chemical Disclosure," *Public Relations Journal,* January 1989, p. 16.
7. "Pollution: Trying To Put the Best Face on Bad News," *Business Week,* July 18, 1988, p. 75.
8. Schultz, p. 16.
9. Robert Tomsho, "Big Corporations Hit by Superfund Cases Find Way To Share Bill," *Wall Street Journal,* April 2, 1991, p. A10.
10. Ibid.
11. Ibid.
12. Ibid.
13. John Woestendiek, *Las Vegas Review-Journal,* November 7, 1991.
14. "What Chernobyl Did," *The Economist,* April 27, 1991, p. 19.
15. Ibid., p. 21.
16. G. Glynn Rountree, "The Current Legal Climate," *Aerospace Industries Association Newsletter* 3 (1990): 4.
17. Ibid.
18. Ibid.
19. Ibid., p. 5.
20. "IFF Puts a Lid on Odors To Aid Community Relations." *Chemical Week,* November 4, 1987, p. 51.
21. Ibid.
22. David Kirkpatrick, "Environmentalism: The New Crusade," *Fortune,* February 12, 1990, p. 47.
23. Ibid.
24. Law Column, *Wall Street Journal,* May 2, 1991, p. B6.
25. Michael Galen, "Turn Exxon into a Model Environmental Citizen," *Business Week,* May 20, 1991, p. 44.
26. Ibid.
27. Ibid.
28. Christopher Manes, *Green Rage: Radical Environmentalism and the Unmaking of Civilization* (Boston: Little, Brown, 1990), p. 9.
29. Ibid., p. 14.
30. Ibid., p. 17.
31. Ibid., p. 248.

7

How Organizations Cope: Training Managers for Worst-Case Scenarios

Control is the first goal of an industrial emergency. The crisis management team must identify what has to be done to contain the emergency, develop the plan, and then muster the resources to get the crisis under control. ❏

Geraldine V. Cox (Vice President, Chemical Manufacturers Association), *New Management*, Summer 1987

S|ometimes you just can't win. Consider first the case described in the *Wall Street Journal* on February 28, 1990. The article reported that General Electric's (GE) secret recipe for making synthetic diamonds had been stolen and allegedly sold to industrial spies in South Korean and Chinese firms. The documents that detailed how these high-quality industrial diamonds could be manufactured had been "zealously protected despite numerous offers from foreign countries," the Journal reported. Behind this case of espionage lay an intriguing plot.

Two men, who were part of an ongoing investigation, approached garbage collectors in an upscale neighborhood in Northboro, Massachusetts, where Chien-Min Sung, a leading research scientist, lived. After paying the workers $25, they searched through Sung's garbage and found the trade secrets, the loss of which could cost GE well over $5 million. Sung, a former GE employee, denied wrongdoing. Yet the paper quoted a source in the case as saying that Sung had removed the GE logo from GE's process instructions and pasted them under his own letterhead. "Before leaving GE," the *Wall Street Journal* reported, "Mr. Sung made off with a virtual library of GE documents, the suit alleges."

This loss occurred despite advanced security at GE and despite background searches on workers who come in contact with trade secrets. How could the company have allowed such a significant breach of security to take place? Could company managers have taken additional management precautions such as role playing or simulation exercises to find gaps in existing security measures?

A different situation engulfed executives at the Clorox Company in spring 1991, when they engaged Ketchum Public Relations to draft a crisis management plan that envisioned a number of hypothetical disasters that could strike the large bleach and chemical manufacturer. Ketchum managers never thought that the document they were preparing was about to become a national embarrassment for its client, Clorox. But that's just what happened.

In developing the draft CMP for Clorox, which the client had never seen, crisis experts at Ketchum did a thorough job. They considered several worst-case scenarios, including a potential boycott of Clorox products by some unspecified group, a scientific report that would link chlorine (an ingredient in Clorox bleach) to cancer in humans, and other possible crises.

One such crisis that Ketchum pondered was the potential response by Clorox if a major environmental group and "unalterably green" journalists attacked the company. If that happened, Ketchum reportedly felt Clorox should accuse them of "environmental terrorism." Although the crisis plan was still in its draft stage, an unknown party leaked the CMP to the leading environmental activist organization, Greenpeace. Within days, the national press had picked up the story.

Now, in newspapers and on television nationwide, Clorox was unwittingly being pitted against an activist group that had never had any intention of boycotting Clorox Bleach, a household product. From its Oakland, California, offices,

Material in this chapter is adapted from Laurence Barton's article in *Industrial Management*, November–December 1991. Copyright 1991, Institute of Industrial Engineers, 25 Technology Park, Atlanta, Georgia 30092.

Clorox issued a statement regarding the Ketchum plan, stating that "Clorox management was not involved in its preparation and is not acting on its recommendations."[1] The best statement in the entire incident was reported by a newsletter, *The Progressive*. Greenpeace's campaigner on toxic threats to the environment, Shelley Steward, was quoted as saying, "They [Clorox] failed to anticipate the worst of worse-case scenarios. That some conscientious person would obtain the plan, and leak it to us."

Several observations can be made about these incidents. First, it is important and encouraging that major corporations such as Clorox are actively planning for crises; the use of crisis experts was virtually unheard of a decade ago. Second, in a very real way the cases provide a lesson to every manager who cares about preserving his or her own reputation: no document is ever private. Assume that anything you write can and will be widely distributed. Third, the Clorox and GE cases illustrate that Murphy's law ("anything that can go wrong, will") is inexorably tied to crisis management.

Whether you work for Clorox, GE, or any other organization, you will find that effective crisis management generally requires that managers consider three important resources:

> Internal and External Resources
> Access to Knowledge
> Planning and Worst-Case Scenarios

These are discussed in the following sections.

THE CRISIS MANAGEMENT TEAM

Every organization should create a crisis management team before the need for such a group becomes obvious. What should such a team look like? Most crisis management experts and practitioners suggest that a small, dynamic team is ideal. With a small group, generally consisting of fewer than ten people, management can generate exciting discussions, learn the frustrations and concerns raised by key executives, and still focus on a workable agenda. Previous chapters have reviewed the role that key executives play in crisis discussions. As an organization moves closer to developing a CMP, executives will want to select a smaller group to help prepare for crisis by staging a series of scenarios.

Chapter 2 discussed the various officers of a company who are typically involved in crisis management planning. Naturally, that group will vary in composition. Factors that could influence its composition are company size, whether the company operates only domestically or in the international environment, whether it is heavily regulated or only moderately so, and whether the organization relies on a large group of consumers or on distributors for most of its business. One multinational corporation with an active sales presence in over fifty countries provided some insight into how it assembled its crisis management team. The team includes an attorney, a media relations manager, several technical experts from various departments of the company, a vice president for finance, the telecommunications manager, and an expert on applicable regulations. The company's CEO chairs the group. Why would a corporation choose these specific managers as the nucleus of its crisis response team? Let's take a brief look at the roles played by each individual.

Attorney

In the event of a crisis, someone who has a background in law is essential. Whether this individual is in-house corporate counsel or serves as an hourly consultant, he or she should help review any crisis plan that is drafted. An attorney can help management consider what statements should or should not be made, whether a statement of apology would be perceived as an admission of guilt or a sincere gesture of goodwill, and whether details of, for example, the nature and severity of a chemical spill or industrial accident may help investigators or complicate matters in the future.

Public Relations Coordinator

As noted in Chapter 2, a communications expert should be an active member of the crisis management team. This individual has ideally worked in media relations and thus understands the needs of reporters in covering a crisis or disaster. In preparing a CMP, the public relations expert will review the many issues discussed in this book regarding news releases and press conference details. She or he may eventually be asked to coordinate rehearsals for managers who speak to the public, regulators, and the press.

Technical Experts

Each organization should designate specific unit managers whose technical preparation and knowledge are superlative and whose personality and experience will enhance overall corporate performance during a crisis. For example, a major electrical utility company may wish to designate as many as five managers to be "on call" and to receive crisis management training in advance. Each of these individuals should have specific, in-depth engineering knowledge not found elsewhere in the company. In an emergency, it would be extremely embarrassing for a company to have to engage an outside consultant to discuss a matter that it should have been able to address with in-house resources. For this reason alone, management needs to study the depth of available expertise far in advance of crisis.

Financial Officer

Although the human aspect of a crisis is always the most important, there is no doubt that a severe crisis can and often does cause fiscal havoc for a company. For this reason, the company treasurer, controller, or financier should be on call in the event of a crisis.

This person should have extensive knowledge of company assets and liabilities, outstanding notes and other debts, how securities and other holdings are held, and the nature of various insurance and contingency policies. The company should ask this person in the drafting stages of a CMP to develop a list of potential credit sources that the company may need to access quickly if extra capital is needed.

Telecommunications Manager

Almost every large company that has experienced a major crisis—and many smaller ones as well—will attest to the fact that telecommunications was the one area they were largely unprepared to handle. When Johnson & Johnson recalled 22 million bottles of Tylenol in 1982, for example, it received hundreds of thousands of phone calls from concerned consumers.

Extra phone lines, multiple fax machines, electronic mail systems, and other facets of modern technology are essential for surviving a major corporate catastrophe. A telecommunications expert can help an organization decide on the layout of a crisis center, and what communications technology—including word processors and copy machines—should be available in that room. Working with a security consultant, a telecommunications manager can also help a company prevent unauthorized access to sensitive information. Long distance carrier MCI offers a crisis center for companies needing immediate 800 numbers.

Regulatory or Public Affairs Expert

Because almost every company or organization is governed by one or more agencies at the local, state, or federal levels, a regulatory expert should be a key member of any crisis team. This person should be fully familiar with all governmental requirements regarding notification of any disaster, accident, or spill. This manager should review the CMP to ensure that protocol is established in terms of who should make phone calls and file various reports and statements. He or she will also want to coordinate follow-up communication with regulators.

CEO or Representative

The CEO of the company should be actively involved in developing a crisis management plan. Because a CEO understands the different roles of employees, stockholders, customers, vendors, and many other publics, this person has an in-depth understanding of what realistically can and cannot be done in a disaster. In addition, this executive should directly address location and geography: in a natural disaster such as an earthquake or flood, where could operations relocate so that basic functions such as payroll and inventory can continue uninterrupted?

For example, ARCO Oil and Gas Company has a long-standing agreement to allow the Employee Information Service (EIS) of Pasadena, California, to relocate its operations to Plano, Texas, in the event of a disaster. A "swat team" of key employees has been designated who would leave California as soon as possible so that operations could resume in Texas within twelve hours. EIS data files are copied each evening in Pasadena and sent by courier to Dallas for storage. Dual computer software and compatible telecommunications equipment is in place in Texas.[2]

PHASE ONE: FACT FINDING

In the fact-finding phase, the CMP managers need to have accurate, relevant information. They will ideally schedule several planning sessions before a single word of a CMP is even drafted. Managers will want to identify what written data they need to prepare for a press conference. These data would typically include

1. How many individuals the company employs, the dollar value of salaries and benefits, and the amount it spends locally or within the region.

2. What multiplier effect the purchasing power of the company has on the economy of the area.

3. Summaries of the company's philanthropy in the past three years, including both cash and in-kind contributions to area charities; also, the extent to which employees volunteer their time to local groups.

4. A master list of all locations where the company does business, the names of plant managers, number of employees who work there, value of the facility for insurance purposes, and whether or not the plant is owned by a subsidiary or in a joint venture with some foreign entity.

5. Tax payments and special assessments the company pays to the local municipality; if a nonprofit organization, what voluntary payments in lieu of tax (PILOTs) are paid annually.

6. A list of awards and citations the company has received in recent years from trade associations, chambers of commerce, state offices of economic development, community and civic organizations, and other such groups.

7. A list of all relevant local, state, and federal laws with which the company must comply on a regular schedule. This would include any inspections required by the U.S. Food and Drug Administration, the Department of Commerce, Occupational Safety and Health Administration, Department of Agriculture, and many others.

8. Profiles of products made or distributed by the company, the type of machinery or equipment used, and the dates of most recent inspections by various state and federal agencies.

9. A written historical overview of the company, including when founded, how the company fared through acquisitions or new ventures launched, and a brief summary of its future plans.

After the crisis management team has requested and received these data from various officers of the company, it should proceed to Phase Two.

PHASE TWO: SCENARIO DEVELOPMENT

With the written data in hand, the team now needs to engage in a robust discussion as to what possible crises could occur in the coming years. As noted in Chapter 1, many types of catastrophes and disasters can strike any organization, and this list should be reviewed to help frame such a discussion. For example, the managers at Arlington Plastics (AP) narrowed their list of crises down to three serious, potential problems; this is a good procedure for all management teams.

Scenario development is not a hit-and-run experiment. Organized properly, scenario development can be a dynamic and extraordinary learning experience for participants. Ideally, the company asks one member of the team to serve as its permanent chairperson. This person first leads the group in a series of provocative discussions that revolve around questions asking "What if . . . ?"

The first scenario meeting might find the chairperson serving as a rotating "judge and jury," prodding managers to react to a series of questions that may get them agitated, defensive, or at least concerned. The entire purpose of a scenario session is to remove managers from the even tempo of traditional staff meetings and to increase their awareness that one significant crisis could cause them the single worst nightmare of their professional career. The chairperson may want to review the list of corporate crises in Chapter 1 to raise awareness of different types of potential crises. To generate discussion, he or she might ask,

1. What if we were sued tomorrow by the National Wildlife Federation because we had just leveled 18 acres of forest in Oregon for our new facility?

2. What if a producer from "60 Minutes" called late today, indicating that the network's team is investigating our company on charges of consumer fraud and that their crew wishes to meet with our CEO tomorrow morning? What should we do?

3. What if an employee leaked our design plans to a foreign competitor?

4. What if our operations were severely disrupted by a natural disaster such as a tornado or earthquake—where could we relocate within a matter or hours or days to maintain some continuity of operations? What cooperative agreements could be made in advance with other companies or facilities so that this transition could be accomplished efficiently?

5. What if a federal agency determined that our product was potentially harmful and the government demanded a recall? Would we seek an injunction order and refuse compliance, or would we comply, possibly laying off workers?

6. What if a plant explosion or chemical leak occurred at our plant? Who would take charge? Who would call local authorities and state agencies? If neighboring homes and businesses suffered losses from our accident, should those parties contact our insurance agent directly without our knowledge? Are we covered in the event of such a calamity?

Each of these cases, and many more that the chairperson might develop in advance, can be explored through role-playing.

The Role-Play in Action

In most mid- to large-sized corporations, several scenario sessions would be scheduled focusing on those crises that the team members agree are most potentially devastating to the organization. The number obviously varies from organization to organization.

In role-playing a scenario, each member of the crisis team should assume a position within the company that is *not* the one he or she traditionally holds. This switch exposes that individual to new thoughts and managerial challenges that he or she otherwise might never be asked to consider.

Let's say that the first scenario session focuses on a major boycott of company products that has just been announced by a leading environmental activist group. The chairperson will want to ask each manager present to assume a different company post for the next two hours, and to respond as if he or she were the designated company officer. The role-players must try to understand the motivations and needs of each character in the scenario.

A realistic list of characters for the group to portray would include

- CEO of the company.
- President of the environmental group.
- A news reporter from Cable News Network (CNN).
- Representative of the company's labor union.
- Press spokesperson for the company.
- Chairperson of the company's board (major stockholder).
- A protester who is carrying a sign outside your headquarters.

For this scenario to generate concrete benefits for all involved, the chairperson needs to *actively* encourage and maintain participation. For example, he or she may first ask the CNN reporter to ask the company CEO a variety of rapid-fire questions about the company, why it has been targeted for a boycott, and so on. The designated CEO should answer as many questions as he or she can, even to the point of making up statistics and situations to keep the conversation flowing. (However, both CEO and reporter should present ideas realistically.) The group should pay close attention to how the CEO's statements and actions reflect the corporate culture of the organization, and note where he or she tends to overstate, overpromise, or oversimplify.

After fifteen to twenty minutes, the CEO is told that a telephone call has come in from the company's largest stockholder, who is deeply concerned about news of a boycott. The stockholder asks a series of questions about what steps the CEO plans to take, how the executive team intends to maintain the value of the company, how major finance houses will be told about developments, and what regu-

CHALLENGE

Schiavone Construction, a firm based in Secaucus, New Jersey, faced one of the more prominent industrial crises of the 1980s. Beginning in 1984, the company endured widespread negative publicity after its managers were indicted for allegedly defrauding the New York City Transit Authority of $7.4 million in a minority business enterprise scandal.

In June 1987, a jury acquitted all the accused company managers, but the company's former executive vice president, Raymond J. Donovan, was not so fortunate. Donovan was then serving as Secretary of Labor under President Reagan, and in the midst of the controversy he was forced to resign his cabinet post. And the lingering doubts about Schiavone, despite the acquittal, were immense. The company's embarrassment not only reached the White House, but triggered other ramifications as well: at least twenty key managers left the company, $500,000 had to be spent on public relations consultants, and more than $100 million was reportedly lost in contracts.[3] It is clear that maintaining the trust of clients is absolutely essential during and after a crisis.

Let's back up to the early period in the Schiavone case. Assume that you are the president of the construction firm, and it is clear that in a matter of days indictments against your executive team will be announced. You believe you are innocent of all charges that will be brought.

Each person in the group should represent a manager at the firm (director of public relations, financial vice president, chief accountant, and so on). Simulate the discussion that you have as you brace Schiavone for the massive national publicity that will result in a few days. Work through the audience, goal, message, and approach, and then ask each manager at the table to reflect on how he or she believes the company can cope—and still function, let alone solicit new clients—in a brewing scandal that could reach all the way to the White House. ✳

latory issues (such as notifying the Securities and Exchange Commission) may be involved.

With that conversation concluded, the group then asks the union officer to meet the company's press spokesperson in the hallway. Naturally, union members are concerned about the impact of a boycott on cutbacks in hours or layoffs of workers. Union members may not want to cross picket lines set up by environmental groups. These and a variety of other union-related issues should be raised in detail.

While the scenario exercise is underway, an administrative assistant should be taking detailed notes so that the reactions, statements, and suggestions of the various group members can be recorded and later evaluated for inclusion in a draft of the crisis management plan. This person will also later be a wonderful resource to the team. Because this individual does not formally participate in the scenarios, he or she can later give the team a clear perspective on the group's process.

Timing and Location

Two-hour scenario sessions are ideal, so that participants remain alert. Several suggestions help the process operate smoothly:

1. The chairperson should never inform the team members in advance about the nature of the crisis they will be facing that day.

2. The chairperson should behave seriously; the purpose of the exercise is not to amuse or entertain the group, it is to challenge them into responding to a threat the company may one day face.

3. As much as possible, the chairperson should seek to create chaos so that team members will have a sense of the urgency and reality of crisis management. This includes phone calls, memos, frantic messages, visits from local officials or regulators, protestors outside the windows—whatever works to realistically dramatize.possible crisis. The chairperson may also want to arrange to have a secretary interrupt the meeting with additional urgent messages and phone calls.

   Technical resources needed to enhance the exercise should be made available in the scenario room before the team gathers. Thus, if the chairperson wishes to have a fax arrive during the session, a fax line should be hooked up and someone elsewhere in the facility should send a printed message at a predesignated time. Similarly, the chairperson may wish to arrange to have a colleague posing as a newspaper reporter call at a particular point during the meeting on a speaker telephone.

4. Team members should agree as a unit in advance that their statements, reactions, and suggestions throughout the scenario sessions are to be kept confidential and are for discussion purposes only.

Ideally, scenarios should be conducted in a crisis control room if one is already established at the company's facility. This lends a degree of seriousness and reality to these sessions. Corporate managers from several industries have mentioned that senior management should anticipate several situations that may develop during scenario sessions. These situations are important because they reflect human nature, ego, and questions of turf; they also reflect the biases that each manager brings to his or her daily duties. These concerns prompt the following suggestions:

1. No one manager or department should be allowed to dominate the planning or scenario sessions. People interested in rapidly climbing the corporate ladder may see these sessions as a unique opportunity to showcase their talents via elaborate or expansive grandstanding that has no intrinsic value for CMP development. There is nothing wrong with politely reminding such people that "We are going astray. Let's get back on track."

2. No one manager or department should be allowed to not participate in discussions; session leaders should work vigorously to encourage participation. Although it is human nature that some people are quieter than others and may feel intimidated by the presence of senior executives, they are being paid to provide insight and guidance into one of the most strategically important series of decisions in the company's history. This is no time for managers to be timid.

3. An anonymous evaluation of the session leader's skills should be held after each session so that she or he can review and improve performance.

4. Questions of budget should be directly addressed. In some cases, managers will not make recommendations to a group because their previous requests for equipment or services have been repeatedly denied. Yet the crisis scenario may provide a unique forum for such managers to convince senior executives that previous requests were in fact reasonable.

Business and industry are using role-playing scenarios more often as planning for crisis assumes greater organizational importance. In Appendix A, you will be asked to role-play in a scenario that involves an ethical dilemma at Johnson & Johnson. Exhibit 7-1 explains how Shell Oil used a variation of role playing to help reduce the potential negative impact that escalating tensions in the Middle East could have on production and distribution. The timing of this exercise, just weeks before the Iraqi invasion of Kuwait in August, 1990, was superb.

EXHIBIT 7-1   Shell Oil Company Scenario Planning

Shell Pioneers Use of Scenarios to Enhance Its Long-Range Planning

Following the onset of the Persian Gulf crisis, several press reports suggested that while other companies were thrown into varying degrees of disarray, Shell International Petroleum Co. was able to pull out a scenario covering such an eventuality.

"Oh, would that we could!" was the response of Tony Wildig, senior researcher in Shell's Group Planning Division, when asked to comment on the truth of this rumor.

The rumor probably arose from the company's reputation as a pioneer in the use of scenarios as long-range planning tools to supplement a regular cycle of strategic and business planning. At Shell, global scenarios are treated as an integral part of the strategic planning process. They represent the fundamental building block of the scenario approach to planning.

In fact, Shell's planning division did not specifically foresee the Iraqi invasion of Kuwait. "It was just one of many potential events that could be considered," says Wildig. "Many others could have the same or similar effect on oil prices, for instance." He says, however, that the global scenario approach did envision several of the important consequences of changes in the Middle East without pointing to their specific cause. "The Middle East is a boiling pot and has been for all of history," says Wildig. "One doesn't need to predict which particular incident may cause the disruption."

Global Scenarios

Shell's global scenarios generally use a 20-year time frame, though in considering certain issues, scenario planners tend to look much further ahead: They review environmental issues, for example, as far as 60 years in the future. The 20-year time horizon is based on the long-term nature of most energy projects. Development of an oil field may

continued

EXHIBIT   7-1

extend 20 years or longer.

Shell compiles global scenarios every two years and supplements them periodically with regional scenarios that look in more detail at the underlying forces at play in particular regions. Recently completed regional scenarios include Europe and the Far East.

The company considers it essential for scenarios to encompass the major issues in the minds of the ultimate users, generally the senior management of Shell. The list of issues will be developed by consultation with outside experts. "The aim is to identify the major shaping forces over the time frame of the scenarios," says Wildig.

Brainstorming and Workshops

As scenarios are being developed, the research team will hold brainstorming sessions and workshops, often with world experts in relevant fields present. The purpose of these sessions is to identify future "branching points" at which there might be significant changes of direction in the unfolding of events.

"We then try to distill two or more different paths along which the world might evolve," says Wildig. "Our aim is to define the challenges underlying each of these paths, with the idea that if your businesses are robust in these worlds, they'll be robust in any of the others, too."

The choice of two possible outcomes out of a range of thousands is of course difficult. "I wouldn't say that we aim to cover 100% or even 80% of possible outcomes," says Wildig. "Rather, we aim for at least 80% of the key issues that have to be addressed in understanding the scenarios." Wildig adds that the selection of more than two scenarios tends to be dangerous: "There's a natural tendency to pick the middle one, as though they were all in a range on the same scale."

The global scenarios most recently selected were "sustainable growth," in which environmental concerns and global coopera-

tion featured prominently; and "mercantilism," in which aggressive trade between the major economies predominates, accompanied by economic collapse in some parts of the world.

Analyzing the Scenarios

"We build right from the bottom up," says Wildig. "We look at the economic and energy situations in each country, and we analyze which way these will develop consistent with the basic assumptions of the scenarios." In the process, the scenario team has deployed econometric models for regional development and energy trends, using systems dynamics techniques to encompass a wide range of variables. "I think the models can get too complex," says Wildig. "But they do help us understand cause and effect."

The scenarios are reviewed by their end users, who provide reactions so that "after a number of iterations we are able to arrive at scenarios that people consider to be appropriate." The aim, says Wildig, is to "ask the operating companies to look at the scenarios and respond with what their strategies should be in relation to them. In the process of looking at the issues, we believe they get a better understanding of their business. The scenarios are really an interpretation of the present."

Final Outlook

The ultimate product of the scenario planning process is a glossy book that runs about 100 pages long. It summarizes the main assumptions of each scenario, their statistical underpinnings and their strategic implications. However, Wildig emphasizes that the book is preceded by as many as 40 background papers, so that users can explore issues in depth. The book is presented to senior managers throughout the group. The planning team has also prepared a video presentation, which is widely circulated.

—Simon Partner

Source: *Business International,* copyright 1990. Reprinted with permission.

Synergy: A Meeting of Minds

A week after the first session, the group gathers again. This time the members come prepared, having reviewed transcripts or summary notes of the sessions. Led by the chairperson, they vigorously debate the ramifications of the "crisis." In particular, the chairperson helps the team conduct a serious postcrisis evaluation focusing in particular on these points:

1. Did we effectively respond to the immediate crisis we faced, or did we react to irrelevant problems and questions?

2. What resources within the company did we use effectively, and which departments or managers did we not adequately utilize? If we were to grade, from "A" through "F" the responsiveness of those we asked for assistance during our mock crisis, what grades would we give, and why?

3. Who was the most effective overall manager on our team during each of the three scenarios, and why? Would this person be an appropriate individual to head a crisis management team in a real disaster? If that person agrees, what tools and resources would she or he need to do this job in the future?

4. Where did we succeed? Where did we fail? What situations did we fail to anticipate?

Postcrisis evaluation is crucial for learning the lessons taught by scenarios.

PHASE THREE: COMMUNICATING OUR MESSAGE

After fact finding and staging and evaluating scenarios, the public relations and public affairs department managers of an organization should address the crisis management team. They should present in detail a plan of action that addresses each major crisis the company has considered. Specifically, the communication specialists need to address the following issues:

1. Given the team experience during the scenario sessions, who is(are) the most appropriate person(s) to speak for the company in a crisis? Should this person be sent to a professional media consultant for training on answering press questions? Would courses in public speaking or managerial communication at an area college or university enhance this individual's presentation style?

2. Where should the central crisis room be located? Should a permanent area be designated and so equipped, or is space so limited that a makeshift situation will need to be considered? If equipment cannot be permanently dedicated for this purpose, what can be borrowed from what departments? What kinds of software and other items will be needed? A series of phone jacks should be installed in this room in advance so that the local phone company can quickly install multiple lines to handle public inquiries.

3. In presenting draft news releases, press kits, and historical data to the crisis team, the communication specialists should inform the team what new communication materials should be developed and held aside to use in the event of a crisis. This might include economic impact information, detailed chemical analysis of materials stored on the property, or other sensitive but not secret data.

4. The communication specialist should tell the team members what media are likely to cover any or all of the three principal scenarios the group has already considered. He or she should also explain how his or her department will monitor the press, and what clipping or video services will provide clips and copies of newscasts for later evaluation by the group and its attorneys.

5. After discussing and evaluating the scenario sessions, the communication team should present a chart that clearly shows the chain of command in a crisis, so there will be no question as to who has what responsibilities. Copies of that chart should be made widely available to all departments so that a lower-level manager who has received no training and little exposure to the entire process will not embarrass the organization, albeit unknowingly.

6. A communication plan to inform employees of the events surrounding a disaster is essential. If employees first learn the details of a company's disaster from the news media before hearing about it from management, the credibility of the senior team will certainly have been impaired. Further, even after the company has spent energy and money for years on programs that build teams and trust in the workplace, a few ill-timed announcements to the press could lead employees to question the sincerity of those in control.

7. The role of clients should not be ignored, even before the crisis management plan has been drafted. The communication specialist should work with the team to determine how the company will keep clients aware of developments as they unfold.

Finally, modern technology must be integrated into both teaching about crisis management and into crisis management itself. Professor Jerry Melching of the John F. Kennedy School of Government has been developing a prototype crisis simulation system using Macintosh computers. Taking the Three Mile Island nuclear accident as his case, Melching asks students to role-play different actors in that crisis. As they sit at their computers, a series of questions, phone messages, and scenarios are presented to them. Each response they provide (for example, "Yes, I'll take the governor's call" or "No, that news release cannot be released at this time") prompts the computer to generate another question or series of problems.

And at the University of Nevada, Las Vegas, the Center on Crisis Management has developed an advanced simulation package, using Hypercard software, that tests participant responses to a series of managerial dilemmas. The first package that has been used by managers in industry and government challenges students to respond to a bomb threat at a hypothetical manufacturing plant in Chicago, Illinois. Two other scenarios, one involving a nuclear facility, and another that traces a surprise scandal that causes trauma for employees at a leading securities firm, are now under development. In the future, additional technological innovations are likely to expand our understanding of managing and communicating during a crisis. (See Appendix D.)

The scenario guidelines offered in this chapter, taken individually and in concert, help the team better understand what motivates various parties in a crisis. By seeking to understand the legitimate needs of reporters, union organizers, employees, stockholders, public interest groups, and regulators, managers become better equipped to face the inevitable crisis.

THE CRISIS MANAGEMENT CONTROL CENTER

A number of major corporations have established crisis communications centers to be used in a major calamity. For major utilities such as Illinois Power Company, a primary focus of management is on providing an auditorium setting so that a large number of newspaper, radio, and television reporters can easily hear crucial information about a loss of electricity. The designers of Johnson & Johnson's crisis center emphasize telephone capacity, so that multiple calls from consumers and other publics can be easily accommodated.

There is no one ideal model, but Exhibits 7-2 and 7-3 offer insight into those issues that management must consider in designing rooms dedicated to crisis coordination. The model shown in Exhibit 7-3 takes into account both the needs of

EXHIBIT   7-2   A Guide to Crisis Center Operations

In operating a crisis center, keep the following points in mind:

- Management must clearly instruct crisis staffers whether they can speak only to consumers, or only to the press, or to anyone who calls in. Giving people at the command center a script is important: as specific questions are posed, the crisis staff can use the script to provide a consistent message. Staff members must be instructed to be candid with callers. If contradictory information is released, or if the news media determines that management has lied about what it knows (for example, about the severity of a spill or accident), the credibility of the entire company could be damaged for years to come.

- All managers who can lend a degree of expertise should be seated near the podium. Particularly if a crisis is complicated by heavily technical questions about chemicals, engineering, or medicine, the media will not expect one person to field all questions. Similarly, the company may wish to invite a state or federal official or regulator who has an obvious interest in the crisis to add further depth to comments made.

- Security needs should be addressed before the press conference. A private security consultant or an internal officer should settle questions of access in advance. Many corporations locate their crisis center toward the rear of factories so that reporters

continued

EXHIBIT   7-2

or curiosity seekers cannot gain undesired entry into other areas of the facility. Other corporations have access cards or badges printed in advance, so that once inside a building, media guests are clearly identified. These badges are then returned when they leave the facility.

- Company logos and signs, as well as any other reminders of the name or identity of the company, should not be readily seen in or near the crisis room. Because photographs will be taken, and because lingering images of this crisis could haunt the company for years to come, it is best to reduce any immediate association people make between the crisis and your company. Although you may be interested and willing to talk on the record about the crisis, there is no need to reinforce public awareness of the fact that the company is in the midst of chaos.

- Don't ignore issues as basic as adequate power supply. During a crisis situation, media crews will be arriving with major equipment; word processors, tape recorders, satellite dishes, and other equipment will all be working simultaneously. If a particular wing in a facility is dedicated to this purpose, the crisis will only become more complicated (and embarrassing) if the power fails. An electrical specialist should evaluate all of these issues in advance.

- Multiple outlets should be installed for telephones and fax machines. Many large companies install at least six telephone lines in the crisis center. Managers should know in advance how to link into a major 800 telephone system with AT&T, Sprint or MCI. Large companies should have at least several, and possibly several dozen, telephone sets in storage for ready use.

- There should be at least three fax machines on site (which can be transferred from other offices) for ready use by reporters and regulators who may be working out of the crisis center. Fill a storage cabinet with reams of 8½ x 11-inch paper. Also that cabinet should contain copies of the company's press kit that gives the history and operations of the company and the names and numbers of press officers, including home numbers. Reporters often request stock photographs of the company CEO and other senior officers, and the public relations department should make a supply available for distribution. Provide at least one copy machine for the use of media representatives and others. Photocopy toner should be easily available.

- Tables and chairs should be ready for use. Reporters appreciate a classroom setting where they can place their pads of paper and other materials in front of them while listening to speakers.

- If possible, a video projection system should be installed and ready for use. Because major crises inevitably lead to lawsuits, countersuits, and thorough reviews by regulators, major stockholders and others, someone in the company should videotape key activities that take place in the crisis center, such as a news conference. This way, the company will have a full and complete record of what was said. In addition, if the company has prepared a five- or ten-minute presentation of its operations and products, that can be easily shown on an overhead system to the audience before questions are taken, thus setting a professional tone for the session.

- Refreshments should be made available at the end of any session with the news media. Be careful not to appear extravagant and wasteful; small sandwiches or doughnuts and coffee always suffice. This gracious step is usually appreciated by visitors.

EXHIBIT 7-3 Recommended Design for a Crisis Management Center at a Corporate Headquarters

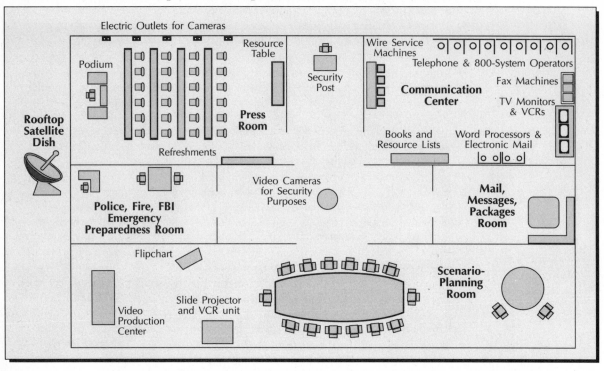

Large corporations often dedicate space to a crisis center. This model features many of the technological and administrative items that can help managers coping with chaos.

management for privacy and coordination of details, and the need of the news media to report directly from their news source.

THE ULTIMATE CRISIS MANAGEMENT CENTER

In December 1991, *Time* magazine provided the first in-depth examination of Mount Weather, the ultrasecret facility in Virginia designed to become the primary headquarters for the entire U.S. government in the event of nuclear attack, chemical warfare, or other major catastrophe. Although the threat of a nuclear holocaust has declined in recent years, the Federal Emergency Management Agency (FEMA) is mandated to maintain the facility, which could house hundreds of key officials, strategists, and military assistants for several months if necessary. Although the government refuses comment on the secret crisis management facility, *Time* reports that Mount Weather, constructed underneath a mountaintop, features a massive computer network, underground pond for drinking water, radio and television studios, cafeterias, power generators, and an extensive telecommunications center. The heavily guarded facility is located 48 miles west of Washington, D.C.

Source: For more information, see "Doomsday Hideaway," *Time*, December 9, 1991, p. 26.

In almost all cases where there is widespread publicity about a crisis, such as a product recall, major explosion, or chemical leak, the control center should be staffed by one or more people around the clock until the crisis situation has been stabilized. Because consumers, employees, and others may work different shifts, and because twenty-four-hour newsradio and cable television programming have proliferated, calls could be made to the center at any hour. The last thing such callers want to hear from the company is a tape recording.

With scenario and communication skills in hand and a control center set up, managers will be prepared to move to the next important phase of crisis management: understanding the trauma that is associated with crisis.

STRESS AND CRISIS: THE INDIVIDUAL RESPONSE

Even thinking about crisis can be stressful. Many managers have admitted that when asked to anticipate an accident or act of terrorism against their company, they felt insecure; a few admitted they became sick to their stomachs. Before moving to the development of a crisis plan, therefore, a word about trauma in the workplace is necessary.

Managers and workers feel the impact of crisis differently because their responsibilities and loyalties to the company are shaded by different needs and desires. So, before a crisis management plan is developed, a company will want to explore how both groups might respond to various calamities that could occur on site.

Dr. Raymond Friedman, an eminent physician, has written on the effects of crisis:

> According to current research, the symptoms of Post Traumatic Stress Disorder (PTSD) occur in 100% of children and approximately 90% of adults who are exposed to a catastrophic event. For example, it was found that all of the children who were involved in a school bus kidnapping in Chowchilla, California, suffered PTSD symptoms. Also, a study of the aftermath of a skywalk collapse at the Hyatt Regency Hotel in Kansas City, Missouri, revealed that approximately 90% of the victims, observers and rescue workers suffered from PTSD.[4]

Therefore, managers should seriously consider engaging a consultant in psychology who can review scenario sessions and planning documents as well as the final CMP. There are several reasons for engaging a consultant before a crisis occurs:

1. CMPs are not merely operational or financial tools; they can also help people survive a traumatic crisis. Because we all experience fears, concerns, and anxiety during a crisis, a psychologist can remind senior management that certain reassurances, statements, or modes of support are needed in the hours and days after a crisis.

2. For a company, a financial motivation underlies any consideration of a psychological component. A leading psychologist specializing in crisis, Mark Braverman of Harvard Medical School, notes that when employees

are in the midst of a crisis, and either personnel are injured or facilities damaged, productivity and job quality decline. It makes good business sense to help people rebound.

3. If a psychologist becomes familiar with the norms and corporate culture of an organization, he or she will not need to quickly learn them when a corporate crisis occurs. If a psychologist is not engaged until *after* a shooting, bomb explosion, or other tragedy, he or she will first need to spend hours talking to managers and workers to get a better sense of the company's operations and history.

Crisis experts agree that even the best planning often fails to identify all potential catastrophes. Exhibit 7-4 describes the case of a laid-off employee whose ultimate revenge led to tragedy for his ex-employer. In the Challenge that follows on page 190, you are asked to assume the role of a company officer whose job it is to deal with employees in the aftermath of the Elgar Corporation killings.

To get professional counseling for personnel, managers can contact their local Mental Health Associations, the American Psychological Association in Washington, D.C., or the psychology department of a local college or university. Dr. Braverman (see interview beginning on page 190) noted in the *Boston Business Journal* that a crisis intervention team often costs from $7,000 to $20,000, but he considers this a sound investment. Writing about corporate crises, he argues, "When a company puts its energies into placating its outside public but ignores its employees and managers, the potential for serious personal and corporate malfunctions increases greatly." [5]

PERSONAL CRISIS AND THE WORKPLACE

For most individuals, the process of solving an unexpected crisis is still "hit or miss." When a serious problem confronts a manager, regardless of its severity, that person must make a number of choices. Some choices will be made quickly but may be issued within a vacuum of information. Or a manager may have adequate information but little or no authority to take certain steps.

How managers cope with both routine daily tasks as well as extraordinary problems is probably influenced by dozens of different factors, especially role models. Literature in the fields of sociology and anthropology suggests that among the most important role models are

- Personal role models, particularly parents and grandparents
- Public role models, including entertainers, sports figures, and political leaders
- Mentors, such as teachers and coaches.

You may have considered one of your parents an especially "strong" individual because he or she displayed courage at a particular moment of crisis or adversity. Or, you may have watched as a friend or acquaintance, stricken with a terminal

EXHIBIT 7-4 A Crisis That Is Difficult To Plan for: Violence in the Workplace

Laid off employee kills two executives

Associated Press

SAN DIEGO — A man detonated bombs and opened fire with a shotgun Tuesday inside the office of Elgar Corporation, an electronics company that had recently laid him off, police said. Two executives were killed.

The man, identified as Larry Thomas Hansel, 41, surrendered three hours later at the Riverside County Sheriff's substation in Palm Desert, about 135 miles northeast.

Hansel acknowledged involvement in the San Diego shootings, San Diego Police Lt. Dan Berglund said. Sheriff's deputies seized several weapons from him.

Company officials said the gunman apparently was targeting three executives and had visited the office earlier in the day asking who was in. One of the three officials was killed and a second hid in his office. It was not immediately known where the third man was at the time.

Witnesses saw the assailant flee the shooting scene on a bicycle with a shotgun and a bandoleer of shells slung over his back. They also said he had a pistol stuffed in his waistband and wore a fannypack.

Bomb experts discovered four "very sophisticated" bombs stockpiled just outside the Elgar building, near a hazardous material receptacle, Berglund said. Employees were forced to leave their cars in the parking lot while experts searched for other explosives.

Sheriff's deputies in Palm Desert said Hansel arrived at the the substation at 510 p.m., nearly three hours after the shooting. A black bicycle was in the back of his blue pickup truck.

Hansel is a technician who had been laid off about three months ago because of company cutbacks, said Chris Kelford, Elgar's chief financial officer.

Other employees indicated Hansel had made some "unsettling statements" in the past, Kelford said.

Police said they haven't determined a motive, although they did indicate the shootings probably had been planned.

"We don't know why he came back but it was apparently to do some harm," Berglund said.

The armed man entered the building at about 230 p.m., set off at least two remote-controlled bombs and blew out the telephone switchboard with a shotgun blast, Kelford said. One of the bombs started a fire with flames up to 15 feet.

The man then went up to second-floor offices in the two-story building and opened fire on two executives, police said. They were later found side by side in a cubicle.

illness, cast away the doubts and fears of physicians and others and pressed on with a rehabilitation program to "beat the odds." At least part of your ability to assess the damage inflicted by a crisis, and to rebound with a methodical plan of response, is thus shaped by experience of crisis management in your formative years. At some point, all families receive a dreaded phone call relaying crisis information: a relative has been involved in an accident, a friend has been killed or injured, or a robbery, rape, or other crime has struck home. Such realities provide even the novice with some working exposure to circumstances in which people manage crises prudently—and sometimes disastrously.

CHALLENGE

Workplace violence has escalated in recent years. In at least four separate incidents, employees of the U.S. Postal Service have shot former co-workers or supervisors. In November 1991, the Postal Service announced that it would begin a psychological profile on each of its more than 700,000 employees. Other shooting incidents have traumatized employees at McDonald's and Luby's restaurants and at hundreds of small and large corporations.

After reading the preceding newspaper account, assume that you are Chris Kelford, chief financial officer for Elgar Corporation. You know little about the situation except the facts that are reported in the story, but it is clear that your employees are traumatized by the killing of the two company officers. You have assembled the group in the headquarters auditorium. Prepare and deliver your remarks. Discuss how you feel, how the organization has been impacted by this event, and what services or counseling that Elgar will provide in the coming days and weeks. You may want to invite a psychologist who specializes in depression and trauma to attend your presentation and to comment on your remarks and questions raised by the audience. ✳

INTERVIEW

Mark and Susan Braverman
Violence and Trauma at Work:
Another Crisis for Management

A bus in California accidentally strikes and kills a pedestrian; the driver is unable to sleep for weeks and finally asks for a medical leave of absence because the trauma of that event haunts him. In the Northeast, several staff members of a leading bank experience mounting anxiety after they are assaulted and robbed by armed gunmen twice in the period of one month; a few later resign from the company because they associate the trauma with their workplace. At a leading stock brokerage firm, the suicide of a senior vice president leads to lingering questions for his immediate staff: What could they have done? Should they have known something was wrong? Was senior management to blame for the manager's ultimate act of depression?

Trauma caused by crises in the workplace is an important and, until very recently, understudied area of management. People coping with crisis may experience severe illness, depression, grief, marital strain, or substance abuse. Treatment often comes too late for a normal recovery to occur.

Crisis Management Group Inc., of Watertown, Massachusetts, is a consulting firm comprised of psychologists, social workers, clergy, and other professionals who offer immediate intervention and on-site counseling for individual workers and groups when an industrial accident, shooting, or other crisis affects a company. Owners Susan and Mark Braverman, a licensed social worker and a psychologist, respectively, bring unique backgrounds to this new field of specialization. Susan worked as an employee assistance program (EAP) provider at Digital Equipment Corporation (DEC) before launching the firm; Mark's experience includes a faculty position at Harvard Medical School. Here the husband-and-wife team discuss their work.

Q *Tell me a little about how you became interested in crisis management. What prompted your decision to help workers on the job?*

A Susan: I'm a clinical social worker and had worked as a psychotherapist; I had long been interested in trauma experienced by workers. At Digital Equipment Corporation, our EAP manager was very forward thinking and believed that when trauma impacted a worker, the company should intervene and support that person. Mark was working at the Harvard Trauma Clinic, and we talked at length about that need; then we jointly developed a program that would help DEC employees and those in other corporations. We wanted to create a protocol so that when a crisis occurred that psychologically affected workers, prompt intervention by experienced counselors could begin. We began the company in 1988. Since then we've worked on over fifty cases where workers or managers have been traumatized in the workplace.

Mark: I'm a clinical psychologist by training and was exposed to the traditional medical model of mental illness. That model assumes that mental distress is caused by factors within the individual, and that when such problems appear they are best treated by therapy or medication. In the course of my training at Harvard Medical School, I encountered some people who challenged that notion. They believed, as I do, that *some* people get ill because stressful situations place them under tremendous strain. These crises lead to a variety of symptoms that negatively affect people on and off the job. We believe that intervening at the point of that impact can help both those individuals and certainly their employers as well.

Q *What kinds of trauma impact workers?*

A Susan: Many of our referrals came after we became involved in assisting a major stock brokerage firm. One morning a worker who had just been fired walked into his Boston office and shot and killed his former boss in front of about 125 workers. The effects on those workers, and hundreds of others in that building, were considerable; some chose to seek counseling right away and were able to cope with this crisis.

Mark: We had another case where an executive with an investment firm killed himself at his home on a Monday morning. Guilt, anger, insecurity—all these emotions haunted his co-workers. We have another client coping with the death of a worker on the job after accidentally inhaling fumes of a poison that had leaked in a lab. Imagine how that person's co-workers felt, especially the more than 2,000 persons whose offices were in an adjoining facility next door. When we met with those workers, they told us that they questioned whether management had been honest with them about what kind of research was being pursued on site. "Can we breathe the air? Is it safe to work here? Why did the accident happen to X and not someone else?" Those are the natural feelings that people experience during a crisis.

Q *How can you help both management and workers in the midst of chaos?*

A Mark: The first thing we do is create an alliance with the company's leadership and plan an immediate response. We ask, "What's the circle of impact? Who are the operational managers? What resources, such as an EAP, exist within the company that we can work with? How do employees work together at present? What are you hearing about employees' feelings and concerns?"

Then we ask management to work with us as a team. It's important that they maintain a high level of visibility, that they stand before their employees as leaders of a crisis response effort. As soon as possible, we arrange with them to gather groups of employees. Top management as well as local management should be there and open the discussion with something like "All of us are having trouble dealing with yesterday's accident. We're all broken up. Here are the facts as we know them. And here are some consultants with special skills to help all of us begin to cope and heal." At that point, we tell the group what people often experience and feel—distrust, fear, isolation, insecurity, depression. Then we encourage employees to speak up and ask questions, to share how they feel, to begin this healing process.

Besides being able to learn what the normal signs of posttrauma stress are, I believe that the most important aspect of this process is the group sharing. Without such a process, led by experts in trauma response and sanctioned and encouraged by management, people seal over. They go into a shell. Work group communication deteriorates rapidly. The group is the most important resource for healing—you have to use it.

Afterward, if people want to meet with us in their offices—or at a restaurant, whatever—we will do that. We also have an 800 number if people want to call us from home after work. You can't deal with a crisis with one single formulated response because people's needs are different; some are public, many are private. But as long as management makes an honest attempt to listen to workers, you can build a reservoir of good-will and loyalty. I'm convinced workers want to like and respect their managers; they want leadership and want to trust their boss. Here's a chance where a lasting impression can be made.

Susan: We've had some cases where the situation surrounding an accident, robbery, or suicide was so sensitive that some information just couldn't be shared with the workers. Management needs to say to employees, "We can't share some details with you (out of respect for the family, or because investigators from OSHA are coming in—whatever). We hope you understand that." Almost always, employees do.

Q *What you're saying is that as a crisis psychologist, you need to build rapid synergy with management. How does that come about? Don't some managers worry that you're going to stir up feelings and issues they would just as soon bury?*

A Mark: Sometimes in our first conversation with management just after a crisis, someone will say, "Aren't you going to stir things up? Do we really want to encourage our people to talk about this?" We tell them, "Things *are* stirred up. Rumors *are* circulating *at this minute.* Productivity *is* waning. Business *has been disrupted.*" You can try to sweep this under the rug, and on the surface things may look fine for a time. Often, we see a false sense of normalcy set it. Eventually, however, problems will surface. These will

include people calling in sick, workers compensation claims, decreased confidence in management, group depression, impaired customer service. When we intervene, we help management give their people the support they need and work to return the group to precrisis status as soon as possible.

Q *How do you measure emotions?*

A Susan: When we first walk in the room and meet with workers after a crisis, you'll often see false smiles; a sense of tension permeates the room. Every time we go into a situation, we ask people to confidentially complete a written feedback sheet. One person will inevitably write, "This is the first time I've had the chance to communicate with my manager. We need *more* of this. Why did it take yesterday's accident to create this kind of communication?"

Q *How do you measure the lingering impact of violence or trauma in the workplace?*

A Mark: Some people will manifest these feelings physically—and their sick time or reduced productivity will cost the company. And of course, a certain percentage of people cope with crisis by trying to self-medicate with alcohol or drugs. Some resort to workaholism. Marital problems are common. It runs the gamut.

Susan: There is a need for much more research on worker's compensation and its relationship to crisis in the workplace. But if there is intervention and counseling up front, the impact can be lessened. A certain level of anxiety is natural; when there is too much anxiety, your ability as a worker to process information, or work the assembly line, and do your job is impaired—there's no question that this happens every day in companies all over the world.

Mark: We set up ground rules when we speak with employees for the first time. We tell them, "Everything you say in here is confidential. Nobody has to talk; you can pass if you want to." But when people do speak about what they are feeling inside, others respond and say, "I needed to hear that. I thought I was the only one."

Susan: We're not suggesting it's always smooth. There are often complications. We were called into a company that experienced a serious loading dock accident where a worker was killed in front of a lot of people. This death occurred just when the company was in the midst of union negotiation. An OSHA investigation team would be coming. And here we were walking around asking people on both sides to talk with us about their feelings. So sometimes external factors mask what is happening, and we are very sensitive to that. My point is that timing is important—you don't want to make things worse. Sometimes you may just have an informational meeting and pursue counseling needs later. *There is no one model that always works;* you adjust to the situation. This is where a specialized trauma consultant is so important.

Q *Banks and almost any retail business with a significant amount of cash on hand are vulnerable to crime. How does your intervention with those organizations differ from the manufacturing sector?*

A Mark: In a typical "takeover" situation, where, for example, two machine-gun wielding people with stockings over their head demand to be taken to the safe and traumatize or injure employees, you have high risk of immediate as well as lingering problems. The bank will call us in, and we will begin to work with employees on site for several days to help them understand their emotions. We have had clients such as this, and we see worker confidence returning. Just then we may get another call "We've been robbed *again*!" That's now a siege situation, and *very* traumatizing.

Those persons cannot and should not go right back into the bank—they may need a different setting, different duties for awhile. People want to feel loyal to their employers, but they also need what's called "reasonable accommodation" and some empathy after that kind of crisis.

Susan: It's been suggested that some 70 percent of large companies have risk and crisis plans, but few if any have taken the time and thought to include the psychological component. We're seeing some progress, but it has taken a long, long time for such an awareness. ❑

The number of missing business executives has escalated in recent years. Possible reasons include foul play, evasion of taxes and/or prosecution, and stress. The Associated Press reported on November 22, 1991, that among the companies surprised by the sudden, unexpected disappearance of executives are Cascade International (perfume and fashion retailer), Hartland Plastics (sports statuettes), and Crazy Eddie (electronics retailer). On April 29, 1992, 57-year-old Sidney Reso, president of Exxon's international business division, disappeared after he had left his Florham Park, New Jersey, home for work. A group calling itself The Rainbow Warriors claimed responsibility and sent ransom notes to Reso's family. The Case Study that follows addresses the problems faced by a Missouri company when its CEO disappeared.

CASE STUDY: WE CAN'T FIND OUR CEO!

Imagine coming to work one day and being given a memo that tells you your boss is missing—not missing from today's staff meeting or company softball game but missing as in *gone*. No one has been able to find him for the past 11 days.

That's precisely what happened at the Y&A Group, a publicly traded Creve Coeur, Missouri, engineering firm. The company's CEO, Malcolm Cheek, was a well liked and successful entrepreneur who enjoyed a reportedly stable family life (a wife of twenty years, two children) and a healthy emotional state.

On March 4, 1991, Cheek checked into a plush New York hotel; his phone call home that evening was the last communication from him. This was unusual: Cheek routinely called his office whenever he was on the road, whether in Alaska or Thailand. FBI investigators learned that he had transferred $24,000 from one of his personal accounts to Atlanta just before he disappeared, but there was no evidence that he knew anyone in Atlanta. Three days after his disappearance, company officials, minus Mr. Cheek, announced they expected that Y&A would incur a net loss of about $7 million for 1990. In the aftermath of that announcement, and with word now spreading in financial circles that the CEO was missing, Y&A's stock price fell an astounding 66 percent in one day. Although a small company with 150 employees, Y&A's first major crisis had become front-page material for the *Wall Street Journal*.

Investigators were baffled because there was no body, no ransom note, no leads, no foul play. A crisis loomed that would affect police, regulatory investigators, stockholders, employees, family members, and certainly colleagues in the corporation.

Assume you are the vice president of Y&A Group and must address the following tasks.

1. Call together the executive staff to reflect on how management should respond to the crisis. How would you open the meeting and lead the discussion? Be sure to focus your initial comments around the themes of audience, goal, and message.

2. Write a memo from yourself to company employees informing them of Cheek's disappearance. Do you want to include the fact that his absence has puzzled police investigators and add that any information would be welcomed? You will also want to update employees on the status of the company and assure them that the disappearance of the CEO will not adversely impact them.

3. How should Y&A inform its clients, which include utility companies and other technical organizations, of Cheek's disappearance? What communications vehicle should be used, and why? What should the content of the message be?

4. Stockholders of Y&A include individual investors, institutional investors, employees, friends, and family members. All of these groups have a vested interest in the financial stability of the company, which—given that the CEO has vanished—hardly seems healthy. What issues must the director of investor relations for Y&A face? Should that person inform Y&A stockholders of Cheek's disappearance, which could cause panic, or should he or she wait until further details are uncovered? What are the business and ethical considerations of that decision? If it is decided to communicate with stockholders, what should be said? What individuals inside and outside

the organization should be consulted in the drafting of any such communication?

5. The press is naturally interested in this corporate crisis. Television programs such as "A Current Affair" seek to interview company officials and employees who knew Mr. Cheek; "Good Morning America!" correspondents want to profile the life and disappearance of the CEO; and a slew of business publications, including *Business Week* and *Fortune,* may smell a very intriguing story in the offing. In reality, a small company such as Y&A is ill equipped to handle the hundreds of phone calls, visits, and inquiries from the national and local media. Should Y&A call a press conference? Why or why not? Should it issue a press release? If so, what should the company say? ❑

Source: Based on "The CEO Vanishes, Leaving a Company Besieged, Perplexed," by Robert Johnson, *Wall Street Journal,* March 15, 1991, p. 1. Used with permission of Dow Jones & Company, Inc. As of publication, Cheek has not been found.

ENDNOTES

1. "PR Firm's Disaster Plan for Clorox Springs Leak," *Las Vegas Review-Journal,* May 13, 1991, p. 3A.
2. Annie Reutinger, "Just in Case," *ARCO Spark Magazine,* August 1989, p. 17.
3. Debra Rubin, Jackie Campbell, et al., "From Collapses to Corruption," *ENR Magazine,* February 11, 1988, p. 29.
4. Robert J. Friedman, M.D., "Early Response to Posttraumatic Stress," *EAP Digest,* October 1988, p. 46.
5. Mark Braverman, "Can Firms Afford Not To Have Crisis Intervention?" *Boston Business Journal,* January 29, 1990, p. 26.

8

The Crisis Management Plan

When most companies are confronted with problems, they simply try to fix them. They fail to use a problem or a crisis as an opportunity to explore a new way to do business. Manager's first instinct is to fix instead of reveal, to solve a problem instead of find an opportunity....

Even in the darkest moments of our crisis, we refused to abandon the things we cared about: our proprietary technology, our alternative to "the standard," our focus on the individual and the future of the personal computer.... It's important in a crisis not to become consumed with expense cutting, but to set aside enough time to work on the company's values, vision, identity and directional goals. This is the company's future. ❑

John Scully, Chairman of Apple Computer, in *Odyssey* (1987)

reparing a comprehensive, written crisis management plan (CMP) is one of the most important challenges any manager can face. The ideas and concepts that follow will help you develop and implement such a plan.

Obviously no written plan should remain stagnant. Because each industry is always changing, organizations should continually review and update their documents with an eye toward identifying emerging problems and threats that could negatively impact operations. Factors such as an increased rate of terrorism, new competitive threats, tougher regulatory penalties, and new scientific findings are all compelling reasons to make the review of crisis plans an ongoing management concern.

This chapter is based on a review of more than forty CMPs that were prepared by companies and nonprofit agencies. Most of these were confidential documents contained in loose-leaf binders; they ranged in length from 2 to nearly 120 pages. These CMPs were for banks, retail companies, pharmaceutical companies, school systems, chemical manufacturers, computer consultants, and other organizations. Specific issues relevant to certain industries will need to be addressed by managers representing different departments of the organization you work for. The following information provides a boilerplate outline for general applicability to business and industry. Much of this material uses as an ongoing example Arlington Plastics, our fictitious company whose officers have been discussing their draft, as the CMP throughout the book. Readers who are managers of organizations in which the necessity of a CMP is being discussed will want to consider how these concepts can be directly applied to the various units and departments that are particularly vulnerable to a crisis.

INTRODUCTION

An introduction to a crisis management plan is usually no longer than two pages. Often the chief executive officer or director of operations of a company writes this section of the document. Its purpose is to greet the reader and explain why crises need to be contained in an immediate and comprehensive fashion. The author may also wish to emphasize that crises can be avoided in many circumstances. Many people assume that small problems do not require concerted response, and such poor judgment frequently leads to a wider and deeper crisis.

The executive writing the introduction may wish to emphasize this point and call on all managers involved in crisis management to work as a team to avoid a lingering and expensive calamity. Some crisis plans include a list of major crises that have occurred in that company's industry in recent years to give credible evidence that the potential for disaster is always present.

If the crisis management plan is confidential, as with some firms in a sensitive industry such as the computer software development, aerospace, chemical, food, or military industries, the heading "CONFIDENTIAL" should be prominently displayed on the cover of the CMP. Each page should be similarly marked with this word, usually in small print as a "footer." In addition, it is not uncommon for an organization to control the number of copies of a crisis plan that are in circulation. Thus the cover of one copy of the plan could be marked "Copy number 20 of 52," as shown in Exhibit 8-1. This is intended to remind employees that copying the data could compromise sensitive material.

EXHIBIT 8-1   Sample Cover Page of a CMP Document

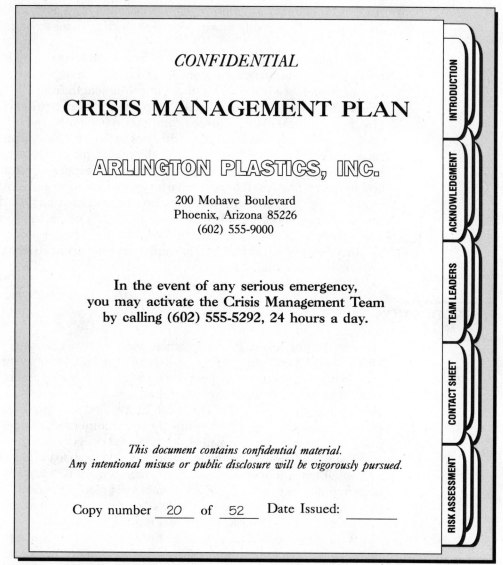

CONFIDENTIAL

CRISIS MANAGEMENT PLAN

ARLINGTON PLASTICS, INC.

200 Mohave Boulevard
Phoenix, Arizona 85226
(602) 555-9000

**In the event of any serious emergency,
you may activate the Crisis Management Team
by calling (602) 555-5292, 24 hours a day.**

*This document contains confidential material.
Any intentional misuse or public disclosure will be vigorously pursued.*

Copy number __20__ of __52__   Date Issued: _____

INTRODUCTION

ACKNOWLEDGMENT

TEAM LEADERS

CONTACT SHEET

RISK ASSESSMENT

The cover of a crisis management plan should prominently display an emergency telephone number that any staff member can access. By placing the word "CONFIDENTIAL" in a prominent position on the cover of the plan, a company mandates that readers protect sensitive information in the document.

A comprehensive plan typically features a list of contents for easy reference. Your CMP should include all pertinent, updated information that could help your key personnel during an emergency. The thirteen sections shown in Exhibit 8-2 are found in many corporate CMPs.

EXHIBIT 8-2 Suggested Contents for Your Crisis Management Plan

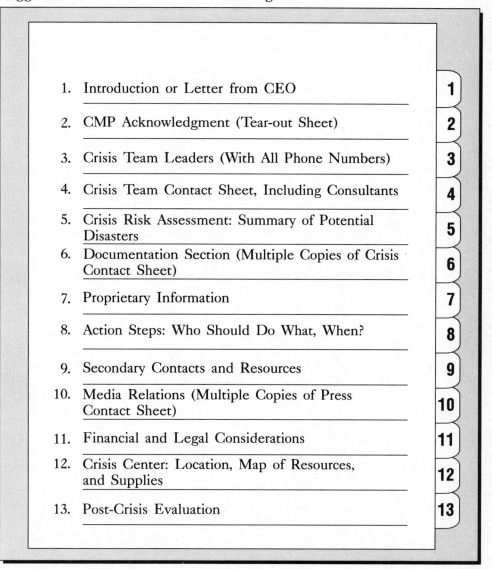

1. Introduction or Letter from CEO | 1

2. CMP Acknowledgment (Tear-out Sheet) | 2

3. Crisis Team Leaders (With All Phone Numbers) | 3

4. Crisis Team Contact Sheet, Including Consultants | 4

5. Crisis Risk Assessment: Summary of Potential Disasters | 5

6. Documentation Section (Multiple Copies of Crisis Contact Sheet) | 6

7. Proprietary Information | 7

8. Action Steps: Who Should Do What, When? | 8

9. Secondary Contacts and Resources | 9

10. Media Relations (Multiple Copies of Press Contact Sheet) | 10

11. Financial and Legal Considerations | 11

12. Crisis Center: Location, Map of Resources, and Supplies | 12

13. Post-Crisis Evaluation | 13

The ideal CMP is logically organized, with names and telephone numbers following the introduction and then progressing into a strategic discussion. Side tabs make these sections easily accessible.

A CEO's letter of introduction to a CMP may contain a message such as the one shown in Exhibit 8-3.

A number of firms ask their managers and supervisors to formally sign a statement that they have read the crisis management plan. There are three specific reasons for requiring this procedure:

1. Because so many managers are busy with a plethora of duties, a signed acknowledgment assures senior management that the plan has indeed been read.

2. When a manager formally signs any document, he or she is more likely to be sure that they are familiar with the contents of that document, which is especially crucial in terms of crisis management.

3. An important signal is sent to managers when an acknowledgment form is attached: this is important!

These forms are usually included in the hiring packet given to senior supervisors and are returned to the human resources office, where they are maintained. Exhibit 8-4 shows an example.

EXHIBIT 8-3   Sample Introduction to a CMP Document

Arlington Plastics
CRISIS MANAGEMENT PLAN: INTRODUCTION

Dear Colleague:

Crises are inevitable in the life of any organization. At AP, our employees work every day to reduce the risk of accident and injury to workers. In addition, the concerted efforts of our workers and supervisors have resulted in an exceptionally strong product line that enjoys wide customer acceptance.

However, life presents many uncertainties to us personally and professionally. In recent years, chemical firms such as ours have been faced with a series of challenging problems: chemical explosions, industrial accidents, railway collisions involving chemical transportation, and crises resulting from industrial sabotage have all been reported. While some crises cannot be avoided, many of these can.

This crisis management plan was developed in late 199_ by our crisis management team, coordinated by Vice President Laurie Shapiro, to strengthen AP's response in the event of a crisis. As a manager, you are expected to read this document thoroughly and to return the completed acknowledgment form to your supervisor. Thank you.

John O'Reilly
John O'Reilly, President

EXHIBIT   8-4   Sample CMP Reader Acknowledgment Form

Arlington Plastics
CRISIS MANAGEMENT PLAN ACKNOWLEDGMENT

I have read and understand Arlington Plastic's crisis management plan dated 9/11/9_ and understand my role in any disaster or crisis containment that may be required.

| _____ | _____ | _____ |
| signature | printed name | date |

THE CRISIS TEAM

The CMP should list all members of the crisis team before it discusses issues and problems. This is important because, in some crises, people need to be contacted before issues can be debated and resolved. First, state who is in charge of plant and department operations in the event of a crisis so that there is no question as to who will be making decisions. Next list backup personnel, in appropriate order. Then list the rest of the team.

Whenever a crisis occurs, the crisis management leader should designate and document who will be responsible for what activities at what times. Because crises can be emotionally difficult and sometimes physically exhausting as well, the leader may designate parties to work in shifts around the clock. This is especially important if the crisis affects a multinational organization, because calls from interested parties around the world may arrive at any hour of the day or night. Many CMPs state early in the document which executive would coordinate a crisis depending on the product or region involved (see Exhibit 8-5).

EXHIBIT   8-5   Sample CMP Listing of Regional Team Leaders

Arlington Plastics
CRISIS TEAM LEADERS

The following managers have been designated as team leaders. The appropriate manager named below should be called immediately by any plant supervisor who suspects or knows that a crisis situation is developing in the region specified.

Region	Manager	Home Telephone	Office Telephone
North America	Jim Letterman	(524) 555-1460	(524) 555-8008
Central America, Asia	Linda Salvo	(524) 555-5113	(524) 555-6134
Europe and Eastern Europe	Dr. Mike Watters	(524) 555-1712	(524) 555-7342
Africa, Australia, All Other Regions	Mark Kawalski	(524) 555-6171	(524) 555-8364

Because the CMP will later be marked a "confidential" in-house document, it is important that key members of the crisis team agree to have their home phone numbers, addresses and other details printed in this limited-circulation document. Many organizations call this the crisis team contact sheet and use the model shown in Exhibit 8-6.

CRISIS ASSESSMENT

The crisis assessment section of the CMP, although not exhaustive, discusses the variety of crises that could occur at an organization. The author(s) of the CMP

EXHIBIT 8-6   A Sample Crisis Team Contact Sheet

Arlington Plastics
CRISIS TEAM CONTACT SHEET

In an emergency, contact the following individuals in the order listed *after* the crisis team leader has been notified or if the team leader cannot be reached. If an individual listed below is not available or cannot be reached, leave a message on the person's answering machine. (MCI and several other long-distance carriers offer a premium service in which they will continue to call a particular party for up to six hours for a flat fee.) In all cases, complete each section of this contact sheet.

Name/Address Title	Home Phone	Office Phone	Cellular Phone	Home Fax	Time Called
Jane Smith, Regulations VP	(524) 555-1212	x4870	555-5859	555-4472	_____
Mike Cotton, Plant Mgr.	(524) 555-1213	x4894	555-3830	555-4942	_____
Carl Moggan, Chem. Dir.	(524) 555-4860	x4893	555-2311	555-3110	_____
Laurie Nuhall, P.R. Dir.	(524) 555-8309	x4403	555-2098	555-8829	_____
Sam Kao, Dir. Safety	(524) 555-3058	x4968	555-3477	555-0822	_____

In the event of a fire, chemical leak, or crisis that involves damage to company property, contact: Susan Liberman, North Insurance Co.—office (800) 555-1274; home (298) 555-3938. If suspicious activity is involved, contact: David Waterhouse, Chemical Investigators, Inc. (745) 555-4923.

Additional Persons to Contact	Addresses	Phone Numbers
_____	_____	_____
_____	_____	_____
_____	_____	_____

should consider the full range of crises discussed in this book, including industrial sabotage, terrorism, a chemical leak, crime committed on company property, natural disasters, and regulatory or product recall problems. Such a listing can be particularly useful in training or educating managers who may be hired at some future date and who have not been involved in crisis planning.

The CMP should discuss each type of crisis, emphasizing those which managers feel have a greater potential for actually occurring. A list for a chemical manufacturer, for instance, would place greater emphasis on the volatility of chemicals, and on the potential damage to the environment from a spill or leak, than on product recall. The recall is important, but the immediate vulnerability of the company relates to damage to life and property. For a toy manufacturer, the recall is of paramount importance because of the threat to children that a defect poses; the actual cause of that defect (such as a manufacturing mistake) assumes secondary importance. The toy company cannot fix the problem in the same way as the chemical manufacturer can fix its product; the toy may have been manufactured and assembled thousands of miles away. The most prudent step is to admit the problem, identify consumers and communicate with them, and then begin to rectify the actual cause of the problem.

DOCUMENTATION DISCUSSION

The CMP should discuss the importance of managers documenting *all* events surrounding a crisis. This is vital not only because future litigation may be involved, but also because any number of parties—regulators, neighbors, the press, and stockholders, for instance—may later demand answers to such questions as

1. When did you first learn of this incident?
2. Where did the accident occur?
3. When did you first contact senior management, or police?
4. How many people were on site at the time of the explosion?
5. Who made the first call to the mayor regarding the need to evacuate the community?
6. What offices in the state house did you contact?

The CMP should state explicitly that formal notes should be taken throughout the crisis, with specific information regarding who called whom, who stated what, and the date and time of all major events. This record will be especially important later, when managers may need to reconstruct events for insurance or liability claims. To this end, many organizations provide multiple blank copies of a crisis contact sheet (Exhibit 8-7) in the CMP. Contact sheets should be used by all managers on the crisis team whenever an important call or visit is made by any internal or external party.

EXHIBIT 8-7 Sample Contact Sheet in a CMP

Arlington Plastics
CRISIS CONTACT SHEET
No. _____ *(in order received)*

Name of Reporting Manager: _____

Call Received at _____ P.M./A.M.   From: _____

Caller's Phone Number: _____   Address: _____

Nature of Inquiry or Call: _____

_____

_____

_____

What Action Was Taken? _____

_____

By Whom: _____

Copies of This Report Sent to: _____

PROPRIETARY INFORMATION

The CMP document should explicitly remind managers on the crisis team that certain information remains confidential and should not be released to *anyone* without the CEO's written authorization. The primary reason for this is not so much to engage in secrecy as to assure accuracy. There have been many cases where credible managers, eager to assist a reporter or inspector, offer information in haste during a crisis, only to later find out that their data were wrong and embarrassment or damage could have been caused to an innocent party. Also, federal or state statutes may preclude the release of certain data.

In the middle of crisis, the telephone can be an indispensable aid to a company, but it can also be the company's worst enemy when hundreds or thousands of callers begin to flood a switchboard. In this regard, remind those who answer phones that confidential information may include (but is not necessarily limited to)

- Net worth of the organization
- Number of government or private-party contracts received

- Assets and liabilities of the firm
- Names of contractors who worked on facility design and construction
- Estimates of damage as a result of an accident
- Salaries or other information regarding company employees
- Home phone numbers of key personnel
- Names of private investors in a firm
- Extent of injuries to personnel (refer to hospital)
- Name of a company's bank or creditors
- Ingredients of certain products
- Whether or not such incidents have occurred in the past
- Blame placed on any individual or party

After the crisis team leader has reviewed the situation, certain information can and should be routinely provided to interested parties. Such information might include

- Acknowledgment that an accident or incident has taken place
- Estimated amount of damage done to a facility (consult with insurance estimators)
- Year company was founded
- Number of employees at the organization
- Name and description of product involved and how it is used
- Action being taken to resolve the problem
- Nature of ownership of the firm (private, public, partnership)
- Nature of the firm itself (for example, financial, travel, sports, manufacturing)
- Name, office, and home phone numbers of director of public relations
- Whether or not area residents should evacuate or take special precautions

ACTION STEPS

The CMP document should raise the following questions, which any member of the crisis team could use in planning responses during a crisis.

1. Has the company CEO or chairperson of the board been contacted?
2. Is there any need to contact police, fire, or arson investigators? The FBI, U.S. Department of Commerce, State Department (on trade or military secrets), the EPA, or a foreign consulate? (If there is any obvious threat to life and property, emergency personnel should be the very first parties contacted— this should be stated explicitly in the CMP.)

3. Who will be responsible for addressing media needs for the next forty-eight hours? Two persons should be named to take rotating shifts of twelve hours each. It is especially important that as few people as possible speak for the company, so that a single, unified message is offered to the press and the public. When too many managers offer opinions, insight, and speculation, the organization can be easily embarrassed, and mismanagement is evident.

4. Should local or regional emergency preparedness officials be contacted? These may include state offices of emergencies, county commissioners, or others.

5. Should the company hire a photographer to document damage or problems immediately?

6. At what point should the organization's attorneys be contacted?

7. Will a press conference be necessary? If so, newspapers and radio and television stations will need to be called, fax follow-ups will need to be sent regarding the time and location of such an event (with directions), and a dress rehearsal of questions and answers will be necessary at least three hours before the actual event.

8. If the crisis involves unionized employees in, for example, a temporary shutdown of the plant, a potential job action, or protests near or at the facility, should a representative of a labor union(s) be contacted?

9. What is the potential for a secondary aspect of the crisis to erupt? This may include circumstances such as more employees being injured or killed, the interaction of different chemicals exploding off site, a secondary fire erupting, or an opponent calling a press conference with new allegations or hard evidence of wrongdoing. Although planning for a secondary crisis is difficult, it is important to recognize that some crises are naturals for breeding this kind of multiple calamity.

10. How can the crisis management team allay the public's fears or panic? If there is no immediate threat to life and property, this reassuring news needs to be emphasized quickly and effectively. This message can be sent via a press conference, news release, or series of interviews with the news media.

11. Have families of any victims been contacted? In many cases, family members have first learned of an accident or calamity from a news report rather than from the organization. On learning of the crisis, the crisis management team should take immediate steps to have a company representative visit the families of those injured or killed. At the end of the meeting this person should offer his or her home and office phone numbers and an assurance that he or she is available for support around the clock.

12. Will a tour of the plant or facility be necessary in the immediate future? If so, certain items may need to be covered or removed so as not to offend the

families of anyone injured during an accident. Who will speak for the company during such a tour? Should the press be allowed or invited to attend?

13. Should parking or access to a particular site or portion of a facility be closed off or restricted to certain personnel?

14. Should all advertising by the firm be canceled until the crisis is further studied? Who will make the call and coordinate these details?

15. What outside parties in addition to the aforementioned need to be contacted immediately by a representative of the firm? What are the names and office or home phone numbers of these important individuals? This information should be listed on a secondary contact sheet, something like the sample shown in Exhibit 8-8.

16. Will a mobile office or crisis communications center be required? In a major industrial accident, company operations and statements may need to be managed from a secondary facility for an indefinite period of time, or until police, arson investigators, or regulators approve reoccupation of the facility. In advance, the crisis management plan should address what area facilities or warehouses may be available on short notice for this purpose.

17. How extensive is the damage? Experts in the various departments of the company (management information services in the event of loss of computer data, inventory control in a fire) should be contacted to see whether additional products or resources can be ordered immediately to avoid major time delays.

EXHIBIT 8-8   Sample Secondary Contact Sheet for CMP

Arlington Plastics
SECONDARY CONTACT SHEET

	Name	Office Phone	Home Phone	Called When?	By Whom?
Key Distributors	Jane Jayson Inc	555-0893	555-3939	_____	_____
	Sam Jewelson	555-7789	555-0096	_____	_____
Key Vendor	Mark Andrew	555-3938	555-2222	_____	_____
	Mike OMalley	555-0440	555-9933	_____	_____
Banker	Susanne Notabe	555-4488	555-9930	_____	_____
Primary Customer	Canadian Foods				
	Jim Payson	(733) 555-4848	(733) 555-9111	_____	_____
Key Consultant	Dr. Ron Gurren	555-4775	555-3900	_____	_____
Local Official	Mayor Sandra Flynn	555-8822	555-0004	_____	_____

This list features some of the primary issues involved in almost any crisis. Special aspects of certain companies will entail additional questions and issues.

MEDIA RELATIONS

As mentioned earlier, one person should speak formally for the organization to the news media throughout a crisis situation. The CEO or other high-ranking individual may wish to call a press conference or issue a brief statement, but the bulk of responsibilities regarding the news media will fall on the shoulders of the director of public relations. This person understands the needs and concerns of reporters, so he or she is often best equipped to help the company develop an effective strategy (although the public relations director is almost never the principal source of quotes).

In drafting a crisis management plan, media relations take on special significance. Consider the following points:

1. The CMP should explicitly state that all calls from the news media be immediately transferred to the director of public relations. This person is likely receiving many calls from the news media and will need to prioritize responses after consulting with senior management on what statements the company can or should make. Of great concern to this spokesperson is the responsibility to be accurate. Misleading, false, or half-true statements to the news media invariably injure the reputation of a company. They could also lead people to act on untrue information, which would cause a host of additional problems. Although a spokesperson can always refuse to answer a question, in any difficult circumstance it is best to tell a reporter that his or her call will be returned by a certain time—and the spokesperson should *keep* that promise. When the spokesperson replies with "no comment," the remark looks bad in print and the public might assume that the organization has something to hide.

   A log of all press-related calls is strongly recommended. This log should be kept long after a crisis has subsided in case documentation is required by outside parties or regulators or a libel suit is filed against the company. A sample press contact sheet is shown in Exhibit 8-9.

2. The spokesperson should immediately retain the services of an area clipping service. These companies monitor area or national radio and network or cable television broadcasts and scan many newspapers and magazines, recording or clipping all relevant coverage of a crisis. For a modest fee, a copy of these tapes and articles is sent to company management and attorneys to review.

3. A spokesperson should always try to maintain a two-way flow of information. In many cases, reporters have already been in contact with state or

EXHIBIT   8-9   Sample Press Contact Sheet in a CMP

Arlington Plastics
PRESS CONTACT SHEET
No. _____ *(in order received)*

Date: _____   Time: _____ P.M./A.M.

Reporting AP Officer: _____

Inquiry Received from: _____ (person)

Reporter/Editor with: _____ (organization)

Question/Inquiry: _____

_____

_____

Response: _____

_____

_____

Is Follow-up Needed? _____   If So, When? _____

Notes: _____

_____

local officials, competitors, or other parties, so the spokesperson may want to ask reporters what they have learned in preparing their stories. This is an appropriate and often helpful approach to take.

4. Speculation is deadly in crisis management. Even if pushed by reporters to attribute a crisis to a particular problem, faulty part, chemical, manufacturing process, or other factor, the spokesperson should insist that he or she cannot make any conclusions until a full investigation has been completed. As mentioned earlier, many public relations professionals have been embarrassed, and their careers impaired, when they made premature statements about victims or conditions, only to be corrected by the truth hours or days later. Their credibility was impaired, perhaps permanently.

5. How will the spokesperson follow up contacts with members of the news media, making sure that all calls are returned and promises for pieces of information are fulfilled? Timeliness is essential. The CMP should emphasize that calls from reporters be returned promptly. Because reporters are

very resourceful at getting the data they need to file a report by deadline, if you do not reply, they will likely find someone, somewhere, willing to talk.

6. The CMP should consider whether company policy favors or precludes any "off the record" comments. For the most part, corporations discourage any of their officers speaking off the record for fear that the statements could be later used anyway.

7. The CMP should discuss what types of "stock" photographs (preshot, ready in multiple copies) can be released and used without permission during a crisis, and what new photographs will be considered by the organization after a crisis has occurred.

8. The CMP should remind the crisis management team that, whenever possible, the spokesperson and others who meet with the press should accentuate the positive in all statements and press conferences. The future viability of the organization could be at stake; indications that the company is handling the crisis competently and in a comprehensive, concerted fashion could go a long way to alleviate the fears of the public and other interested parties.

9. The CMP should detail resources the spokesperson may need at his or her disposal to effectively represent the company during crisis. This list may include additional telephone operators and administrative assistants, and access to photocopying and fax equipment. In addition, permission to use certain facilities for a press conference or other activity may be needed.

10. The CMP should highlight the fact that a dress rehearsal of a press conference is a must. The spokesperson can role-play a reporter during such a session, helping the management team refine answers to remove accusations, presumptions, or unwarranted anger and blame. Although some organizations ask their official spokesperson (usually the public relations director) to speak at press conferences, the majority of crises that were handled well in this survey featured a senior executive other than that director behind the podium. The main reason for this is not that the public relations director is unable to handle the situation, but rather that he or she is sometimes perceived to be too "media savvy," too clever or slick in answering questions and presenting the company's perspective. Regardless of who the spokesperson is, a careful rehearsal of questions and answers is necessary. At a formal press conference, the public relations director should stay near the senior executive to provide necessary clarifications or additional information.

11. The CMP should discuss what written materials about the firm would be released at a press conference. This might include copies of the organization's annual report, fact sheet, biographies of senior management, and a statement on the nature and resolution of the crisis. Usually management provides a contact sheet with the spokesperson's name and home, office, and fax numbers.

12. Any comments or questions by reporters regarding the potential liability of the company in a crisis calls for consultation with the company's legal counsel. In many cases when a press conference is necessary, counsel should be present (but not conspicuous) to assist the person speaking if a particularly sensitive question is raised. If an attorney is known to reporters and actively participates in the press conference, journalists may justifiably report that the company is visibly concerned about its legal vulnerability. The attorney should also sit in on the dress rehearsals for any press conference.

13. The CMP should address the subject of advanced communications technologies, which are becoming increasingly important as satellites continue to reduce the costs of international transmissions between news organizations. If the company is large or prominent enough that calls for a press conference might come from around the world, can the company arrange for a private network feed in several locations? Has the company previously produced a five- or ten-minute video on the organization that could be easily distributed on three-quarter-inch broadcast tape to news organizations? Is there any need or use for a video news release (discussed earlier in this book)? If the organization routinely uses electronic mail, are there any messages, statements, or pieces of data in the company's files that could be improperly accessed and later distributed to the news media? Questions about these and related technologies should be discussed in the crisis plan.

14. The CMP should remind the spokesperson that a routine follow-up evaluation of effectiveness should be undertaken within thirty days after the crisis. Learning lessons is one of the few rewarding aspects of crisis management, and the lessons may be invaluable in a future calamity.

FINANCIAL AND LEGAL CONSIDERATIONS

The CMP should discuss what options are open to the company if a serious mishap should cause widespread harm to the company's assets and viability. Thus the CMP should discuss

- How to temporarily suspend trading of the firm's stock, if necessary
- How to acquire stock in large volumes in the event of a massive sell-off by investors
- How to address various audiences (there are usually many, each with specific information needs)
- How to communicate with managers of pension plans and other institutional investors who have a vested interest in the company

- How to communicate with major brokerage firms, who recommend investments, effectively and rapidly
- How to reach consumers (through paid advertisements, mailings, a press conference)
- How to reach employees, whose employment and potential retirement income could depend on the satisfactory handling of the crisis

The financial and legal section of the CMP needs to be thoroughly reviewed and approved by legal counsel and by the company's major underwriter and insurance carrier. Some major corporations that have taken these preventive steps in anticipating and planning for disaster report that this risk assessment has helped them reduce business insurance costs.

LOGISTICS OF CRISIS MANAGEMENT

As mentioned, most organizations should designate a crisis management center. The CMP should discuss the location of such a center, how it will be staffed and by whom, and what resources are needed to respond well. Exhibit 7-3 shows such a model center.

EVALUATION METHODS

In the aftermath of a crisis, the executive team will want to evaluate all facets of the crisis, those managed successfully, as well as those that failed. In some organizations, managers complete evaluation forms and then copies of all forms received are shared with the crisis management team, which meets shortly after the crisis to compare notes and make recommendations to strengthen the existing CMP. Then new pages and recommendations can be distributed to appropriate managers for inclusion in their copies of the CMP. A sample evaluation form is shown in Exhibit 8-10 on page 214.

These suggestions should be actively integrated with the information provided in Chapter 5, "Communication as a Management Tool," in developing a crisis management plan.

RISK MANAGEMENT: THE LIABILITY FACTOR IN A POOR PRODUCT OR DESIGN

Any crisis management plan must also envision questions of product liability. Small and large corporations increasingly find that the issue of risk contributes in a major way to the costs of doing business. In fact, three risk categories—health insurance, product liability, and workers compensation—can easily cost a mid-sized company several million dollars a year or more.

In April 1992, a major flood caused widespread destruction of property throughout downtown Chicago after an old tunnel near the Chicago River collapsed, allowing the river to flow into the whole underground system. The estimated cost in terms of actual damage caused to private property, costs to repair underground systems, and the loss of income suffered by area businesses may exceed $1.5 billion. Complicating this picture is the fact that many of those businesses which lost assets in the flood did not hold the specific insurance necessary to protect themselves because the area was not situated in a designated flood district. Lawsuits against many parties—the designer of the tunnels, construction companies which built them, city workers who supervised the system, and other parties—may take nearly a decade to resolve through litigation.

The Chicago flood is only one example of potential faulty product design. Toy, pharmaceutical, heavy equipment and numerous other manufacturers are increasingly concerned about product liability. Risk expert Donald Hardigree of the UNLV Institute on Risk and Insurance Management reports that product manufacturers often fail to understand that they are vulnerable in a successful lawsuit if they breach any warranty that is stated or implied, if they produce a product later found faulty under tort law, or if a court determines that strict liability exists.

Manufacturers also face exposure to a product liability suit if

- they sell or manufacture a defective product.
- it is alleged that there is negligence in product design, construction, packaging and/or assembly.
- there is unsufficient, inaccurate or misleading warnings, labels and/or instructions that accompanied, or should have accompanied, the product.
- the manufacturer fails various tests of reasonable judgment, including failing to foresee unintended use of the product by consumers; the manufacturer must also design against these uses.

One recommended defense in protecting a manufacturer from a crisis in terms of injuries, deaths or economic hardship incurred by the end user is to insure that the product is manufactured, tested and labelled *properly.* Private laboratories and consulting firms can assist with these functions. Increasingly, insurance underwriters are insisting that these requirements be documented if the producer is to secure adequate insurance.

Source: For more information, see *Commercial Liability, Risk Management and Insurance* by Donald Malecki, Ronald C. Horn, Eric A. Wiening and James H. Donaldson, American Institute for Property and Liabilities Underwriters (Malvern, Pennsylvania), second edition, 1986, pp. 92–96. For information on the 1992 Chicago flood, see "A Flood of Questions," *Business Insurance,* April 20, 1992, p. 1.

EXHIBIT   8-10   Sample Post-Crisis Evaluation Form

Arlington Plastics

POST-CRISIS EVALUATION

Please complete this evaluation honestly and thoroughly. If you request, your response will be kept confidential. Be as specific as you can regarding incidents, people, and issues that merit attention. Evaluation is a necessary and important step in planning how to prevent or mitigate future problems.

Your Name (optional): _____ Date: _____

Department: _____ Extension: _____

What was your role in this crisis? _____

How did you first learn of the incident? _____

Were you satisfied with how you were notified? _____

Why or why not? _____

_____

How could the notification system be improved? _____

Approximately how many hours did you spend exclusively in managing an aspect of this incident? _____

On a scale of 1 (very poorly) to 10 (excellently), how would you rank the way the company managed this crisis? _____ Using this same scale, how would you rank your department's management of this crisis? _____ How would you rank the company's public relations response? _____

What specific comments about certain managers or departments can you offer? If you noticed particularly outstanding or deficient service, please tell us more:

_____

_____

_____

How can the company's CMP be improved? _____

_____

_____

CASE STUDY: THERE ARE NO FATALITIES
ON FLIGHT 30 ... OOPS ....

World Airways was a potentially strong contender in the airline industry in the early 1980s. New routes on both the East and West coasts were being added every few months. At the same time, passenger reservations were up. Management was confident that rivals such as Eastern Airlines and Delta Air Lines would lose market shares once World had established a firm foundation with its customers.

On the evening of Saturday, January 23, 1982, however, a World Airways DC-10 jetliner carrying 208 passengers and crew skidded off an icy runway at Boston's Logan International Airport. The plane broke into several pieces, landing both in the water and on the runway. Despite the fact that the crew and many passengers were hurled into freezing waters during a heavy fog, it appeared that no one was killed. The next morning, the *Boston Globe* reported on the front page,

> No one was killed or critically injured, although at least 40 people, including the pilot and copilot, were taken to area hospitals. "Everybody is accounted for," Sgt. Herbert Hall of the State Police at Logan said late last night. "There are no bodies floating around or anything like that. We are missing two, but they missed the flight," which originated in Los Angeles.

Although passengers complained in the hours immediately following the crash that the crew appeared confused and uninformed, World Airways spokesperson Michael Gunn told the *Globe*, "Everything was fantastically quiet. It was a matter of minutes before everybody got off the plane."

Not quite.

World Airways officials refused to discuss the plane crash in the days following the crisis. They also refused to release a list of the 195 passengers and 13 crew members on the flight. Three days after the crash, the press reported that the wife of one of the passengers had been trying unsuccessfully to have officials of either the airline or airport determine the whereabouts of her missing husband and son. Within a week it was confirmed that Walter Metcalf, age 60, and his son Leon, 40, of Dedham, Massachusetts, were front-row passengers on the plane. Passengers later recalled that they were thrown into the water, but they were never seen or heard from again. It was now evident that this remarkable story of a crashed jetliner, seemingly *without* major incident, was becoming a crisis for World Airways.

Assume that you are the chief spokesperson for World Airways. Up until now your company, based in Oakland, California, has ordered you to remain silent on the accident. Now that the television networks and the print media are reporting a major gaffe, a myriad of publics—the traveling public, investors, and the National Transportation Safety Board—will certainly demand public accountability.

Develop a detailed plan of response for your corporate officials in terms of what the company should say to whom, and when. Keep in mind the following considerations:

Speaking too quickly in the heat of chaos can cause embarrassment for an organization. World Airways learned that lesson on January 23, 1982, when it told the press that all passengers were safe after its airliner crashed at Boston's Logan Airport. In actuality, two passengers drowned. The airline no longer exists.

1. The press has been embarrassed. They reported, based on World Airways statements, that there had been no fatalities. Reporters and editors are not likely to trust your future statements and assurances.

2. Passengers with existing reservations may choose to cancel their plans now that the credibility of World Airways has been impaired. What can you do or say to reassure these individuals?

3. The entire process by which attendants of World Airways take their "number counts" before each flight is likely to be questioned. Discuss what management steps you will suggest to guarantee the integrity of this important process. What will you do regarding the records of past flights?

4. A number of lawsuits will probably be filed against your company. What steps, if any, can or should the airline take to ameliorate the ill will caused by the accident of Flight 30? Should the airline send flowers or representatives to those who remain in the hospital? Should airline representatives travel to the homes of the passengers to personally apologize for any injury or inconvenience? Should the airline offer to pay for any medical bills incurred as a result of the crash? ❑

APPENDIX

A

Test Your Crisis Management Skills: You Won't Believe What I Received in Today's Mail

What would you do if an employee whom you fired months ago decided that the best retribution was to send some of your trade secrets—or a product in the final stages of research and development—to one of your competitors?

Three crises now emerge. There is one for your company, which may have invested years of effort and significant capital in developing the product. There is a second crisis for managers of the company receiving the trade secret, because they must decide whether they should look at the plans and possibly take advantage of the data, or send them back. The third crisis is for law enforcement officials, who for the most part have had little experience in dealing with such cases.

Throughout the 1980s and into the early 1990s, a see-saw for some industries caused a number of layoffs throughout the U.S. economy. Most employees whose positions are eliminated move on without causing their former employers any significant problem. Others, however, may seek to take advantage of the computer software, manufacturing secrets, blueprints, or other data that they had access to in the past.

In 1985, for instance, a contract employee for 3M, Philip A. Stegora, sent some samples of a new casting tape, which doctors would use in casting broken bones, to four rivals of 3M. Stegora was later convicted of mail fraud and transporting stolen property across state lines; he served twenty-two months in prison for his

crime. But the crisis he created poses a significant number of challenges for management.

Let's assume you are director of research and development for Johnson & Johnson, one of 3M's principal rivals in the health care industry. For many years, Johnson & Johnson has dominated the market for plaster-of-paris bandage rolls, and your brand name further enhances your market share. Yet the introduction of a stronger 3M fiberglass product in 1980 threatened Johnson & Johnson's position.

Using an alias, let's say Stegora sends you samples of 3M's new fiberglass product and says that for $20,000 he will explain the technology behind this breakthrough. Stegora uses a Minneapolis post office box and asks that he be contacted to arrange a meeting.

There are a variety of dynamics at work in this case: consider the legal, ethical, competitive, profit, and human issues. In order to address them, assemble a group of managers at Johnson & Johnson. Each person in your group should role-play a different manager in the company (product research and development, security, public relations, fiscal, and so on). These managers have read industry reports about the mailing of proprietary documents, and they wish to use a scenario-based exercise to test how they would respond. The following questions will guide that staff meeting:

1. You are director of research and development at Johnson & Johnson and you have just received the letter and samples from Stegora. What would you do? Whom would you contact within your company, if anyone?

2. Would you send the sample fiberglass tape to your chemists for further analysis? If your lab-

oratory personnel have been unable to develop a similar prototype after years of trying, and an examination of this sample could further your research (and potentially your career), would you take this step?

3. Are you breaking any law by examining or conducting tests on the samples? Are you breaking any law by not contacting a law enforcement agency such as the FBI? Could you potentially be guilty of a crime just for examining the sample?

4. Would you communicate with 3M? If so, what level of manager at that competitor would you contact? Would you telephone or write this individual, and what would influence that decision? Would you contact your corporate counsel before making any such communica-

tion, or could that complicate the situation? Two individuals should separate themselves from the group and role-play, one the role of a Johnson & Johnson manager and the other a manager from 3M.

5. If you decide that writing your competitor is the most appropriate avenue, write that piece of communication. If you decide to call the competitor, write down the principal points you wish to emphasize in that conversation.

Note: An excellent article on trade secrets and industrial espionage is by Michael A. Epstein and Stuart D. Levi, "Protecting Trade Secret Information: A Plan for Proactive Strategy," *Business Lawyer* 43 (May 1988): 887–914.

Source: For further information on this case, see Kevin Kelly and Joseph Weber, "When A Rival's Trade Secret Crosses Your Desk," *Business Week,* May 20, 1991, p.48.

B

The Role of the Federal Emergency Management Agency (FEMA) in Preparing for Crisis

Thus far we have concentrated mostly on the role of corporate crises. Yet business and industry is also impacted by the forces of nature that cause calamities such as floods, earthquakes, hurricanes, or other disasters. As a manager, you may one day be called upon to coordinate the disaster operations of a particular department, store, or entire company. What agencies of the government can help you in such a massive undertaking? Here are some answers.

FEDERAL EMERGENCY MANAGEMENT AGENCY (FEMA)

When creating congingency plans as part of a comprehensive crisis management program, most businesses might not think to turn to the federal government for planning assistance. And yet the Federal Emergency Management Agency (FEMA) was created for just that purpose and is a valuable and practical resource for today's corporation. In the agency's own words, its mission is to provide "emergency management information . . . spanning the full spectrum of emergency preparedness and response concerns, techniques and information."

FEMA is based in Washington, D.C.; the agency also maintains ten regional offices, each servicing between four and eight contiguous states. These offices disseminate information to businesses and individuals alike through a series of publications. These publications range from cards on hurricane survival (designed to fit in a wallet) to a booklet on limiting the effect of nuclear attack on electronic equipment.

WHY FEMA?

FEMA has a considerable number of sharply focused publications designed for highly technical professionals; the agency also excels at public consciousness raising.

Year after year, evening news programs show major disasters throughout the United States that have taken a heavy toll on people and facilities. Often, the damage involved might have been reduced had those affected been given even a small amount of prior education and some basic skills.

FEMA's baseline disaster guides are invaluable. Each addresses a specific threat to personal safety or operations and is liberally sprinkled with clear examples, illustrative graphics, and detailed diagrams. These publications are backed by equally comprehensive guides for administrative use within companies.

FEMA'S VALUE TO THE CORPORATION

Many new and developing companies are perceptive enough to spend time and effort into developing disaster contingency plans from the start. But developing a company sometimes precludes such an investment. Many companies only turn to disaster planning once crisis has struck. Either way, FEMA is there.

Publications from the agency step through the following essential tasks:

- Creating contengency policies
- Writing a crisis manager's job description
- training a crisis manager
- Forming and conducting classes for in-house training of employees in disaster planning
- Obtaining financial assistance from government agencies following a disaster

DISASTER SCENARIOS

At one time or another, every corporation experiences pressure or damage from natural emergencies or disasters. The likely key to motivating management to act *before* a crisis is to identify the potential damage and show how cost-effective preventive measures can be.

Even something as seemingly trivial as inclement weather can shut down plants. Heat waves can bring power failures as air conditioners work harder. Frigid temperatures, besides freezing equipment and water, often brings snow and ice that can keep employees from reporting to work.

A backhoe mistake can cause termination of telephone service for all but those fortunate companies with their own microwave or satellite links, and even they may be left without local service. For most companies, this is crippling, but for direct marketers whose income is entirely derived from telephone sales orders, a week without an 800 number could mean insolvency.

Not only do companies have to worry about fire accidentally starting within the company's facilities, but crisis managers must also consider the potential liability from other sources such as brush fires and arson.

Floods and hurricanes can force evacuation of work areas, threaten computer and telephone systems alike, and submerge everything in their path when they strike. Like many natural disasters, one danger of floods is they are not absolute. A company may be torn between trying to

mop up water as it arrives and evacuating personnel for safety, abandoning hope of saving equipment and records in the process.

Earthquakes and volcanic activity have received closer attention in recent years following the devastating 1989 Loma Prieta earthquake in northern California and the 1991 eruption of Mount Pinitubo that forced evacuation of both U.S. military bases in the Philippines.

The spill of hazardous materials is an increasing risk as more and more sites are discovered. Contamination of water supplies, the atmosphere, and the workplace is a particular risk for those companies not already handling such materials themselves, as they may not be aware of the issues involved. Such contamination need not be manmade. For example, scientists are increasingly aware that radon, a natural gas, sometimes seeps from the ground into buildings and creates a health risk.

As remote and entirely catastrophic as it may seem, nuclear radiation and explosion can and should be planned for. Modern nuclear weapons, particularly the neutron variety, can be targeted precisely and reliably. In addition, nuclear plants and U.S. military weapons are vulnerable to failure and destruction or contamination of the surrounding area. In either event, though, there is a reasonable chance of survival. Both explosive damage and the effects of radiation on people and electronics can be prepared for.

THE CRISIS MANAGER'S RESPONSIBILITIES

FEMA suggests there are four distinct stages of disaster handling for crisis management professionals:

- *Mitigation* involves minimizing the window of opportunity for disaster. This can include site selection, facilities design, and astute production management techniques. Larger companies may find dividing operations among different geographical regions helps to isolate possible natural disasters.

- *Preparedness* means having adequate resources to meet the remaining risk after mitigation. Companies with integral MIS departments can make cross-alignments with similar-size companies. In the event of a disaster affecting one company, the other can provisionally perform data processing functions for both.

- *Response* to an actual crisis follows. By the time a crisis actually strikes, absolutely everything possible to minimize the effect should already have been performed, and most actions should simply be conforming to prescribed policy. If the disaster's extent is unpredictable, even during the event, the crisis manager might have to do some quick thinking.

- *Recovery* involves dealing with the aftermath of a crisis and preparing for the next one. A crucial part of that preparation is analyzing the disaster just past for areas needing improved management. In the events of psychological trauma or death, crisis counseling may be in order. Returning employees may need flex-time for a short period to help restore their personal affairs.

RESOURCES

FEMA produces a wide assortment of publications. A select few that may be of particular interest to industry are

- FEMA-20
  FEMA Publications Catalog
  This catalogue lists FEMA publications designed to help citizens plan for and respond to disasters and emergencies of all types.

- #6-0339
  Emergency Program Manager An Orientation to the Position
  A home-study course designed primarily for emergency program managers, it provides an introduction to the four phases of comprehensive emergency management: mitigation, preparedness, response, and recover.

- #8-0855
  Disaster Mitigation Guide for Business and Industry
  This guide provides basic information useful for developing site-specific disaster mitigation plans for business and industry. Emphasis is placed on those disasters likely to affect industries throughout the United States, including natural (earthquake, fire, flood, and severe storms) and manmade (hazardous materials incidents and nuclear war).

- #8-0721
  Digest of Federal Disaster Assistance Programs
  This handbook is designed to serve as an initial source of information for state and local governments, and private citizens and public officials who need disaster assistance. It is a compendium of federal programs that are specifically designed to supplement state and local relief and recovery efforts of major disasters or emergencies. It includes both programs that require a presidential declaration of an emergency and those which do not.

- #8-0691
  Habitability and Human Problems in Shelters
  This civil preparedness guide contains instructional guidance to be used by pre-trained congregate lodging facility and fallout shelter managers and by untrained but capable people who may be designated as facility or shelter managers when

an emergency situation develops. The concept of "habitability" is developed and integrated into the management of human problems. It refers to all those factors that influence the comfort, safety, general well-being, or behavior of people in facilities or shelters prior to, during, and (in some cases) following an emergency. This preventive approach to the management of human problems is intended to augment reactive capability.

■ #07644
Transportable Telecommunications for a Sur-

vivable Crisis Management System
Provides a nontechnical explanation of the concept of transportable telecommunications for a survivable crisis management system.

For copies of the preceding publications, or other information, FEMA may be contacted at the following address:

FEMA
P.O. Box 70274
Washington, DC 20024

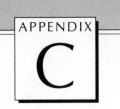

Sample Crisis Management Plan

As seen in the case of Arlington Plastics, most CMPs contain proprietary information and are rarely shared with the public. Although such diverse companies as General Electric, Gillette, and Land's End all confirm that they have such plans, they will not release them for review. One organization where confidential information is not a concern, and that was willing to share its CMP, is the Westside Community School District of Omaha, Nebraska. Their brief and insightful plan follows.

Westside Community Schools
Omaha, Nebraska

CRISIS COMMUNICATIONS PLAN
Guidelines for News Media Relations in Emergency Situations

This plan is intended to supplement other administrative procedures and guidelines for dealing with emergency situations. It should be reviewed on an annual basis, and should be distributed to all members of the District who could be affected.

Emergency Situations

It is always to the District's advantage to cooperate with news media, but never more so than during a crisis situation. Our schools are always open to public scrutiny, and that includes the media. But not all news is good news. But no news often has a far more negative effect on the public, so we will try to provide information in a timely fashion at all times. This plan is intended to be used in situations which, because of their scope or seriousness, become the focus of much media attention. The 1975 tornado is a case in point. The actual implementation of the plan should be determined by the size and nature of the emergency.

Situations can include:
- Serious accidents involving students or staff
- Acts of violence involving staff or students and/or non-district persons
- Natural disasters striking any district property
- Fires, explosions
- Strikes

Before an Emergency

- Designate an Emergency Communications Coordinator (ECC) and an alternate ECC. The Coordinator should not be directly involved in efforts to resolve the emergency situation itself, e.g., the superintendent, but should be someone who is familiar with working with the news media on a regular basis. (In most situations, the Director of Communications may be designated.) A back-up person should be selected to act when the ECC is unavailable. Technical or other experts may be designated as spokespersons as well. *All employees should know that the ECC, alternate, and designates are the only employees authorized to speak with the media.*

continued

- Members of the EC Team will hold organizational and review meetings.
- Select one primary and one or two secondary locations to be emergency newsrooms (point of assembly for reporters), apart from the area designed for dealing with the crisis itself. The room(s) designated should be able to accommodate news conferences, with multiple telephones, electrical outlets and typewriters, and even refreshments. (The Board Rooms of the ABC Building are obvious first choices. Other locations should be designated in the event that those rooms are made unaccessibly by the emergency.)
- News media identification badges should be made available for distribution by the ECC.
- A brief version of the plan should be distributed to all area news media.

During an Emergency

- The emergency should be reported at once to the superintendent who will inform the ECC, who will activate the plan. The ECC will inform the other members of the team of the nature of the emergency. The superintendent will notify the Board of Education members and keep them up-to-date on a timely basis (they may be sought out for interviews).
- Employees should refer all news media inquiries to the ECC. Reporters should be directed to the Emergency Newsroom. Reports will be issued at the newsroom. Interviews will be arranged and updates gathered by the ECC and EC team.
- All members of the team should be helpful and courteous at all times to the news media, but should refer all questions to the ECC. Depending on the situation, persons other than the ECC (e.g., the principal of the school where the emergency occurred) may be designated as spokespersons, and should then respond to all questions to the best of their ability. Answer honestly, but do not speculate or guess. If you don't know, say so ... then get the answer as soon as possible. Be prompt in your dealings with the media; they have pressing deadlines. Always call the media back when you say you will, usually immediately after you have gathered the facts. Don't use educational jargon. Do not speak "off the record." Do not ask to see the story before it is used. Always inform the ECC or Communications Department whenyou have talked with a reporter. This eliminates possible contradictory statements. Do not give "exclusives" to members of the media. All should have an equal chance for gathering information, which is a key reason for having a media center and news conferences.

continued

- The media should be provided with the following information:
  Facts—no speculation, and no cover-ups. In laymen's terms, tell the key facts who, what, when, where, why, and how:
  - What happened? When? And Where?
  - How and Why did it happen? (Do not speculate if you don't know; say so.)
  - Who was involved?
    Provide names only after next of kin have been notified of death or injury, and only according to the District's other policy on releasing confidential information.
  - Extent and nature of injuries, property damage (no dollar amounts), continuing damage, and insurance coverage.
- Photographers (and others) should not be allowed at the scene if there is still danger in the area, but should be allowed in when the immediate danger has passed. They should be provided with stills of the facilities from the Crisis Plan Preparedness file.
- Employees should be informed of the details of th situation as soon as possible, by the fastest means possible.
- Key community and political leaders should also be informed as soon as possible on an individual basis by designated personnel if the situation is serious enough to warrant it.

After the Emergency

- If the situation warrants it, make arrangements for the media to be personally escorted to the site.
- Arrange for other photographs if confidentiality prevents photographing the scene or people.
- Release to the news media, as soon as possible, company decisions relating to the incident, whenever it is deemed necessary. Where appropriate, express gratitude to the community, police and fire departments, emergency crews, and employees for their help. This places a positive ending on what could have been a negative story.
- The ECC or delegate should follow up by compiling a file of clippings, and a summary of how the Crisis Plan operated during the emergency, and what might improve the Plan. This should be accomplished within two weeks, while the information is fresh.

New Avenues in Disaster Planning: The UNLV Center for the Study of Crisis Management

To help prepare for a crisis in a more timely and effective manner, many organizations are using innovative management tools that focus on decision making during a business disaster. As you saw in Chapter 7, companies such as Shell Oil often hold "worst-case scenario" planning meetings where executives are briefed on a fictitious economic, political, or environmental disaster. Then they are asked to role-play and decide, for example, how to best deploy Shell resources in designated regions of the world.

Technology is playing an increasingly important role in disaster planning. At the University of Nevada, Las Vegas, the author directs the Center for the Study of Crisis Management. This facility, diagrammed on page 228, features advanced Macintosh technology that can project several simulated business disasters onto individual computer screens.

University students and visiting industrial managers utilize Center facilities to better understand the many complex issues that arise during a crisis. After a briefing on a particular disaster, each participant must decide how to respond to news reporters, nervous employees, government regulators, and others with a stake in the outcome. Then a series of important strategic decisions are posed; each response is recorded using Authorware® and later evaluated by teams of company representatives for the most accurate, timely, and complete managerial response.

The use of this technology in crisis planning can be invaluable. In a typical scenario session, each of some 20 managers in a room is pre-assigned a management role, usually one that does not parallel his or her actual position. In addressing several dozen critical questions during the computer-generated crisis, a significant amount of learning takes place. Managers leave the session with a broadened perspective of the issues and parties with which their colleagues must grapple, and they also understand the need for coordination of company response in the event of a disaster. For senior management, having the entire scenario video-recorded for later evaluation is equally valuable: they can identify gaps in their existing crisis plan and improve upon it.

The Center offers participants access to the UMI Database, which scans and prints copies of articles and/or abstracts that have appeared in some 800 business journals since 1983. In addition to a reference library on crisis and risk management issues, the Center is scheduled to dedicate a classroom for crisis seminar purposes. Each summer the Center hosts a national conference on crisis management that brings together scholars in the field of crisis and risk management. They are joined by CEOs, public affairs and public relations managers, and other corporate executives.

For more information on the Center for the Study of Crisis Management, please write to the author at the address shown in the preface.

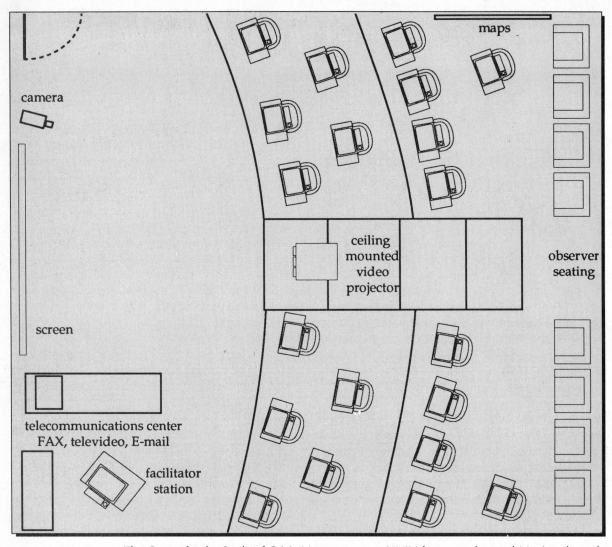

camera

screen

telecommunications center
FAX, televideo, E-mail

facilitator
station

maps

ceiling
mounted
video
projector

observer
seating

The Center for the Study of Crisis Management at UNLV features advanced Macintosh work stations where managers gain experience in crisis management by participating in computer-generated crises such as bomb threats and industrial accidents. Dr. Regan Carey and the author developed a program, using Authorware and Hypercard software packages, that allows managers to view how their colleagues are responding to different aspects of the crisis. They then make a series of important choices regarding the news media, regulators, consumers, insurance issues, and a myriad others. Initial funding for the Center has been provided by the U.S. Department of Energy.

BIBLIOGRAPHY

Readers interested in more detailed information on the subjects covered in this work may wish to consult the following articles, monographs, and books that span the subjects of crisis management, crisis communications, and organizations coping with chaos. Many of these articles were helpful in researching this book.

Environment

Badolato, Edward V. "Environmental Terrorism: A Case Study." Paper presented at the Symposium on Social and Psychological Profile of Terrorists, George Mason University, May 3, 1990.

Badolato, Edward V. "Vulnerability of the Oil and Gas Transportation and Storage System." Paper presented to the Joint Government-Industry Symposium on Transportation Security," March 21–22, 1990.

"Big Corporations Hit by Superfund Cases Find Way To Share Bill." *Wall Street Journal*, April 2, 1991, p. 1.

Carney, James, and Cramer, Jerome. "Who Knows How Many Will Die?" *Time*, April 29, 1991, p. 64.

"Environmentalism: The New Crusade." *Fortune*, February 12, 1990, pp. 44–54.

"Explosions Spew Toxic Cloud over City." *Las Vegas Review-Journal*, May 5, 1991, p. 16A.

"Fleeing the Love Canal." *Newsweek*, June 2, 1980, pp. 56–57.

"Huge Cost of Removing Asbestos Causing Concern on Campuses." *Chronicle of Higher Education*, December 7, 1988, p. 1.

"IFF Puts a Lid on Odors to Aid Community Relations." *Chemical Week*, November 4, 1987, pp. 61–65.

Kunreuther, Howard. "Problems and Issues of Environmental Liability Insurance." Geneva Papers on Risk and Insurance 12, (1987): 180–197.

"Love Canal Court Papers To Be Opened," *Wall Street Journal*, May 15, 1991, p. B5.

Manes, Christopher. *Green Rage: Radical Environmentalism and the Unmaking of Civilization*. Boston: Little, Brown, 1990.

Otway, Harry, and Cannell, William. "Risk Communication in Europe after Chernobyl: A Media Analysis of Seven Countries." *Industrial Crisis Quarterly* 2, (1988): 3–15.

Otway, Harry. *Communicating with the Public about Major Accident Hazards*. London: Elsevier, 1990.

"Pollution: Trying To Put the Best Face on Bad News." *Business Week*, July 18, 1988, p. 76.

"The Town of Dow." *Business Month*, December 1987, pp. 59–68.

"Toxic Chemical Disclosure." *Public Relations Journal*, January 1989, pp. 13–20.

"What Chernobyl Did." *The Economist*, April 27, 1991, pp. 19–21.

Sabotage

"Chicago's Poisoned Tylenol Scare." *Wall Street Journal*, November 29, 1989, p. B1.

Glorioso, John E., and Mattocks, Gerald B., Jr. "Teaming Up Against Crises." *Security Management*, October 1989, pp. 49-52.

"Sudafed Capsules Examined." *Las Vegas Review-Journal*, March 6, 1991, p. 8A.

"Sudafed Capsules Recalled; At Least 2 People Die." *USA Today*, March 4, 1991, p. 1.

"Sudafed Maker Faulted for Failing To Follow Through after Recall." *Wall Street Journal*, March 11, 1991, p. 16.

"Sudafed's the Last Thing to Be Afraid of," *Wall Street Journal*, March 13, 1991, p. 19.

Terrorism

Alali, A. Odasuo, and Eke, Kenoye Kelvin. *Media Coverage of Terrorism* . Newbury Park, CA: Sage Publications, 1991.

Badolato, Edward V., and Snyder, Rodney. "The Future of Terrorism." *Counterterrorism and Security,* March–April 1991, pp. 26–32.

"Business Copes with Terrorism." *Fortune,* January 6, 1986, pp. 47–55.

"Coping with the Fear of Terror." *Fortune,* May 26, 1986, pp. 57–59.

"Ex-Marine Provides Security to Vital U.S. Energy System." *Insight,* April 10, 1989, pp. 16–17.

Glorioso, John E., and Mattocks, Gerald B., Jr. "Teaming Up Against Crises." *Security Management,* October 1989, pp. 49–50.

Greenwald, Judy. "Global Firms Must Cope with Terrorism." *Business Insurance,* May 14, 1990, p. 48.

"Hijacking Raises New Questions on Los Angeles Airport's Security." *New York Times,* May 30, 1989, p. A19.

Hoffman, David. "A Week of Crisis Management" (Middle East hostages). *Washington Post,* August 6, 1989, pp. 1–27.

"How to Cope With Bomb Threats in the Mailroom," The Office, Vol. 104, No.4, October 1986, 54–85.

Littlejohn, Robert E. "When the Crisis Is Terrorism." *Security Management,* August 1986, pp. 38–41.

Maddox, Robert C. "Terrorism's Hidden Threat and the Promise for Multinational Corporations." *Business Horizons,* November–December 1990, pp. 48–51.

"The New and Growing Management Problem of Terrorism." *IM,* May–June 1987, pp. 2–3.

Nudell, Mayer, and Antokol, Norman. "Contingency Planning for Terrorism: Part 2." *Risk Management,* August 1986, pp. 30–36.

Pattakos, Arion, CPP. "Trends in Terrorism: The Experts Comment." *Security Management,* October 1985, pp. 121–122.

"Terrorism on High Street." *Management Today,* January 1990, pp. 36–59.

Vance, Charles F. "When Trouble Strikes." *Security Management,* January 1988, pp. 27–29.

General Crisis Management

Bennett, Steven J., and Snell, Michael. *Executive Chess: Creative Problem-Solving by 45 of America's Top Business Leaders and Thinkers.* New York: NAL Penguin, 1987.

Bernstein, Jonathan. "The Ten Steps of Crisis Management." *Security Management,* March 1990, pp. 75–76.

Charles, Michael T., and Kim, John Choon K. *Crisis Management: A Casebook,* New York: C.C. Thomas, 1988.

"Coping with a Corporate Crisis." *Canadian Business Review,* Autumn 1986, pp. 17–20.

"Crisis Management: Looking for the Warning Signs." *Management Solutions,* January 1987, pp. 5–10.

Feinberg, Mortimer, and Serlen, Bruce. "Crash Course in Crisis Management." *Working Woman,* January 1987, pp. 24–28.

Fink, Steven B. "When The Crisis Hits." *Chief Executive,* Winter 1986–1987, pp. 34–36.

Hartley, Robert F. *Management Mistakes and Successes,* 3rd ed. New York: Wiley, 1991.

Herman, Martin B. "How To Survive a Strike." *Security Management,* September 1990, pp. 145–147.

"How To Safeguard Your Reputation in a Crisis." Paper presented by Roger Mountford and Anne Forest to IIR Public Relations Seminar, March 3, 1989.

James, Ralph C. *Hoffa and the Teamsters: A Study of Union Power.* New York: VanNostrand, 1965.

Janis, Irving L. "Problems of International Crisis Management in the Nuclear Age." *Journal of Social Issues* 42 (1986): 201–220.

Jenkins, John. A. *The Litigators: Inside the Powerful World of America's High-Stakes Trial Lawyers.* New York: St. Martin's, 1989.

Lerbinger, Otto. Managing Corporate Crises: Strategies for Executives. Boston: Barringer Press, 1986.

Littlejohn, Robert F. *Crisis Management: A Team Approach.* New York: AMACON Books (American Management Association, Publications Division), 1983.

Marcus, Alfred. "The Deterrent to Dubious Corporate Behavior: Profitability, Probability and Safety Recalls." *Strategic Management Journal* 10 (1989): 233–250.

Meyers, Gerald. *When It Hits the Fan—Managing the Nine Crises of Business.* Boston: Houghton Mifflin, 1986.

Mitchell, Michael. "Crisis Management: Handling Public Relations in a Disaster." *Professional Safety,* January, 1987, pp. 28–31.

Mitroff, Ian, and Pauchant, Thierry. *We're So Big and Powerful Nothing Bad Can Happen to Us.* New York: Carol Publishing, 1990.

Mitroff, Ian I., Shrivastava, Paul, and Udwadia, Firdaus E. "Effective Crisis Management." *Academy of Management Executives,* November 1987, pp. 283–292.

Mitroff, Ian I., Pauchant, Terry C., and Shrivastava, Paul. "Crisis, Disaster, Catastrophe: Are You Ready?" *Security Management,* February, 1989, pp. 101–108.

Mitroff, Ian. "Teaching Corporate America To Think About Crisis Prevention." *Journal of Business Strategy* 6 (1986): 40–47.

Muller, Rainer. "Corporate Crisis Management." *Long Range Planning,* October 1985, pp. 38–48.

Nelkin, Dorothy. "Risk Reporting and the Management of Industrial Crises." *Journal of Management Studies* 25 (1988): 341–351.

Nelson-Horschler, Joani. "We Were Wrong: Acts of Contrition Brighten a Company's Tarnished Image." *Industry Week,* April 16, 1990, pp. 20–25.

Nudell, Mayer, and Antokol, Norman. *The Handbook for Effective Emergency and Crisis Management.* Lexington, MA: Lexington Books, 1988.

Nudell, Mayer, and Antokol, Norman. "Before the Going Gets Rough." *Security Management,* March 1988, pp. 49–51.

Nudell, Mayer, and Antokol, Norman. "Crisis-Free Crisis Management." *Risk Management,* April 1989, pp. 31–34.

Oates, Martha. "Responding to Death in the Schools." *TACD Journal,* Fall 1988, pp. 83–96.

Pinsdorf, Marion K. *Communicating When Your Company Is under Siege.* Lexington, MA: Lexington Books, 1987.

Reilly, Anne H. "An Organization Ready for Crisis? A Managerial Scorecard." *Columbia Journal of World Business,* Spring 1987, pp. 79–88.

Rosenthal, Uriel, Charles, Michael T., and Hart, Paul T., eds. *Coping with Crisis: The Management of Disasters, Riots and Terrorism.* New York: Charles C. Thomas, 1989.

Shrivastava, Paul, and Mitroff, Ian. "Strategic Management of Corporate Crises." *Columbia Journal of World Business,* Spring 1987, pp. 5–11.

Stack, Jack. "Crisis Management by Committee," *Inc. Magazine,* May 1988, p. 26.

Weick, Karl E. "Enacted Sensemaking in Crisis Situations." *Journal of Management Studies,* July 1988, pp. 305–317.

Natural and Other Disasters

Badolato, Edward L., Bleiweis, Julius, Craig, Julie, and Fleming, Horace, Jr. "Hurricane Hugo: Lessons Learned in Energy Emergency Preparedness, Executive Summary." Paper presented to the Strom Thurmond Institute of Government and Public Affairs at Clemson University, February 1990.

Bresnick, Alan. "When the Event Is a Natural Disaster." *Adweek,* June 17, 1986, p. 10.

Brown, Donna. "A Tale of Two Cities." *Management Review,* February 1990, pp. 31–35.

Lukaszewski, James E. "Corporate and Private Sector Communications Responsibility: Transborder Disaster Situations." *Vital Speeches of the Day,* March 1, 1987, pp. 305–310.

Quarantelli, E. L. "Disaster Crisis Management: A Summary of Research Findings." *Journal of Management Studies,* July 1988, pp. 373–385.

Rosenthal, Uriel, Charles, Michael T., and Hart, Paul T., eds. *Coping with Crises: The Management of Disasters, Riots and Terrorism.* New York: C.C. Thomas, 1989.

Shrivastava, Paul, and Siomkos, George. "Disaster Containment Strategies." *Journal of Business Strategy,* September–October 1989, pp. 26–30.

St. Clair, Scott T. "How Hugo Hit Charleston." *Security Management,* August 1990, pp. 73–75.

Toubiana, Josef H. "Crisis Intervention in a School Community Disaster: Principles and Practices." *Journal of Community Psychology* 16 (April 1988): 228–240.

Financial and Insurance Crisis Management

"Bank Security Today: Surprise Package and Close Up on Fraud." Booklets and video series for banks. Bank Administration Institute, Rolling Meadows, Minnesota, 1989.

Boyce, Brian. "The Brink's Bullion Robbery: A Study on Money Laundering Operations." *The World of Banking,* September–October 1990, pp. 8–9.

Braverman, Mark. "Post-Robbery Damage Control: The Human Factor." *Bottomline,* March–April 1991, pp. 23–25.

Buccino, Gerald P. "Crisis Management, as Tricky As 1, 2, 3." *The Secured Lender,* November–December 1986, pp. 67–78.

Buccino, Gerald P. "Crisis Management: Dealing with the Organization." *The Secured Lender,* May–June 1988, pp. 34–69.

"Clutch Management in a Crisis," *Risk Management,* April 1988, pp. 72–74.

"Crisis Management: How Commercial Credit Handled the Ohio S&L Crisis." *Credit Magazine,* March–April 1986, pp. 10–12.

"Crisis Plans Ease Corporate Disasters." *Business Insurance,* May 14, 1990, p. 24.

"Crisis Plans Ensure Companies' Future." *Business Insurance,* May 28, 1990, p. 39.

Dunkin, Michael. "Crisis Communication. " *Credit Union Management,* March 1990, pp. 12–13.

Hammonds, Keith, and Friedman, Jon. "Dean Wittter Braces for a Backlash in Boston." *Business Week,* March 6, 1989, p. 86.

"How Risk Managers Cope with Political Risk." *National Underwriter,* June 27, 1986, pp. 3–4.

Jaben, Jan. "When Disaster Strikes." *United States Banker,* July 1986, pp. 52–58.

Kessler, Karen. "Communicating in the Eye of the Crash." *IABC Communication World,* March 1988, pp. 28–29.

Marcus, Alfred. "Corporate Adjustments to Catastrophe: A Study of Investor Reaction to Bhopal." *Industrial Crisis Quarterly* 3 (1989): pp. 213–234.

Marcus, Alfred, Bromley, Philip, and Goodman, Robert. "Preventing Corporate Crises: Stock Market Losses as a Deterrent to the Production of Hazardous Products." *Columbia Journal of World Business,* Spring 1987, pp. 33–42.

Marcus, Alfred A., and Goodman, Robert. "Victims and Shareholders: The Dilemmas of Presenting Corporate Policy During a Crisis." *Academy of Management Journal* 34 (1991): 281–305.

Miller, Danny. *The Icarus Paradox: How Excellent Companies Bring About Their Own Downfall.* New York: Harper Business, 1990.

"Public Relations Didn't Hurt Bank, Management Did." *Boston Globe,* March 26, 1985, p. 68.

Rosenthal, Beth Elyn. "PR Nightmare Stuns Texas Bank." *IABC Communication World,* September 1988, pp. 40–41.

Sayles, Michael C. "When It Hits the Fan." *CLU,* April 1990, pp. 16–17.

Soper, Richard H. "Foresight Must Be 20/20 When Creating a Crisis Management Program." *Risk Management,* September 1989, pp. 38–40.

Sutton, Robert. "The Stigma of Bankruptcy: Spoiled Organizational Image and Its Management." *Academy of Management Journal* 30 (1987): 542–69.

"Three Fire Losses May Top $500 Million." *Business Insurance,* May 9, 1988, p. 1.

"What Should We Tell the Press?" *ABA Banking Journal,* July 1987, p. 58.

Industrial Accidents and Crises

Addis, Karen K. "The Night the Lights Went Out in San Francisco." *Security Management,* February 1990, pp. 26–3

Ansberry, Clare. "Oil Spill in the Midwest Provides Case Study in Crisis Management." *Wall Street Journal,* January 8, 1988, p. 23.

"Beating Victim King Depressed, Scared." *Las Vegas Review-Journal,* April 15, 1991, p. 10B.

"Bridge Building in the Kanawha Valley." *Chemical Week,* March 25, 1989, pp. 2223.

Charlier, Marj. "Adolph Coors Has Spill into Creek of at Least 150,000 Gallons of Beer." *Wall Street Journal,* May 13, 1991, p. A9.

"Crisis Management: A New Twist on Teamwork." *Dow Corning World, Third Quarter Review,* 1989, pp. 11–15.

Geyelin, Milo. "Dalkon Shield Trust, Hailed as Innovative, Stirs a Lot of Discord." *Wall Street Journal,* June 3, 1991, p. 1

"How Toxic Shock Galvanized a Market." *Business Week,* April 15, 1985, p. 90.

Jackson, Ron. "Prevention's the Backbone in the Anatomy of a Recall." *Marketing News,* August 6, 1990, p. 10.

Jacobs, Bruce A. "Beating Back a Crisis." *Industry Week,* March 23, 1987, pp. 93–96.

Kabak, Irwin, and Siomkos, George. "How Can an Industrial Crisis Be Managed Effectively?" *Industrial Engineer,* June 1990, pp. 18–21.

Kelly, Kevin, and Weber, Joseph. "When a Rival's Trade Secret Crosses Your Desk." *Business Week,* May 20, 1991, p. 48.

McCarthy, Michael J. "MagiCan'ts: How Coca-Cola Stumbled." *Wall Street Journal,* June 4, 1990, p. B1.

Mitroff, Ian. "The Complete and Utter Failure of Traditional Thinking in Comprehending the Nuclear Predicament—Why It's Impossible To Formulate a Paradox-Free Theory of Nuclear Policy." *Technological Forecasting and Social Change* 29 (1986): 51–72.

"Now Comes the Fallout: The White House and Congress Reappraise Nuclear Safety." *Time,* April 16, 1979, pp. 22–26.

"Organizational Design for Hazardous Chemical Accidents: A Public Inquiry into a Major Industrial Accident." *Columbia Journal of World Business* 22 (1987): 51–58.

Rodgers, Warren. "My Terrible Vacation," *Inc. Magazine,* February 1988, pp. 116–117.

Simurda, Stephen J. "Starting Over From Ground Zero." *Family Business,* June 1990, pp. 18–23.

Starks, Roy M., Jr. "Preparation: The Key to Crisis Control." *Chemical Engineering,* June 1989, pp. 171–174.

"Videotape of Beating by Officers puts Full Glare on Brutality Issue." *New York Times,* March 18, 1991, p. 1.

White, Tom. "Nerve Gas Controversy: While Cambridge and Arthur D. Little Argue in Court, Protesters Demand Answers." *The Arlington (MA) Advocate,* December 6, 1984, p. 1.

The *Challenger* Shuttle Disaster

Moffett, Matt, and McGinley, Laurie. "NASA, Once a Master of Publicity, Fumbles in Handling Shuttle Crisis." *Wall Street Journal,* December 14, 1986, p. 22.

"Morton Thiokol: Reflections on the Shuttle Disaster." *Business Week,* March 14, 1988, pp. 82–91.

"NASA's Troubled Flight Plan." *Newsweek,* February 10, 1986, p. 35.

"Report to the President: Actions to Implement the Recommendations of the Presidential Commission on the Space Shuttle *Challenger* Accident." NASA, Washington, DC, July 14, 1986.

Schwartz, Howard. "On the Psychodynamics of Organizational Disaster: The Case of the Space Shuttle Disaster." *Columbia Journal of World Business* 22 (1987): pp. 5967.

Starbuck, William H., and Milliken, Frances J. "Challenger: Fine-Tuning the Odds until Something Breaks." *Journal of Management Sciences,* July 1988, pp. 319–340.

"What Went Wrong? Zeroing In on a Faulty Booster—and a Devastating Blowtorch Effect." *Newsweek,* February 10, 1986, pp. 33–34.

Crisis Management Planning

Braverman, Mark. "Can Firms Afford Not To Have Crisis Intervention?" *Boston Business Journal,* January 29, 1990, p. 26

Friedman, Raymond J., M.D. et al. "Early Response to Posttraumatic Stress." *EAP Digest,* October 1988, pp. 45- 49.

Hales, Thomas, M.D. et al. "Occupational Injuries Due to Violence." *Journal of Occupational Medicine* 30 (June 1988): 483–487.

"Planning for the Worst: Crisis Planning." *Management Review,* August 1988, pp. 7–8.

"Why Crisis Management Plans Are Essential." *Los Angeles Times,* December 29, 1989, p. D3.

Public Relations and Crisis Management

Ansberry, Clare. "Forgive or Forget: Firms Face Decision Whether to Apologize for Their Mistakes." *Wall Street Journal,* November 24, 1987, p. B1.

Calbreath, Dean. "In a Crisis, These Are the Guys To Turn to." *Washington Business Journal,* October 22, 1990, p. 1.

Cooper, Michael. "Planning the Big Media Event." *Public Relations Journal,* July 1983, pp. 13–15.

"Crisis Management: Handling Public Relations in a Disaster." *Professional Safety,* January 1987, pp. 28–31.

D'Aveni, Richard. "Crisis and the Content of Managerial Communications: A Study of the Focus of Attention of Top Managers in Surviving and Failing Firms." *Administrative Science Quarterly* 35 (1989): 634–657.

Dilenschneider, Robert L., and Forrestal, Dan J. *Public Relations Handbook.* Chicago: Dartnell, 1987.

Feucht, Frederic N. "It's Symbolic: Is Your Corporate Logo Sending the Right Message to the Right People?" *American Demographics,* November 1989, pp. 30–33.

Fisher, Lynn, and Briggs, William. "Communicating with Employees During a Time of Tragedy." *Communication World,* February 1989, pp. 32–35.

Fishman, Donald A. "Public Relations and Point-Shaving: The Anatomy of a PR Crisis." Academic package, Boston College Department of Speech Communication, May 1981.

Guzzardi, Walter, Jr. "How Much Should Companies Talk?" *Fortune,* March 4, 1985, pp. 64–68.

Hammer, Joshua. "Calling Mr. Crisis Control." *Newsweek,* October 22, 1990, p. 54.

"How Corporations Are Learning to Prepare for the Worst." Business Week, December 23, 1985, pp. 74–76.

Lagadec, Patrick. "Communications Strategies in Crisis." *Industrial Science Quarterly* 1(1987): 1926.

Leary, Dennis P. "Crisis Communications: A Planning Check-List." *Credit,* March–April 1988, p. 13.

McCue, Lisa J. "Averting PR Disasters: Smart Managers Have Contingency Plans." *Bottomline* 3 (July 1986): 15–20.

Plummer, Diane M. "Crisis Communication." Cadbury Schweppes Ltd., Paper presented to IABC London Conference, July 16, 1987.

"PR Firm's Disaster Plan for Clorox Springs Leak." *Las Vegas Review-Journal,* May 13, 1991, p. 3A.

Reinhardt, Claudia. "How to Handle a Crisis." *Public Relations Journal,* November 1987, pp. 43–47.

Runenstone, Catherine. "How to Ace a TV Interview." *Working Woman,* November 1986, p. 75.

"Trouble on the Team: A Foreign Policy Power Play Leads to Talk of Haig's Resignation." *Time,* April 6, 1981, pp. 8–11.

"Who's Minding the Store?" *Newsweek,* April 13, 1981, pp. 39–40.

Wilson, Steve. "When the News Hits the Fan." *Business Marketing,* November 1987, pp. 92–94.

Union Carbide/Bhopal Crisis

"A Backlash Is Threatening Chemical Makers." *Business Week,* December 24, 1984, pp. 50–51.

Bowander, B. "The Bhopal Accident." *Technological Forecasting and Social Changes* 32 (1990): 169–182.

"Calming the Public Fears: It's Up to the Chemical Makers." *Business Week,* August 26, 1985, p. 33.

"Carbide Chief Called Candid and Humane." *Boston Sunday Globe,* December 9, 1984, p. 26.

"Gas Fears Cause New Panic in India City." *Boston Herald,* December 15, 1984, p. 4.

Hall, Alan. "The Bhopal Tragedy Has Union Carbide Reeling." *Business Week,* December 17, 1984, p. 32.

Helm, Leslie et al. "Bhopal, a Year Later: Union Carbide Takes a Tougher Line." *Business Week,* November 25, 1985, pp. 96–101.

Jackson, Stuart. "Union Carbide's Good Name Takes a Beating." *Business Week,* December 31, 1984, p. 40.

Kirkland, Richard J., Jr. "Union Carbide: Coping With Catastrophe." *Fortune,* January 7, 1985, pp. 50–53.

Kunreuther, Howard. "Post-Bhopal Behavior at a Chemical Company." *Journal of Management Science* 25 (1988): 387–403.

"Rumors Stir Panic in India." *Boston Globe,* December 12, 1984, p. B1.

Shrivastava, Paul. *Bhopal: Anatomy of a Crisis.* Cambridge, MA: Ballinger, 1987.

"Union Carbide Fights for Its Life." *Business Week,* December 24, 1984, pp. 52–56.

Perrier and the Benzene Crisis

Lander, Mark, and Driscoll, Lisa. "You Can Lead a Restaurateur to Perrier, But . . ." *Business Week,* June 25, 1990, pp. 25–26.

"Perrier Battling Back One Year After Recall." February 18, 1991, p. 29.

"Perrier Expands North American Recall to Rest of Globe." *Wall Street Journal,* February 15, 1989, p. B1.

"Perrier's Recall Drives Down Its Stock Price." *Wall Street Journal*, February 12, 1990, p. B2.

"Perrier's Strategy in the Wake of Recall: Will It Leave Brand in Rough Waters?" *Wall Street Journal*, February 12, 1990, p. B1.

Toy, Stewart, and Driscoll, Lisa. "Can Perrier Purify Its Reputation?" *Business Week*, February 26, 1990, p. 45.

The *Exxon Valdez* Crisis

"The Alaskan Oil Spill: Lessons in Crisis Management." *Management Review*, April 1990, pp. 9–21.

"Exxon Settlement Won't Heal Scars on Alaskan Coast." *Las Vegas Review-Journal*, March 24, 1991, p. 6A.

"Exxon's Future: What Has Larry Rawl Wrought?" *Business Week*, April 2, 1990, pp. 72–76.

"The Exxon Valdez's Insidious Legacy." *Washington Post*, national weekly edition, March 4–10, 1991, p. 33.

Gilson, Tom. "Impacts of an Environmental Disaster on a Small Local Government: The Valdez, Alaska Oil Spill." *Government Finance Review*, June 1989, pp. 27–29.

Holusha, John. "Exxon's Public Relations Problem." *New York Times*, April 20, 1989, p. B1.

Newman, Lloyd N. "Exxon's Lessons for Other Managers." *Business and Economic Review*, July–September 1989, pp. 8–10.

Olive, David. "In The Wake of the Exxon Valdez." *Management Ethics*, Summer 1989, pp. 48–49.

Ashland Oil Crisis

Ansberry, Clare. "Oil Spill in the Midwest Provides Case Study of Crisis Management." *Wall Street Journal*, January 8, 1988, p. 21.

"Ashland Responded with Responsibility to Crisis Caused by Diesel Oil Spill." *The Oil Daily*, February 10, 1988, p. 4.

Smith, Gene. "Ashland Oil Getting High Marks for Handling of Diesel Oil Spill." *The Oil Daily*, January 25, 1988, pp. 11–12.

Stricharchuk, Gregory, and Green, Wayne E. "Ashland Oil Ordered To Pay $10.3 Million." *Wall Street Journal*, June 1, 1990, p. 87.

Stricharchuk, Gregory, and Green, Wayne E. "Ashland Ordered To Pay Damages for Discharge from Oil Refinery." *Wall Street Journal*, June 1, 1990, p. B4.

Widner, Melissa. "Ashland Grades Out High for Oil Crisis Handling." *MidAmerican Outlook*, Spring 1988, pp. 8–9.

Individual Crises

"AT&T Bares Its Teeth; It Says It Will Make a Hostile Bid for Balky NCR." *Business Week*, December 17, 1990, pp. 24–26.

Beveridge, Dirk. "AT&T, NCR Reach Merger Agreement." *Las Vegas Review-Journal*, May 7, 1991, pp. 1F–2F.

Carton, Barbara. "In Case of Catastrophe." *Boston Globe*, March 26, 1989, p. A5.

"Cleared for Takeoff: United Cuts a Deal with Pan Am—And Lays a Gutsy Bet on Global Growth." *Business Week*, November 5, 1990, pp. 46–49.

Donlan, Thomas G. "Still a Lousy Idea: The Odometer Imbroglio Haunts Chrysler." *Barron's*, March 6, 1990, pp. 24–25.

Freedman, Alex M. "Rumor Turns Fantasy into Bad Dream." *Wall Street Journal*, May 10, 1991, pp. B1, B4.

Gantz, John. "AT&T, NCR Alliance May Never Celebrate the Honeymoon." *Infoworld*, December 17, 1990, p. 41.

Hall, Carla. "Milli Vanilli's Mega-Hit Meltdown." *Washington Post*, November 17, 1990, p. D1.

Hammer, Joshua, and Rosenberg, Debra. "Fear in the Back Room: Charges of Extortion at Cumberland Farms." September 24, 1990, p. 64.

Leon, Mitchell. "Tylenol Fights Back." *Public Relations Journal*, March 1983, pp. 10–14.

Mehegan, David. "A Search for Answers in a Daughter's Death." *Boston Globe* Magazine, September 16, 1984, pp. 22–28.

"P&G Rubs in Rumor Suit." *Wall Street Journal*, March 20, 1991, p. D4.

Shrager, Carl A. "Three Strikes and You're Out—Why the UAL Employee Buyout Failed." *Corporate Growth Report*, October 1990, pp. 17–18.

Sutton, Robert. "Managing Organizational Decline: Lessons From Atari." *Organizational Dynamics* 14 (1986): 17–29.

Toubiana, Josef H. et al. "Crisis Intervention in a School Community Disaster: Principles and Practices." *Journal of Community Psychology*, April 1988, pp. 228–240.

Trow, George W. S. "A Reporter at Large: Devastation." *The New Yorker*, October 22, 1990, pp. 54–79.

Travel and Tourism Industries

"Bomb on 1988 Flight Was a Transferred Bag, Investigator Says." *Washington Post*, March 25, 1991, p. C16.

"Bomb Safely Disarmed at Tahoe Casino." *Las Vegas Review-Journal*, February 3, 1991, p. 8B.

Brewton, Charles. "Managing a Crisis: A Model for the Lodging Industry." *Cornell Hotel and Restaurant Administration Quarterly*, November 1987, pp. 10–15.

"Crisis Management: Sobering Thoughts." *Marketing* (UK), November 10, 1988, pp. 30–31.

Davidson, Wallace. "Large Losses, Risk Management and Stock Returns in the Airlines Industry." *Journal of Risk and Insurance* 54 (1987): 162–172.

"Death Trap in Kansas City." *Newsweek*, July 27, 1981, pp. 30–31.

Gomez, Herman. "Cruise Ship Security Stays Afloat." *Security Management*, April 1988, pp. 50–55.

Higgins, Richard. "Jet Skids into Water at Logan." *Boston Sunday Globe*, January 24, 1982, p. 1.

Higgins, Richard, and Fox, Wendy. "World Airways Flight 30: Now Two Are Missing." *Boston Sunday Globe*, January 27, 1982, p. 1.

Lehman, Celia Kuperszmid. "When Fact and Fantasy Collide: Crisis Management in the Travel Industry." *Public Relations Journal*, April 1986, pp. 25–28.

Mildon, Lloyd. "Porpoisiningh—What Does That Mean? The Lack of Media Education at the Sioux City Crash of United Flight 232 Created Confusion and Misunderstanding." *IABC Communication World*, December 1989, p. 54.

Nash, Tom. "Nightmare in Cologne." *Director* (UK), October 1990, pp. 77–82.

"On a Wing and a Prayer." *CFO: The Magazine for Chief Financial Officers*, November 1990, pp. 32–40.

Sawyer, Judith H. "When Crisis Strikes: How Do You Avert Disaster—Or Cope with It—At Your Meetings?" *Successful Meetings*, September 1989, pp. 64–78.

Stolberg, Sheryl, and Lieberman, Paul. "Crisis Management: Fatal Collision at LAX Becomes a Public Relations Nightmare for SkyWest, USAir Officials." *Los Angeles Times*, February 1, 1991, p. B1.

Individuals Coping with Crisis: Profiles

Cohen, Daniel. "Bill McGowan: To the Edge and Back." *Business Week*, March 4, 1991, pp. 46–49.

Fins, Antonio N. "This Bogey Has Arnie's Name on It." *Business Week*, March 4, 1991, p. 28.

French, Desiree. "Boston's Crisis Psychologists." *Boston Globe*, August 22, 1989, p. 41.

Heller, Robert. *The Decision Makers: The Men and the Million-Dollar Moves Behind Today's Great Corporate Success Stories*. New York: Truman Valley Books/Plume, 1989.

"He's an Asset When Crisis Hits." *Las Vegas Review-Journal*, February 18, 1991, p. B1.

Johnson, Robert. "The CEO Vanishes, Leaving a Company Besieged, Perplexed." *Wall Street Journal*, March 15, 1991, p. 1.

"Los Angeles Police Chief Taunted at Hearing; U.S. Plans Wide Inquiry on Brutality." *New York Times*, March 15, 1991, p. A10.

McGreevy, Brian. "Trauma Victims Learn To Cope with Emotional Scars." *Atlanta Constitution*, August 9, 1990, p. K3.

"Press Wears Out a Hero's Welcome Mat." *Washington Journalism Review*, May, 1982, pp. 10–11.

Smith, Geoffrey, and Driscoll, Lisa. "Victor Kiam, the Self-Sacking Quarterback." *Business Week*, February 25, 1991, p. 46

Stuller, Jay. "When The Crisis Doctor Calls." *Across the Board* 25 (May 1988): 45–51.

Crisis from a Historical Perspective

Abel, Elie. *The Missile Crisis*. New York: Bantam Books, 1966.

Allison, Graham T. *Essence of Decision: Explaining The Cuban Missile Crisis*. Boston: Little, Brown, 1971.

Blaisdell, Thomas C., and Selz, Peter, eds. *The American Presidency in Political Cartoons, 1776-1976.* Salt Lake City: Peregrine Smith, 1976.

Brightman, Harvey J. "Crisis! Managerial Lessons from Pearl Harbor." *Business,* January–March 1989, pp. 3–10.

Fussell, Paul. *The Great War and Modern Memory.* Oxford, England: Oxford University Press, 1975.

Halberstam, David. *The Powers That Be.* New York: Knopf, 1979

Herzstein, Robert Edwin. *The War That Hitler Won.* New York: Putnam, 1978.

Kaplan, Justin. *Lincoln Steffens, An Autobiography.* New York: Touchstone Books, 1974.

Kearns, Doris. *Lyndon Johnson and the American Dream.* New York: Harper & Row, 1976.

Kendrick, Alexander. *Prime Time: The Life of Edward R. Murrow.* Boston: Little, Brown, 1969.

Manchester, William. *The Last Lion: Winston Spencer Churchill Alone, 1932–1940.* Little, Brown, 1988.

Sperber, Ann M. *Murrow: His Life and Times.* New York: Freundlich Books, 1986.

Tebbel, John. *The Media in America.* New York: Crowell, 1974.

Crisis Management Theory

Fink, Stephen. "Crisis Forecasting: What's the Worst That Could Happen?" *Management Review,* 1986, pp. 53–56.

Gladwin, Thomas N., and Kumar, Rajesh. "The Social Psychology of Crisis Bargaining: Toward a Contingency Model." *Columbia Journal of World Business,* Spring 1987, pp. 23–31.

Janis, Irving L. "Problems of International Crisis Management in the Nuclear Age." *Journal of Social Issues,* Summer 1986, pp. 201–220.

Kuklan, Hooshang. "Managing Crises: Challenges and Complexities." *SAM Advanced Management Journal,* Autumn 1986, pp. 39–44.

Mintzberg, Henry. "The Strategy Concept II: Another Look at Why Organizations Need Strategies." *California Management Review,* Fall 1987, pp. 25–32.

Mitroff, Ian I., Shrivastava, Paul, and Udwadia, Firdaus E. "Effective Crisis Management." *Academy of Management Executive* 1 (1987): 283-292.

Ramee, John. "Crisis Management: Looking for the Warning Signs." *Management Solutions* 32 (January 1987): 5–10.

Weich, Karl E. "Enacted Sensemaking in Crisis Situations." *Journal of Management Studies* (UK), July 1988, pp. 305–317.

Wisenbilt, Joseph Z. "Crisis Management Planning among U.S. Corporations: Empirical Evidence and a Proposed Framework." *Advanced Management Journal,* Spring 1989, pp. 31–41.

Real Estate and Community Crises

DeGeorge, Gail. "Disney Is Souring Its Neighbors." *Business Week,* August 8, 1988, pp. 48–49.

"From Collapses to Corruption: Managing Company Crises." *ENR,* February 11, 1988, pp. 28–37.

Hornblower, Margot. "Not in My Backyard, You Don't." *Time,* June 27, 1988, pp. 44–45.

Hurt, Harry, III. "Donald Trump Move Over." *Newsweek,* February 5, 1990, p. 43.

Lee, Cynthia. "(Bob) Hope Deflects Pleas To Sell or Donate Land." *Las Vegas Sun,* February 26, 1990, p. 32.

Mickadelt, Frank. "Battle Threatened in Sam Clemente over Seaside Village Plan." *Orange County Register,* April 9, 1990, p. B8.

Pell, Eve. "The High Cost of Speaking Out." *California Magazine,* November 1988, pp. 88–146.

Stevenson, Richard. "Debate Grows on Development Fees." *New York Times,* February 16, 1989, p. B1.

The Persian Gulf Crisis: Managing a War

Dowd, Ann Reilly. "George Bush as Crisis Manager." *Fortune,* September 10, 1990, p. 55.

Duffy, Brian. "The 100-Hour War." *U.S. News & World Report,* March 11, 1991, pp. 11–22.

Duffy, Brian et al. "Desert Storm." *U.S. News & World Report,* January 28, 1991, pp. 20–22.

Gergen, David. "The President's Finest Hour." *U.S. News & World Report,* March 4, 1991, p. 64.

"Global Fallout: The Iraq Mess Will Clobber World Economies." *Business Week*, September 10, 1990, pp. 30–31.

Harbrecht, Douglas et al. "Managing the War." *Business Week*, February 4, 1991, pp. 34–37.

Hazelton, Jared. "The Iraqi Oil Crisis and Texas." *Texas Banking*, September 1990, p. 20.

Hymowitz, Carol. "Companies Make Plans for Emergencies." *Wall Street Journal*, January 24, 1991, p. B1.

Johnson, Robert. "Crisis Management: FMC Moves To Keep Clients Like the Army Supplied During War." February 11, 1991, pp. 1–6.

Konrad, Walecia, and Hawkins, Chuck. "The Scoop on CNN's Bottom Line." *Business Week*, February 4, 1991, pp. 70–71.

Kowet, Don. "Instant Journalists in Time of Crisis: With All the Big News in the Middle East, Plenty of People Are Getting into the Act of Trying to Report It." *Insight*, October 15, 1990, pp. 46–48.

Lander, Mark. "Publicity? Why, It Never Even Occurred to Us: Companies Are Vying To Donate Products to the Troops." *Business Week*, September 24, 1990, p. 46.

Miller, Michael, and Carrol, Paul. "The Gulf War Gives Computer Buffs Use for Their Machines." *Wall Street Journal*, February 25, 1991, pp. 1–5.

Nelson, Milo. "Desert Fox No Match for Desert Fax." *Information Today*, November 1990, pp. 35–36.

Pennar, Karen et al. "The Toll That War Could Take on the Economy." *Business Week*, January 28, 1991, pp. 32–33.

Peterson, John. "Europe and the Crisis in the Gulf." *Europe*, November 1987, pp. 24–27.

"Reactions to War." *Business Insurance*, January 21, 1991, pp. 1, 30.

Seib, Gerald. "Military Reform Has Given Field Commanders Decisive Role and Reduced Interservice Rivalry." *Wall Street Journal*, January 24, 1991, p. A12.

Shapiro, Stacey, and Alfred, Carolyn. "Conflict Triggers War Risk Rate Hikes for Airlines, Shippers." *Business Insurance*, August 13, 1990, p. 101.

Siler, Julia Flynn. "The Iraq Crisis: The Fear Factor." *Business Week*, October 1, 1990, pp. 38–39.

Snow, Nick. "U.S. Better Prepared for Present Mideast Crisis." *The Oil Daily*, August 27, 1990, p. B5.

COMPANY INDEX

A

A. H. Robins, 32, 48–49
Alcoa Aluminum, 25
Alsys, 68
Alyeska, 9
American Cancer Society, 138
American Diabetes Association, 138
American Home Products, 49
American Red Cross, 138
American Telephone and Telegraph (AT&T), 18, 74, 78–79, 94
Ammerman Enterprises, 133
Amoco, 152
AMTRAK, 42–43
Anjou, 86
Apple Computer, 152, 196
ARCO Oil and Gas, 174
Arthur D. Little, 11
Associated Press, 80, 93
Audi, 32, 83

B

B. F. Goodrich, 82
Bally's, 74
Bank of America, 33
Bank of Boston, 33
Bank of Credit and Commerce International (BCCI), 95
Bank of Tokyo, 61
Bellevue Hospital, 67
Bethlehem Steel, 152
Blockbuster Entertainment, 96
Borden, 152
Brinks, 32
Brooklyn Bottling, 147
Browning-Ferris, 152
Burroughs Wellcome, 11, 85–86

C

Cable News Network (CNN), 15, 73

Cascade International, 193
CBS, 25
Chesebrough-Ponds, 157
Chrysler, 15, 74–76, 83, 92
Cincinnati Bell, 95
Citibank, 27, 64, 95–96
Clorox, 86, 171–172
CNBC, 35, 73
Coca-Cola, 118–119, 147
Consolidated Natural Gas, 152
Continental Airlines, 96
Coors Brewing, 31, 158
Crazy Eddie, 193
Cumberland Farms, 69–71

D

Dean Witter Reynolds, 32
Digital Equipment, 191
Dow Chemical, 156–157
Dow Corning, 33
Dow Jones, 80
Drexel Burnham Lambert, 32, 97, 139
Du Pont, 17, 161
DuPont Hotel, 32

E

Eastman Kodak, 152
Edison, 17
Elgar, 189
Equitable Life Assurance Society, 5
Equitable Life Insurance, 96
ESL, 32, 66, 98–99
Evian, 86
Exxon, 5, 8–10, 41, 152, 162, 193

F

First National Bank (Minneapolis), 117

Ford Motor Co., 17, 72, 83, 91
Franklin Research & Development, 152

G

General Electric, 93, 152, 171–172, 223
General Mills, 51, 93
General Motors, 77–78, 152
General Public Utilities Service Corporation, 38
Gillette, 223
Greyhound, 32, 112
Grucci, Inc., 28–29

H

H. B. Fuller, 152
Hartland Plastics, 193
Harvard University, 112
Heinz, 51
Hershey, 17
Hertz Rent-A-Car, 112
Hitachi, 32, 61
Holiday Rambler, 82
Hooker Chemical, 153–154
Hormel, 32, 112
Hyatt Regency Hotel (Kansas City), 32, 187

I

IBM, 32, 152
Illinois Bell Telephone, 115
Illinois Power Co., 184
International Flavors & Fragrances, 161
Irvine, 105
Ishikawajima-Harima Heavy Industries, 61

J

Japan Air Lines, 61
Jefferson Smurfit, 152
Johns Manville, 154
Johnson & Johnson, 3–4, 11, 32, 72,
    84–85, 95, 174, 184, 217–218

K

Kellogg, 17, 51
Kimberly-Clark, 32
Korean Airlines, 66
Kraft Foods, 36

L

Land's End, 223
Levi Strauss & Co., 82, 151
Liberator, 82
Lincoln Federal Savings and Loan,
    32, 136
Lloyds Bank International, 11
Louisiana-Pacific, 152, 163
Louisville Gas & Electric, 152
Luby's Cafeterias, Inc., 33, 99, 100,
    103, 190

M

McDonald's, 35, 66, 96, 161, 190
MCI, 94
McKesson, 86
Medialink, 137–138
MGM Hotel (Las Vegas), 32
Mitsubishi, 61
Mitsui, 61
Monsanto, 152
Morton Thiokol, 32

N

Nabisco, 27
NASA, 4
National Cash Register (NCR), 74,
    78–79
Nestlé, 27

New England Patriots, 45
Nike, 28
Nissan Peru, 61
Nix Used Car Center, 139
Norelco, 45
Northwestern National Bank, 115–118
Nucor, 152

P

Pan Am, 32, 66
Panhandle Eastern, 152
Parkway, 82
Pennzoil, 32
Pepsi, 147
Perrier Group, 32, 86, 88–89, 130
Petrus, 82
Pfizer, 162
Polaroid, 152
Procter & Gamble, 32, 85, 92, 95–97

R

R. H. Macy, 96–97
Reebok, 28
Remington, 45, 47
Reuters, 80
Rohm & Haas, 156

S

Safety-Kleen, 152
Safeway Stores, 167–168
Sandoz Chemical Plant, 32
Schiavone Construction, 178
Shell Oil, 12, 180–181
Sony France, 61
Southern, 152
Spartan, 82
Special Metals, 157
Sperry Rand, 45
Sprint, 94
St. Elizabeth's Hospital, 42
Standard Oil, 17
Starkist, 27
Stratton, 82
Suntory, 86

Superior, 82
Suzuki, 83

T

Target Department Stores, 151
Texaco, 156
Texas Eastern, 158
3M, 217–218
Tokyo Engineering, 61
Toshiba Air Conditioning, 61
Twin City Federal Bank, 117

U

U.S. Postal Service, 190
Union Carbide, 32, 59–60, 126
United Airlines, 112–113, 119
Universal Silk, 61

V

Vance International, 114
Veryfine Products, 33

W

W. R. Grace, 152
Wal-Mart Stores, 152
Walt Disney Corp., 105
Waste Management, 152
WCVB-TV, 144–146
Wellman, 152
Westside Community School District, 223–226
Weyerhauser, 163
World Airways, 215–216
WPRC-TV, 137

Y

Y&A Group, 193–194

NAME INDEX

A

Abramson, Richard, 42
Allen, Robert E., 79
Allison, Graham T., 21, 30
Amin, Idi, 15
Ammerman, Dan, 133
Arnett, Peter, 24
Aronoff, Craig, 63, 71, 75, 120

B

Badolato, Edward, 60
Barton, Laurence, 59, 86, 110–111, 171, 227–228
Baskin, Otis, 63, 71, 75, 120
Berglund, Dan, 189
Bernays, Edward L., 17, 43
Berrand, Steven, 96
Biden, Joseph, 41
Bogdanovich, Walt, 67
Bradley, Thomas, 64
Braverman, Mark, 187–188, 190–193, 195
Braverman, Susan, 190–193
Bren, Donald, 105
Briggs, William, 99, 120
Burson, Harold, 84, 120
Bush, George, 40–41

C

Campbell, Jackie, 195
Canan, Penelope, 108
Carey, Regan, 228
Carter, Jimmy, 39, 154
Carter, Tommy, 139
Cheek, Malcolm, 193–194
Chien-Min Sung, 171
Churchill, Winston, 21, 23–24
Clark, M., 169
Cleary, Fran, 50
Coors, Peter, 158

Cox, Geraldine V., 170
Crivello, Frank, 167
Curtis, John, 101

D

Davidson, Art, 10, 13
Davis, Ronald V., 130
Dinkins, David, 148
DiSalvo, Shirley, 70
Dissmeyer, Virgil, 115–116
Donaldson, James H., 213
Donlan, Thomas G., 120
Donovan, Raymond J., 178
Dorfman, Dan, 96
Douglas, John, 7

E

Epstein, Michael A., 218
Erben, Ralph "Pete", 99–100, 103
Exley, Charles E., 79

F

Farley, Richard, 98
Ferris, Jerry, 101
Fisher, Lynn, 98–99, 120
Fletcher, Meg, 115
Fonda, Jane, 153
Foreman, Dave, 163
Friedman, Raymond, 187
Friedman, Robert J., 195
Fryar, Irving, 46
Fussell, Paul, 30

G

Galen, Michael, 169

Gates, Daryl F., 63–64, 133
Gibbs, Geoffrey Taylor, 63, 71
Gibbs, Lois, 153–154
Glaberson, William, 120
Glen, Peter, 27, 30
Goodman, Robert, 72
Gorbachev, Mikhail, 33
Govoni, Stephen J., 96
Griffin, Merv, 61
Grucci, Felix, Sr., 28
Gunn, Michael, 215

H

Hager, M., 169
Haig, Alexander, 40–41
Halberstam, David, 19, 30
Hale, Jim, 101
Hales, Thomas, 13
Hall, Herbert, 215
Hansel, Larry Thomas, 189
Hansen, Rick, 28
Hardigree, Donald, 213
Hartley, Robert F., 49, 71
Hazelwood, Joseph, 1
Hearst, William Randolph, 19
Hector, Gary, 168
Helmsley, Leona, 61
Hennard, George, 103
Heppe, Karol, 63
Hermann, Charles F., 71
Heyman, Lori, 68
Hicks, Karen, 50
Hinnant, Kathryn, 67
Holland, H. Russel, 10, 162
Holusha, John, 13, 47, 58
Horn, Ronald C., 213

I

Iacocca, Lee, 15, 61, 75–76
Iarossi, Frank, 41

J

Johnson, Robert, 195

K

Keating, Charles, 32, 136
Kelford, Chris, 189
Kelly, Kevin, 218
Kennedy, John F., 20–23, 132
Kennedy, Joseph P., Sr., 24
Khrushchev, Nikita, 21
Kiam, Victor, 45–46
King, Martin Luther, Jr., 20
King, Rodney, 62–63
Kirkpatrick, David, 169
Klovstad, Richard, 115
Knight, Herbert, 100, 103
Kohler, Robert, 98

L

Lahourcade, John, 101
Lee, Ivy, 18
Levi, Stuart D., 218
Levy, Phil, 144–146
Light, Larry, 13
Lipman, Joanne, 13, 120
Lippmann, Walter, 14
Loeb, Marshall, 150
Lord, Miles, 48
Louganis, Greg, 28

M

Magner, Denise K., 169
Malecki, Donald, 213
Manchester, William, 30
Manes, Christopher, 1, 163, 169
Mao Tse Tung, 15
Marcus, Alfred, 72
Mathews, Mark, 103
McCarter, Judy, 103
McCarthy, Joseph, 24–26
McCarthy, Michael J., 119
McGinley, Laurie, 13
McKee, Kenneth C., 38, 47

McKinley, George, 120
Medvedev, Grigori, 160
Melching, Jerry, 183
Merlino, Doreen, 157
Metcalf, Leon, 215
Metcalf, Walter, 215
Meyers, Gerald, 58
Milken, Michael, 32
Miller, Eric, 147
Mintzberg, Henry, 49, 71
Mitchell, Leon, 120
Mitchell, Mark, 85
Mitroff, Ian I., 4, 13, 50–51
Moffett, Matt, 13
Morris, Edmund, 16, 29
Moy, Frank M., Jr., 42–43
Murrow, Edward R., 24–26
Murrow, Janet, vi, 24
Mydans, Seth, 71

N

Nader, Ralph, 77–78, 109, 166
Nixon, Richard, v, 41

O

Oates, Joyce Carol, 121
Oizumi, Kiochi, 60
Olson, Lisa, 46–47

P

Page, Arthur, 18
Paley, William S., 25
Partner, Simon, 181
Pell, Eve, 120
Pemberton, John Styth, 118
Perdue, Frank, 126–127
Peters, Thomas J., 28
Pflaumbaum, Madeline, 28
Pinsdorf, Marion K., 3, 120
Plater, Zygmunt J. B., 164–166
Plummer, Diane, 13
Portney, Kent, 105
Pring, George, 108
Pugh, Theresa, 156

Pulitzer, Joseph, 19

R

Rather, Dan, 139
Rawl, Lawrence G., 5, 41, 162
Reagan, Ronald, 40
Reilly, Anne, 52, 71
Remington, Frederick, 19
Reso, Sidney, 193
Reutinger, Annie, 195
Roosevelt, Eleanor, 24
Roosevelt, Franklin D., 24, 135
Roosevelt, Theodore, 16, 19
Rountree, G. Glynn, 13, 169
Rubenstein, Howard, 46
Rubin, Debra, 195
Rubin, Paul H., 120
Rynearson, Dr., 102

S

Sadat, Anwar, 20
Salinger, Pierre, 132
Schenkler, Irv, 97
Schrader, Vernon, 101
Schultz, David L., 169
Scully, John, 196
Smith, Steven, 67
Sperber, A. M., 30
Stalin, Joseph, 15
Steffens, Lincoln, 16, 19
Stegora, Philip A., 217
Stephenson, David, 161
Sterling, Phyllis, 106
Stevens, William, 41
Steward, Shelley, 172
Swanson, Carl L., 120

T

Tebbe, John, 29
Thornburgh, Richard, 38
Tomioka, Shiniricho, 60
Tomsho, Robert, 169
Trump, Donald, 61

Tsongas, Paul, 146

U

Unti, George, 167

V

Vance, Charles F., 114, 120

W

Wallace, Mike, 84
Weber, Joseph, 218
Weinberger, Marc, 91–92, 120
Weingarten, Pam, 96
Weld, William, 146
White, Theodore H., 22, 30
Wiening, Eric A., 213
Wildig, Tony, 180–181

Wisenbilt, Joseph Z., 47, 57, 71
Woestendiek, John, 158, 169
Woliver, Jim, 100, 103
Woolard, Edgar, 161

Z

Zukowski, Joseph, 110–111

SUBJECT
INDEX

A

accidents, visibility of, 141–142
accountants, in communication channel, 64
acquisitions
    and debt of UAL, 112
    of NCR by AT&T, 78–80
activist groups, 161
    as audience of company communication, 123
    company lawsuits against, 108–109
    emergence of organized protests, 27
    and environmental issues, 156, 160, 161, 165–166
    Love Canal homeowners, 153–154
advertising
    on TV programs with violence or sex, 93
    Perrier campaign for reintroduction, 88, 89
    planning message before crisis, 94
    program at time of crisis, 70–71, 80, 207
    role of director of, 36
Agriculture, Department of, inspections by, 175
air pollution. See pollution
air traffic controllers, strike by and firing of, 111
airline crashes
    Korean Airlines flight 007, 66
    Pan Am flight 103, 32, 66
    World Airways, 215–216
alar, apples treated with, 33
Alaska
    and Exxon oil spill, 9
    and prevention of environmental crisis, 165
Alcoa Aluminum, 25–26
Allen, Robert E., 78–79
Allison, Graham, 21–22
Alsys, crises at, 68–69
Alyeska, and Valdez oil spill, 9–10
American Home Products, 49

American Stock Exchange, requirements on dissemination of information, 74–75
American Telephone & Telegraph (AT&T), acquisition of NCR, 18, 78–80
Ammerman, Dan, 133
Ammerman Enterprises, Inc., 133
AMTRAK, train collision, 42–44
annual reports, role of, 18, 36, 73
ARCO Oil and Gas Company, relocation contingency plans, 174–175
Arlington Plastics (AP)
    CMP for, 197–198, 200–202, 204, 207, 209, 214
    communication strategy on possible recall, 124, 127, 140–143
    crisis planning case study, 52–56, 176
    plant expansion, 104
arrest of company official, 32
asbestos, danger and removal of, 154–155
AT&T. See American Telephone & Telegraph
attorneys
    in communication channel, 64, 206
    in crisis planning, 173, 212
    role in press conference, 210–211
Audi, acceleration problem in, 32
audiences
    communicating with, 29, 64, 74, 122, 211–212
    coordinating company responses to, 113–114
    identifying, 122–126
    in role-play of scenario development, 177–178
    understanding information needs of, 36
    See also communication strategy; information
audits, as preventive action, 51

B

Bangladesh, natural disasters in, 33

Bank of America, branch closings, 337
Bank of Boston, accusation of money laundering, 33
Bank of Credit and Commerce International (BCCI) scandal, 95
bankruptcy, 5, 32
banks
    crisis plan for, 115–117
    risk of crisis in, 65, 193
Bay of Pigs invasion, 21
behavior, organizational, 12, 37
behavioral profiling as preventive action, 51
benzene
    in Perrier Water, 32, 86–90
    release into air, 156
Bernays, Edward L., 17, 43
Berrard, Steve, 96
Better Business Bureau, monitoring complaints from, 94
Bhopal, India, gas leak and explosion in, 32, 59–60
birth defects, rates of near mining and factories, 151
blackmail of Japanese businesses, 61
Blockbuster Entertainment Corporation, 96
boat renting, risk of crisis in, 65
bomb threat, simulation of, 184
bombings
    of IBM offices, 32
    of Japanese businesses, 61
    likelihood of, 11
Boston Herald, harassment of female sports writer from, 45–47
boycotts
    consumer
        contingency plan for, 171–172
        as crises for corporations, 27
        organized, 92–93
        of Procter & Gamble products because of logo, 97
Bradley, Thomas, 64
brainstorming, in scenario development, 181

brand loyalty, change in Coke formula, 118
brand recognizability, of Tylenol, 85
Braverman, Mark
    interview, 190–193
    trauma and employee productivity, 187–188
Braverman, Susan, interview, 190–193
Bren, Donald, 105
Briggs, William, 99
Brinks robbery, 32
Brooklyn Bottling, effects of rumor on, 147–148
budget issues, addressed in role-play, 180
building industry, risk of crisis in, 65
Burrell's clipping service, 135
Burroughs Wellcome, Sudafed tampering and recall, 11, 85–86
Burson, Harold, 84
Bush, George, 40–41
Business Week, on Kiam and Remington, 47

C

Cable News Network (CNN), 15
cancer
    breast, at Love Canal, 153
    link, contingency plan for, 171
    lung and throat, from asbestos exposure, 154
    rates of near mining and factories, 151
Carter, Jimmy
    and Love Canal crisis, 154
    on TMI communication crisis, 39
case studies
    Brooklyn Bottling rumors, 146–148
    Coca-Cola's MagiCans promotion, 118–119
    Cumberland Farms' treatment of employees, 69–71
    explosion of Grucci, Inc. plant, 28–29
    Safeway in earthquake, 167–168
    sexual harassment charges, 45–47
    World Airways accident, 215–216
    Y&A Group, missing CEO, 193–195
CBS, Murrow and McCarthy, 25, 26

"CBS Evening News with Dan Rather," use of VNR, 139
Center for the Study of Crisis Management, 183, 227–228
Centers for Disease Control (CDC)
    on Dalkon Shield, 49
    on tampons and TSS, 85
    on tap water, 88
chain of command
    assessing as preventive action, 51
    planning for crisis, 183
Challenger explosion, 4–5
    Morton Thiokol role in, 32
Cheek, Malcolm, disappearance of, 193–194
chemicals
    disclosure of, 156
    evaluation of, 163
    identification and storage of, 141–142, 161
    penalties for dumping of toxic, 156
    reporting of release into environment, 155–156
    storage and testing of hazardous, 164
    transport of hazardous, 156
Chernobyl explosion, 33, 159–160
Chesebrough-Ponds, cleanup liability of, 157
Chicago flood, and liability, 213
chief executive officer (CEO)
    contacted in crisis, 205
    involvement in CMP, 174, 197, 200
    missing, 193–195
    press conference by, 208
    resignation of, 68–69
    training in press relations, 132–133
Chien-Min Sung, 171
China Syndrome, The, 38
chlorofluorocarbons (CFCs), suspension of use, 161
Chrysler Corporation
    celebrity of Iacocca, 60–61
    loan guarantee program for, 15, 75
    steering problem in Plymouth Horizon/Dodge Omni, 83, 92
    tampering with odometers, 61, 75–76
    Ultradrive transmission, 83
churches
    neighborhood opposition to, 105
    scandal in, 62
Churchill, Winston, 21, 23

Citibank
    communication channels in, 64
    rumors about, 95–96
clients
    informing of crisis, 183
    loss of major, 142–143
Clorox Company, contingency plan of, 171–172
Coast Guard, U.S., and oil spill, 9
Coca-Cola
    changing formula for, 118
    MagiCans promotion, 118–119
    rumor about competitor, 147
Commerce, Department of, inspections by, 175
communication
    with employees, about disaster, 98–99, 102, 183
    legality of, 139–140, 172
    message of, 126–127, 140
    with stockholders, vehicles for, 73, 74, 76, 80–81
communication channels
    formal, necessity of, 64
    identification of before crisis, 10, 29
communication strategy, 122–128
    in acquisition attempt, 78–79
    to combat rumors, 147–148
    goals of, 124–126
    in investment crisis, 80–81
    for loss of major client, 142–143
    managing elements of, 122–128
    for product recall, 87, 88, 94, 95, 140, 142
    of school district in emergency, 224–226
community relations
    company contributions, 107, 108, 109, 175
    dealing with community protests, 103–109
    education about chemicals and emergency response, 161, 164
    methods for company outreach, 106–108, 110
    planning for environmental crisis, 156
    See also activist groups; neighborhood protests
community relations manager, handling a NIMBY crisis, 104, 106–108, 109
companies
    local, publicity for crises in, 67

privately owned, risk of crisis in, 60–62
publicly traded, risk of crisis in, 59–60
risk exposure of, 62, 66–67
competition
  of recalled product, 88
  as source of rumors, 147
  strategy to outsmart, 49
complaints
  documentation of, in product recall, 90
  patterns and trends in, 53, 64, 93, 94
computer software
  dual equipment in distant location, 174
  simulation of crisis, 183–184
confidentiality
  of CMP, 197–198
  of proprietary information, 204–205
Congress, U.S., Chrysler loan guarantee, 15, 76
consumer affairs manager, role of, 35
consumer confidence
  effect of strike, 112
  impact of recall on, 84–85, 90–92, 95
  in reintroduced product, 88, 89
  See also information
consumer movement
  growth of, 10, 19
  Nader's attack on GM, 77
  product investigations, 81–82, 83
  See also boycotts, consumer
Consumer Product Safety Commission (CPSC), role of, 81
Consumer Reports, 81
  corporate executives' attitude toward, 83
  on Plymouth Horizon/Dodge Omni, 83
Consumers Union of the United States, 81
contacts
  emergency
    in CMP, 198, 201–202, 204
    secondary, in CMP, 207
contingency planning, uses for, 51
Controller of the Currency, U.S., and bank fire, 115, 117
Coors Brewing Company, fines against, 158

counseling, on-site for traumatized employees, 98, 187–188, 190–191
Count Chocula cereal, 93
crisis
  anticipation of, 5, 52, 54–56, 202–203
  definition of, 2
  major types, 32–33
  preparation for, 8, 10, 17, 52, 54
  public perception of imminence of, 7
  secondary, potential for, 206
crisis control center
  conducting scenarios in, 179–180
  in coping with bank fire, 115, 116
  designation and preparation of, 213
  location of and equipment in, 174, 182
  in Luby's Cafeteria crisis, 101–102
  mobile, 207
  operation of, 184–187
  See also telecommunications
crisis management
  chronology of response, 103
  containment and control, 3, 58
  emergence of attention to, 57
  federal help in disasters, 219–222
  organizing by management areas, 56
  planning in advance, 3, 12, 56
  as strategic challenge, 3, 37, 161
  strategies, 49–50
  training in, using simulation, 183
Crisis Management Group Inc., 190
crisis management plan (CMP), 2, 12–13, 41–42, 57, 187
  action steps, 205–208
  audience-specific, 123–124
  content and format of, 197–214
  development in advance, 10, 12, 115–118
  fact-finding phase, 175
  introduction to, 197–200
  lack of preparedness, 167
  leaked contingency plans, 171–172
  of Luby's Cafeteria, 101–102
  preparation for product recall, 94–95
  preparation for strike, 114
  scenario development, 176–182
  for school district, 223–226
Crivello, Frank, 167

Crystallizing Public Opinion (Bernays), 17
Cuban missile crisis, 21–22
culture, corporate, psychologist's knowledge of, 188
Cumberland Farms case study, 69–71
customers
  as audience segments, 123
  communication with by publicly traded company, 73, 76
  evacuation plans for, 163
  inquiries about product satisfaction, 83
  service to to avert crisis, 93–94
  serving in crisis, 8, 29, 167–168
  See also clients; consumer confidence

D

Dalkon Shield Information Network, 50
Dalkon Shield IUD
  company response to complaints about, 48, 49, 50
  and Robins bankruptcy, 32
Davidson, Art, 10
Dean Witter, charges against stockbroker, 32
decision making in crisis, 2, 50
definition of organization, forming, 49
departments, involvement in crisis management, 33–36
deregulation. *See under* government regulation
developers, and community relations, 105
Digital Equipment Corporation (DEC), EAP manager, 191
dimension-control matrix, 58
Dinkins, David, 148
disasters
  coordination of plan for, 157
  natural, 3, 33, 219–222
Dissmeyer, Virgil, interview, 115–118
documentation
  control of in product recall, 91
  of events in crisis, 203, 206
  of testing and labeling of products, 213
Dodge Caravan, 83

Dodge Omni, 83, 91–92

Donovan, Raymond J., 178

Dorfman, Dan, 96

Dow Chemical, environmental policies, 156–157

Drexel Burnham Lambert
rumors about, 97
use of VNR, 139

Du Pont, environmental commitment, 161

Dukakis, Michael, press conferences of, 146

DuPont Hotel, Puerto Rico, fire, 32

E

Earth First!, 163, 166

earthquakes
banks damaged in, 116, 118
meeting customer demands in, 5–6
relocation of operations, 174

econometric models, for scenario development, 181

Economist, The, on Chernobyl disaster, 159

economy, national, as factor in strike negotiations, 113

ecoterrorism, 163, 166

Elgar Corporation, killings at, 188, 189, 190

emergency preparedness
local and regional, 206
See also contacts, emergency

emergency response programs, 157, 161

emissions
Dow on compliance with standards, 256
reporting of chemicals released, 155–156

emotional preparation, internal, 51

employee assistance program (EAP), 191

Employee Information Service (EIS), 174

employees
arrest of for drug dealing, 145
classes for, as preventive action, 51
communication with after workplace violence, 98–99, 102, 103
communication with in crisis, 183, 194, 212

community activity of, 107, 175
death of on job, 191
evacuation plans for, 163–164
extortion of by employer, 69–71
group sharing after workplace crisis, 191–192
instruction on answering inquiries, 184
leak of design plan, 176
need for "reasonable accommodation," 193
nonstriking, security concerns for, 114
status of after bank fire, 115, 117
theft of trade secrets by former, 171, 217
trauma in workplace, 187–193
violent crimes by former, 97–98, 188, 189, 190, 191

entertainment industry, risk of crisis in, 65

environmental crimes
costs to company for cleanup and legal battle, 162
prosecution of, 10–11, 160, 162

environmental impact
audit of, 51
of corporate operations, 151
of developments, 105
influence on corporate policies, 11
and litigation against companies, 59
prevention of disaster, 160, 163–164

environmental law, ethic and effectiveness of, 165

environmental movement
company outreach to, 161
protests of corporate activities, 9–10, 104, 105, 164, 171
radical, 163, 166
science and technology in, 166
sophistication of about publicity, 166

Environmental Protection Agency (EPA)
civil penalty against Texas Eastern, 158
enforcement of environmental crimes, 10–11, 160
and Love Canal, 153, 154
regulation of allowable damage, 151

environmental regulation. *See under* government regulation

environmental responsibility, 151, 156–157, 160–163

the economic argument, 166
judging a company on, 150, 151, 152

Equitable Life Assurance Society, rumors about, 5

Erben, Ralph "Pete," 99
interview, 100–103

ESL, workplace shooting at, 32, 66, 98–99

evacuation
of Love Canal residents, 154
plan for employees and customers, 163, 164

evaluation
by employees after violent crisis, 98–99
of communication strategy, 127–128, 135, 136
of crisis management methods, 212, 214
of leader of scenario development, 180
postcrisis, 3, 118, 182, 211

executives
contact with in crisis, 81, 167, 168, 201–202
disappearance of, 193
indictment of, 178
personal liability for environmental crimes, 11
role in crisis management, 34
suicide of, 191
See also chief executive officer (CEO); managers

Exley, Charles E., 78–79

explosions
Bhopal Union Carbide plant, 59–60
Chernobyl nuclear power plant, 33, 159–160
crisis planning for plant, 176–177
Grucci fireworks plant, 28–29
state investigation of plant, 29
visibility of, 141–142

Exxon, *Valdez* oil spill, 5, 32
costs of to company, 162
prevention of, Alaska study of, 165
as public relations failure, 3, 5, 8–10, 41

F

Farley, Richard, 98

Federal Bureau of Investigation (FBI), and environmental crimes, 160
Federal Emergency Management Agency (FEMA), 187, 219–222
financial officer, role in crisis team, 173–174
fires
    deaths of MOVE members, 33
    DuPont Hotel, Puerto Rico, 32
    elements of crisis to manage, 8
    MGM Hotel, 33
    rebuilding after, 117
    service disruption at bank, 115–118
Fisher, Lynn, 99
floods
    in Bangladesh, 33
    Chicago downtown, 33, 212
    likelihood of, 11
    relocation of operations, 174
Fonda, Jane, 153–154
Food, Drug, and Cosmetics Act, classifications of recall, 83
Food and Drug Administration (FDA)
    and Perrier recall, 87, 88
    responsibility of, 81, 175
food producers and distributors, risk of crisis in, 65
Ford Pinto
    and Ford reputation, 72
    loss of consumer confidence, 83, 91–92
Foreman, Dave, 163
France, Perrier production in, 86–87
Franklin Research & Development, 152
fraud, indictment of Chrysler, 75–76
Friedman, Raymond, 187

G

Gates, Daryl F.
    handling of complaints, 63–64
    and press relations, 137
General Electric (GE)
    nuclear weapons research of, 93
    theft of trade secrets of, 171
General Motors (GM), relations with stockholders, 76–78
General Public Utilities Service Corporation, and TMI crisis, 38–39

Gibbs, Lois, 153–154
goals, organizational
    awareness of in crisis, 34
    consistency with societal expectations, 64
    defining, 49–50
goodwill
    in community relations, 109
    role of public affairs manager, 34
    See also community relations
government, federal
    corporate relationship with, 51
    energy policy, 165
    growth in, 17–18
    intervention in public interest, 19
    risk of crisis in, 65
government regulation
    compliance with, 36
    crisis plan required of banks, 116
    deregulation's impact on labor unions, 109
    environmental, 155–156, 160, 162, 164
    expert on in crisis planning, 174
    growth in, 26–27
    of product recalls, 81–83, 90, 91, 94
government regulators
    contact with in crisis, 94, 123, 124–125, 141, 205
    EPA officials held hostage, 154
    presence at press conference, 184
    regular communication with, 64, 73
Green Rage (Manes), 163
Greenpeace, and Clorox contingency plan, 171–172
Greyhound, strike against, 32, 112
group homes, neighborhood protests of, 106
Grucci, Inc., fireworks plant explosion, 28–29
Gulf War (1991), press coverage of, 15–16
Gunn, Michael, 215

H

Haig, Alexander, 40–41
Halberstam, David, 19
Hansel, Larry Thomas, 189
Hardigree, Donald, 213

hazardous chemicals. *See under* chemicals
hazardous waste, liability for cleanup, 157–158
hazards
    classifications of in product recall, 83
    unknown, liability for, 155
Hearst, William Randolph, 19
heart disease, at Love Canal, 153
helicopter renting, risks in, 65
Hennard, George, 103
Heyman, Lori, interview, 68–69
Hitachi, indictment of officials, 32
Holland, H. Russel, 162
Hooker Chemical Company, dumping at Love Canal, 153–154
Hope, Bob, 105
Hormel, strike against, 32, 112
hospitals, vulnerability of, 7
hostage crises, 98, 154
hotels, risk of public crises in, 65
House Un-American Activities Committee (HUAC), 24–25
human resources. *See under* resources
Hyatt Regency Hotel, Kansas City, skywalk collapse, 32, 187

I

Iacocca, Lee
    apology for odometer disconnecting, 76
    as Chrysler spokesperson, 75–76
    press coverage of, 61
    shaping public opinion, 15
Iarossi, Frank, 41
IBM
    bombing of office, 32
    trade secret theft, 32
Illinois Bell Telephone Co., service disruption, 115
Illinois Power Company, press conference space, 184
image, company
    impact of Bhopal leak and explosion, 59–60
    and public relations tools, 128–139
In Search of Excellence (Peters), 28
In the Wake of the Exxon Valdez (Davidson), 10

indictment of company officials, 32, 178

Infact, documentary on GE nuclear research, 93

information

allaying fears or panic, 206

inaccurate or misleading statements, 37, 123, 134–135, 204–205, 208, 209, 215–216

managers' access to, 52

on environmental issues, 156–157, 161

on product recall, 11, 83, 90

in postcrisis routine, 205

required of company by stock exchange, 74–75

tours of facility by media and others, 206–207

See also documentation

insurance

annual updates for visible companies, 62

contact with carriers in crisis, 90, 101

health and workers compensation, 212

knowledge of company coverage, 8

review of CMP by carriers, 212

settlement after bank fire, 115, 117

International Atomic Energy Agency (IAEA), 159

International Bottled Water Association, 88

international events, as factors in strike negotiations, 113

International Flavors & Fragrances (IFF), 161

international location, expansion to, 52

interviews

Braverman, S. and M., 190–193

Dissmeyer, 115–118

Erben, 100–102

Heyman, 68–69

Levy, 144–146

Moy, 43–44

Plater, 165–166

intimidation of employees, 49, 70–71

inventory

losses of, 167–168

reduction of as preventive action, 51

investment crisis, 75–78, 78–80, 80–81

investor relations

communication strategy, 73, 78–79, 80, 211

loss of confidence, 73–80

role of manager of, 36

Investor Relations Service Bureau, 129

Iraq

invasion of Kuwait, impact on labor negotiations, 113

war with U.S. and allies, press coverage of, 15–16

Irvine Company, and community protests, 105

issue audit, to monitor emerging problems, 62–64

issues management, as preventive action, 51

It's Not My Department! (Glen), 27–28

J

Japanese companies, violent acts against, 60, 61

Japanese competition, and Chrysler loan guarantee, 76

Jewish organizations, protest by, 93

job loss, threat of

in AT&T acquisition of NCR, 78

and Chrysler loan guarantee, 76

John M. Langston Black Lawyers Association, 63

Johns Manville Company, asbestos lawsuits, 154–155

Johnson & Johnson

crisis center, 184

role-play of ethical dilemma, 180

TSS crisis, 32

Tylenol tampering and recall, 3–4, 72, 84–85, 95, 174

journalists. *See* reporters

Justice, Department of

prosecution of environmental crimes, 160, 162

settlement with Exxon, 162

K

Keating, Charles, 32

Kennedy, John F.

as communicator, 23

crises in presidency of, 21–22

press conferences of, 132

Ketchum Public Relations, 171–172

Kiam, Victor, as spokesperson, 45–47

kidnappings, of Japanese businesses' employees, 61

Killeen, Texas, mass killings in, 99, 100–103

Kimberly-Clark, TSS crisis, 32

King, Rodney, videotaped beating of, 33, 62–64

Klovstad, Richard, 115

Kohler, Robert, 98

Korean Airlines flight 007, 66

Ku Klux Klan, rumor of link to product, 147–148

L

labeling

and product liability, 212–213

warning, 85, 94

labor unions

contacting in crisis, 206

decline of in U.S., 109, 111

as possible source of rumors, 147

in United Airlines strike, 112–113

See also strikes

landfill, cleanup liability of users of, 157–158

law enforcement

communicating company policy to, 71

contact with in crisis, 101, 102, 205, 217, 218

lawsuits. *See* litigation

layoffs and firings, branch closings, 33

Lee, Ivy, 18

legislation, impact of, 51

leukemia

and benzene, 156

at Love Canal, 153

Levy, Phil, interview, 144–146

liability

news media questions on, 210–211

product, and risk management, 212–213

libel, 139, 140

Lincoln Savings and Loan, federal takeover of, 32

litigation

after Exxon oil spill, 10
against advocacy groups, 108–109
by families of Tylenol victims, 84–85
by homeowners after plant explosion, 29
community or individual suit against companies surveyed, 57
documentation of events surrounding crisis, 203
documented inspections and testing, 94
on environmental pollution, 157
on worksite fire, 115, 117
and product liability, 212–213
Robins' attack on Dalkon Shield complainants, 48
for service disruption, 114
Texaco and Pennzoil, 32
Lloyds Bank International, study of location, 11
location, and need for CMP, 57, 59
logging, 163–164
logos
  Satan-worshipping seen in, 32
  visibility of in crisis, 134, 185
Lord, Miles, 48
Los Angeles, air quality of, 151
Los Angeles Police Department
  chief and the press, 133
  verdict in King beating trial, 33, 64
  videotaped beating of King, 62–64
losses
  in contracts and clients, 178
  financial, 117
  of inventory, 167–168
  See also sales; stock value
Louisiana-Pacific, costs of ecoterrorism, 163
Love Canal Homeowners Association, 153–154
Love Canal, New York, environmental damage in, 153–154
Luby's Cafeteria, mass killings at, 33, 99, 100–103, 190

M

McCarthy, Joseph, 24–26
McDonald's
  recycling and public education, 161
  rumors about, 32

shootings at, 66, 190
McKee, Kenneth, 38–39
Macy, R. H., rumors about, 97
MagiCans, Coca-Cola promotion, 118–119
management as academic discipline, 17
managers
  access of to crisis plans and resources, 52
  acknowledgment of CMP, 200–201
  contact information on in CMP, 201–202, 204
  involvement in serious crises, 58
  knowing how to delegate, 36
  personal crises of, 7–8
  See also executives
Manes, Christopher, 163
manufacturing
  chemical and pharmaceutical, risk of crisis in, 65
  heavy, litigation against firms in, 57
  need for product recall plan, 90
market share, impact of recall on, 91–92
marketing, MagiCan promotion, 118–119
meat-packing houses, conditions in, 16, 18
Medialink, 137
Medvedev, Grigori, 160
meetings
  annual and periodic, 73
  as communication vehicle, 123
  with community groups, 106, 109, 110, 111
  informational, in investment crisis, 80
Melching, Jerry, 183–184
mergers, communication strategy for, 80–81
MGM Hotel fire, 33
Midland, Michigan, Dow's social contract with, 157
military information, in wartime, 24
Miller, Eric, of Brooklyn Bottling, 147–148
Milken, Michael, 32
mobilization of citizenry, as wartime press role, 20
money laundering, bank accused of, 33
monopolies, break-up of, 17–18
Morris, Edmund, 16

Morton Thiokol, role in *Challenger* accident, 32
Mount Weather, Virginia, 186
MOVE, deaths in fire in Philadelphia, 33
Moy, Frank M., Jr., 42
  interview, 43–44
multinational organizations, crisis team designation in, 201
Murrow, Edward R., 24, 25–26

N

Nader, Ralph
  challenge to GM, 77–78
  legal defense for advocacy groups, 109
NASA, press information on *Challenger*, 4–5
National Association of Manufacturers, on chemicals reporting, 156
National Cash Register (NCR), acquisition by AT&T, 78–80
National Environmental Policy Act, 166
National Wildlife Federation, 176
natural resources, waste and destruction of, 165
neighborhood protests
  and gains for environmental law, 165–166
  and plant explosion, 29
  power of NIMBYs, 104–106
  See also activist groups
New England Patriots, losses of, 45
news, "spins" on by sources, 23
news clipping services, 135, 208
news media
  access to building, 184–186
  accuracy of company information, 215–216
  after bank fire, 115, 117
  communication with on workplace killings, 98, 100, 101, 102
  coverage of Love Canal hostage crisis, 154
  and disappearance of CEO, 194
  expansion of role of, 16, 17, 19, 22–23, 25–26
  handling of calls from, 208, 209
  improving relations with, 23, 110, 111

local, 23, 70, 107
needs of in crisis, 173, 185, 206
"off the record" comments, 210
on plant explosion, 29
predicting coverage of hypothetical crisis, 183
preparation for dealing with, 23, 52, 67, 94, 208–211, 224–226
and TMI crisis, 38–39
training in relations with, 51, 133
use of by management and labor in strike, 112, 113
use of VNRs, 136–139
viewpoint of in covering crisis, 144–146
See also press coverage; reporters
newsletters, use of, 73, 106–107
NIMBY syndrome, 103–106
combating with litigation, 108–109
managing crisis, 106–108
nonprofit institutions, "payment in lieu of taxes" (PILOT), 108
Norelco, challenge to Remington, 45
Northeast
likelihood of NIMBY crises, 106
litigation against first in, 57, 59
Northwest, environmental litigation against firms in, 59
Northwestern National Bank (Norwest Bank), fire, 115–118
"Not In My Back Yard." *See* NIMBY, syndrome
nuclear industry
public suspicion of, 159–160
unprepared for accident, 39
nuclear plants
explosion at Chernobyl, 159
planned, impact of TMI on, 160
radiation release, 38–39
risk of crisis in, 65
simulation of crisis in, 183–184
Nuclear Regulatory Commission (NRC), and media affairs in TMI crisis, 39
nuclear weapons research, consumer boycott to protest, 93

O

Occupational Safety and Health Administration (OSHA)
inspections by, 175

reporting of hazards to, 154
oil spill from *Exxon Valdez*, 32
company in chaos, 8–10
settlement and public outrage, 162
Olson, Lisa, and the New England Patriots controversy, 46–47
operations
knowledge of in crisis management, 34
vice presidents of, survey of on crisis management, 57
organizations
needs for crisis preparation, 52
public view of, 15
ownership
by celebrities, 60–62
employee, 112, 113
private, risk in companies with, 60–62

P

packaging
double- or triple-sealing of products, 84, 94
improvement in, 51
liability for negligence in, 212
Page, Arthur, 18
Paley, William S., 25
Pan Am flight 103, explosion, 32, 66
"payment in lieu of taxes" (PILOT), 108, 175
Pemberton, John Styth, 118
Pennzoil, court battle with Texaco, 32
Pepsi-Cola
and Coke's formula change, 118
as possible source of rumor, 147
Perdue, Frank, as spokesperson, 126–127
Perrier water
distribution of, 87–88
recall of water with benzene, 32, 86–90
reintroduction of, 87, 88
personal crisis, in workplace, 188–189
persuasiveness, of managers in working well to handle crisis, 36
pesticides, apples treated with, 33
Pfizer, environmental penalty, 162
plants
access to in crisis, 207
design improvement, 51

expansion or relocation of, 52, 104, 108
Plater, Zygmunt J. B., interview, 165–166
Plymouth Horizon, 83, 91–92
Plymouth Voyager, 83
police conduct, videotaped beating of King, 62–64
Police Misconduct Lawyers Referral Service, 63
political action committees (PACs), use of by company, 108
political corruption, news media coverage of, 18–19
pollution
air, from business and industry, 151, 155–157
air and water standards, Nader demands on GM, 77
costs of lawsuits, 157–158
effectiveness of environmental law, 165
monitoring levels of, 160
Postal Service, U.S., shootings by former employees, 190
Powers That Be, The (Halberstam), 19
press, business and financial
news leaks to, 95
responding to in investment crisis, 74
press conferences
advantages of, 124, 129, 132
company statements at, 87, 208
considering need for, 132, 206
fact sheets for, 210
in investment crisis, 80
planning and running, 94, 133–136, 145
rehearsal for, 132, 210
use of by news media, 146
press coverage
of documentary attacking GE, 93
of employee intimidation, 70–71
of fires and explosions, 4–5, 8
of GM stockholder meeting, 77–78
impact of celebrity owner, 60–61
monitoring, 135
of monopoly break-ups, 17–18
of police handling of King beating, 63–64
of product recalls, 3–4, 84, 85–86
of scandals, 60–62
of well-known companies, 67
press kits

assembled in advance, 80–81, 94, 183
contents of, 129, 210
objective of, 67
press officers, in companies, 18
press releases
defined, 128–129
during strike, 113
in investment crisis, 80
to local news media, 107
on Perrier recall, 130–131
planning in advance, 183
role or function of, 67, 128–129
preventive actions, types of, 50, 51
problem solving
role models for, 188–189
training in, 2
Procter & Gamble
false rumors about logo, 32, 96–97
proprietary information, 95
recall of Rely Tampons, 32, 85, 92
product defects
Coca-Cola's MagiCans, 118–119
and communication strategy, 80–81
Dalkon IUD, company's defensive reaction, 48
negligence in design, 212
Perrier water, 86–90
redesign after recalls and criticism, 83
sampling of, 81
product liability, 82, 212–213
product recall. *See* recall
product safety. *See* safety, product
product tampering
government role in cases of, 82–83
in Hormel strike, 32
Sudafed capsules, 33, 85–86
Tylenol capsules, 3–4, 32, 84–85, 92, 95, 174
productivity, and workplace trauma, 187–188
products
launching new or modified, 52
risk associated with types of, 65–66
property destruction, during strike, 112
proprietary information
guarding in crisis, 204–205
Procter & Gamble concern about disclosure of, 95
See also trade secrets
psychological consulting

after workplace trauma, 6–7, 98, 190–193
in preparing for crisis, 187–188
public affairs
departments, 27
managers, on crisis team, 34, 57, 93, 174
NASA emergency plan for, 4–5
public confidence
after bank fire, 116, 117
in NASA, 4
undermined by rumors, 96
See also consumer confidence
public opinion, 14–30
continual assessment of, 28
Exxon customer reaction to oil spill, 9–10
importance of to corporations, 12, 15, 17
managing in product recall, 82
shaping of by Iacocca, 15
public relations
as concern of corporations, 17, 18
coordination of after bank fire, 117
damage to in Nader's attack on GM, 77–78
definition of, 63–64, 122
Exxon's failures in oil spill, 5, 10
handling of Tylenol scare, 84–85
projection of positive image, 128–139
as rumor control, 96, 97
strategy for Perrier reintroduction, 88
public relations managers
dealing with media, 145–146, 208
Heyman interview, 68–69
role in crisis team, 35, 93, 172
publications, company, available in community, 107
publicly traded companies
publics of, 73–74
risk of crisis in, 59–60
publics. *See* audiences
Pugh, Theresa, 156
Pulitzer, Joseph, 19

Q

quality control, 94

R

Rawl, Lawrence G., handling of oil spill crisis, 5, 41, 162
Reagan, Ronald
assassination attempt on, 40–41
firing of air traffic controllers, 111
real estate development, risk of crisis in, 57, 65
recalls
communication strategy for, 80–81, 124, 140, 142
evaluation of program, 90–91
preparing response to, 94–95
products susceptible to, 93
See also Perrier water; Rely Tampons; Sudafed ; Tylenol
recycling
by McDonald's, 161
economic argument for, 166
relocation
after bank fire, 116–117
after natural disaster, 174, 176
Rely Tampons
association with TSS, 85
Procter & Gamble's recovery from recall, 92
Remington Corporation, CEO's crises, 45–47
reorganization of parent company, 69
repair design, internal, 51
reporters
environmentalist, hypothetical attack by, 171
expansion of role of, 18
muckraking, 18–19
skill at getting story, 132, 134–135
as source of information, 208–209
stonewalling of, 68
training in objectivity, 23, 135
wartime, ethical dilemmas faced by, 24
resources
allocation of, in developing a crisis plan, 52
identifying those needed to achieve goals, 49
natural, destruction of, 165
in product recall program, 94
use of in crisis, 3
Rhine River contamination, 32
riots

on acquittal of Los Angeles police officers, 33, 64
at soccer stadium, 33
risk
   analysis, dimension-control matrix for, 58
   assessing, 59–67
   management of, 212–213
   susceptibility, 52–53, 65–66
robbery, Brinks, 32
Robins, A. H., handling of Dalkon Shield crisis, 32, 48, 49
Roger and Me, 77
Rohm & Haas Company, 156
role-play
   of press conference, 210
   in scenario development, 177–180, 227
Roosevelt, Franklin D., and the press, 135
Roosevelt, Theodore
   and power of muckrakers, 19
   press coverage of, 16–17
rumors
   as a crisis, 95–97
   about financial condition, 95–96, 97
   about Klan link to soft drink, 147–148
   about logo, 32, 97
   about McDonald's hamburgers, 32
   control of, 97

S

sabotage, during strike, 112
safety
   product
      agency monitoring, 81
      and company reputation, 82–83
      improving as preventive action, 51
      link to health problem, 33, 85, 92, 171
      Nader demands of GM, 77
Safeway, meeting customer demands in earthquake, 5–6
sale of company, as crisis, 68, 69, 78–80
sales, impact of recalls on, 84–85, 87, 90, 91–92
Salinger, Pierre, 132

Sandoz Chemical plant, contamination by, 32
scandal, computer simulation of, 184
scenario development in crisis planning, 52, 176–182, 227
   global and regional, by Shell, 180–181
Schenkler, Irv, 97
Schiavone Construction, indictment of managers, 178
school buildings, asbestos in, 155
school district, CMP of, 223–226
scientific or technological project, and risk susceptibility, 52–53
secrecy, about Chernobyl's effects, 159–160
security
   employee background searches, 171
   location of crisis center, 184–185
   for telecommunications, 174
   theft of trade secrets, 171
   vulnerability during strike, 112, 113, 114
   and workplace violence, 102
security agencies, in communication channel, 64
"See It Now," 26
service disruption
   assessing extent of damage, 207
   and bank risk of financial loss, 115–118
   Safeway in earthquake, 167–168
sexual harassment, 46–47
Shell International Petroleum Co., scenario planning, 180–181
Sherman Antitrust Act, 26
shootings
   of Japanese businesses' employees, 61
   at offices of well-known company, 66, 98
   at Texas cafeteria, 33, 99, 100–103
   at workplace by former employee, 32, 97–99, 188, 189, 190
simulations, computer, in crisis planning, 183–184, 227
"60 Minutes"
   Murrow's influence on, 26
   on Ford Pinto, 83
slander, defined, 139
SLAPPS (strategic lawsuits against public participation), 108–109
snail darter, protection of, 165

social organizations, scandal in, 62
social responsibility, 4, 12, 156–157, 161
   charitable contributions, 151, 175
   GE nuclear weapons research, 93
   of multinational companies, 8
   stockholder demands of GM, 77
   See also community relations; environmental responsibility
social workers, intervention of in workplace trauma, 190–193
soil contamination, by Coors, 158
Soviet Union
   coup in and international investments, 33
   coverup of Chernobyl disaster, 159–160
Spanish-American War, role of newspaper publishers, 19
Special Metals Corporation, cleanup liability of, 157
spokesperson
   activities of, 208–211
   assigned to deal with media, 117, 206, 208
   choosing appropriate one for audience, 123, 126–127, 132, 182
   identifying in advance, 64, 94
   resources needed by, 210
   in stock crisis, 73
Standard Oil, break-up of, 17
state governments
   bank regulators' action after fire, 115, 116, 117
   complaints from departments of public safety, 94
   environmental safeguards of, 151–152
   Exxon's dealing with in oil spill crisis, 9
   federal help for Love Canal through, 154
   fine for wastewater discharge violations, 158
   and nuclear accident, 38, 39
Steffens, Lincoln, 16, 18, 19
Stephenson, David, 161
Stevens, William, 41
Steward, Shelley, 172
stillbirths, at Love Canal, 153
stock market scandal, Japan, 33
stock value
   and disappearance of CEO, 193–194

impact of crisis on, 59–60, 72, 73, 211

and Nader campaign against GM, 78

of Perrier in recall crisis, 87

rumors about drop in, 96

suspension of trading, 101, 211

stockbroker, charges of bilking investors, 32

stockholders

enhancing communication with, 62, 73–80

protest of corporate policy by, 77–78

reaction to Bhopal explosion, 59–60

strategic management, definition of, 6

stress

as cause of illness, 191

in employees and managers, 187

organizational behavior fueled by, 36

strikes

by air traffic controllers, 111

factors affecting negotiations, 113

at Greyhound, 32, 112

at Hormel, 32, 112

preparing for, 113–114

at United Airlines, 112–113

Sudafed, product tampering and recall, 11, 33, 85–86

sunshine laws, and dumping of toxics, 155–156

Superfund law

Community Right to Know amendment, 155–156

liability of users of landfill, 157–158

violation of, 10–11

suppliers, contacting in product recall, 90

Supreme Court, decisions affecting large industries, 17

survey, preparedness of firms, 57

synagogues, neighborhood opposition to, 105

T

takeover, federal, of Lincoln Savings and Loan, 32

tampons, TSS crisis, 32, 85, 92

tax, payments in lieu of (PILOT), 175

team

crisis

contact information on, 198, 201–202, 204, 207

responsibilities of members, 36, 42–44

size and composition of, 12, 33–36, 172–174

technical experts

in crisis planning, 173

at press conferences, 134, 184

technical operations managers, role in crisis management, 34

technological firms, risk of crisis in, 65

telecommunications

backup equipment in distant location, 174

crisis center requirements, 174, 182, 185

lack of preparation at TMI, 39

planning role of manager of, 174

setting up after bank fire, 116

TV arrangements, 211

use of 800 number, 51, 81, 84, 86, 87, 94, 119, 174

and workplace violence, 98–99

Tennessee Valley Authority, Tellico Dam, 165

terrorism

attacks on Japanese businesses, 61

Pan Am flight 103 explosion, 32

threat of against corporations, 7, 11

See also ecoterrorism

Texaco, Inc.

judgment in Pennzoil case, 32

reporting of chemicals released, 156

theft

employee, Cumberland Farms' handling of, 70

of trade secrets, 32, 171, 176, 217–218

Thornburgh, Richard, as Pennsylvania governor, TMI, 38

Three Mile Island

accident at, impact on other projects, 160

nuclear power plant, release of radiation (1979), 38–39

software simulating crisis at, 183

timber industry, costs of ecoterrorism, 163

toxic shock syndrome (TSS), link to tampons, 32, 85, 92

trade secrets, theft of, 32, 171, 176, 217–218

train accident, AMTRAK in Boston, 42–44

training

for asbestos removal workers, 155

in crisis management, 2, 12, 183

of local officials on chemicals and storage, 161

in media relations, 133, 182

in prevention of environmental crisis, 160

for technical experts, 173

in waste management, 163

transportation, public, risk of crisis in, 65

trauma, from workplace crises, 6–7, 187–193, 190

Tropical Fantasy, rumors about, 147–148

Truth About Chernobyl, The (Medvedev), 160

Tsongas, Paul, press conference of, 146

tuberculosis, rates of near mining and factories, 151

"20/20", and product rumor, 147

Tylenol

managing recall of, 84–85, 174

product tampering, 3–4, 32

restoring consumer confidence, 92, 95

U

UAL, acquisitions by, 112

Underwriters' Laboratories (UL), role of, 81

Union Carbide, Bhopal accident, 32, 59–60

United Airlines, strategies in strike, 112–113

United States and allies, press coverage of Gulf War, 15–16

University of California at Berkeley, asbestos removal costs, 155

University of Virginia, asbestos removal costs, 155

unknown hazards, liability for, 155

UNLV Institute on Risk and Insurance Management, 213
utilities
  public and private, risk of crisis in, 65
  service disruption, 114

V

values, threat to in crisis, 50. *See also* goals, organizational
Vance, Charles F., 114
Veryfine Products, use of apples treated with alar, 33
victims, notifying families of, 206
video clip services, 135
video news releases (VNRs)
  news media use of, 136–137, 146
  objectives of, 136–139
violent crimes
  against Japanese businesses, 60, 61
  in the workplace, 97–99, 188–190
  trauma from, 192–193
voluntary organizations, participation in, 107, 175
vulnerability, assessing, 52–53, 203

W

wage and benefit concessions, 112–113

Wall Street Journal, as source of rumors, 95
Walt Disney Corporation, as Florida neighbor, 105–106
war
  as factor in labor negotiations, 113
  and scenario development, 180
warning labels, 85, 94
warning systems
  monitoring problems, 53, 62–64, 107
  as preventive action, 51
Washington, D.C., as opinion center, 17–18
waste
  hazardous, liability for cleanup, 157–158
  management training, 163
  reduction of, 156
  treatment facility, community concern about, 161
wastewater discharge, penalties for, 158
water
  bottled, revenues of, 86
  contamination, 88, 157, 158
WCVB-TV, covering company in crisis, 144
Weingarten, Pam, 96
Weld, William, press conference of, 146
West
  litigation against firms in, 57
  NIMBY crises in, 106

Weyerhauser, costs of ecoterrorism, 163
whistleblowing, and preventive action, 51
White, Theodore H., 22
White House, crisis management in, 40–41
Wildig, Tony, 180–181
Woolard, Edgar, 161
workers compensation, 213
workplace violence, 97–99, 188–190
  trauma from, 7, 187–193
World Airways accident, 215–216
World Crisis, The (Churchill), 21
World War I, press mobilization of citizenry, 20
World War II, Murrow's plea for U.S. help, 24
WPRC-TV, on use of VNRs, 137

Y

Y&A Group, missing CEO of, 193

Z

zoning
  community protests of permits, 104
  monitoring laws on, 107